working your way th...

WORDSTAR®

Sally Graham

Instructor, Office Personnel Program
De Anza Community College
Cupertino, California

WordStar Consultant

Published by

W10U   SOUTH-WESTERN PUBLISHING CO.

CINCINNATI   WEST CHICAGO, IL   DALLAS   PELHAM MANOR, NY   PALO ALTO, CA

COVER PHOTO: Manfred Kage/Peter Arnold, Inc.

Preface

You are about to discover a new way to produce and edit documents on a computer using the WordStar®[1] program. Together, your computer and WordStar will enable you to produce letter-perfect documents—no matter how many changes and revisions are made—much faster than on an electric typewriter.

Each lesson in this text-workbook contains

- a list of objectives the lesson will cover.

- a step-by-step guide through each WordStar command providing hands-on instruction for every edit function introduced.

- a discussion section explaining each WordStar command.

- end-of-chapter questions to check your mastery of the lesson.

- computer exercises to provide you with material on which to try out the commands learned in each lesson.

Who Should Use This Text-Workbook?

This text-workbook is written for the novice computer user. Secretaries who find a computer on their desk one day with instructions from the boss to "type all my documents on our new computer"; students learning word processing concepts; and computer owners who want to use WordStar word processing software will all find this text-workbook to be an easy step-by-step guide. The instructions are applicable to all versions of WordStar except WordStar 2000® and WordStar 2000 Plus®.

This text-workbook is designed to be a self-teaching guide through WordStar and can be used as a successful learning tool by itself; however, a teacher's manual which contains additional tests and exercises for the classroom is available.

Before proceeding to learn the WordStar commands, it is necessary for you to understand just exactly what word processing is and to know some basic information about your computer. The first lesson in this book will teach you some of the basic concepts of word processing.

In addition to having some background information on word processing, you will want to know how to prepare diskettes for your computer. Consult Appendix A for disk formatting procedures.

Sally Graham

---

[1]MicroPro, WordStar, MailMerge, and SpellStar are registered trademarks of MicroPro International Corporation. Any reference to MicroPro, WordStar, MailMerge, or SpellStar refers to this footnote.

Contents

1. Word Processing and WordStar _____

OBJECTIVES:

1. Describe the elements of a word processor.

2. Define word processing.

3. Describe the keyboard.

4. Describe differences between a typewriter and a word processor.

5. Explain how a WordStar page setup will look.

ELEMENTS OF ALL WORD PROCESSING COMPUTER SYSTEMS

There are five elements of a word processing system. They are the

1. keyboard.

2. disk drives.

3. printer.

4. central processing unit.

5. video display terminal.

You communicate or direct the computer through a **keyboard** by entering words and commands. The computer (shown in Figure 1.1) receives your words and answers your commands through the **central processing unit** and displays this input on a **video display terminal** better known as a **VDT** or a screen. The **printer** produces a hard copy of your words. A **hard copy** is the printed copy.

1

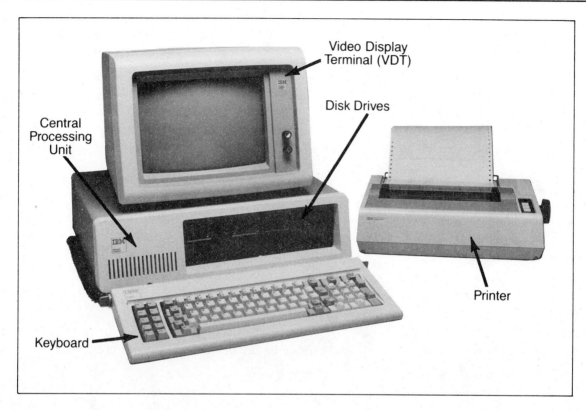

Figure 1.1   An IBM Personal Computer System

The **disk drives** save keyed material on disks when requested and also activate computer software programs like WordStar. The disk drives use a **floppy disk,** (shown in Figure 1.2) to store material. A floppy disk looks like a 45 rpm phonograph record. Disks used can be 5 1/4 inches or 8 inches, depending on the disk drive.

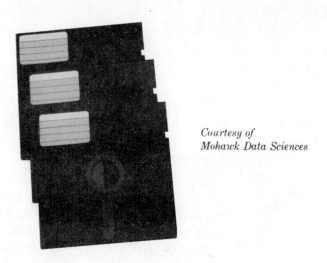

*Courtesy of
Mohawk Data Sciences*

Figure 1.2   Floppy Disks

WORD PROCESSING DEFINED

Word processing is a way to create, edit, store, and print text on a computer or word processor. Word processors are computers. Some word processors can only perform word processing tasks; other word processors can perform tasks in addition to word processing, such as business forecasting, accounting, and game playing.

COMPUTER KEYBOARD

The computer keyboard looks like a regular typewriter keyboard except that it has additional keys. WordStar needs only four special keys to execute its commands. These keys are the

1. Ctrl (control) key.

2. Esc (escape) key.

3. Del (delete) key.

4. ENTER or RETURN key.

The ENTER or RETURN key may have an arrow pointing to the keyboard and is used to send information to the processing unit in the computer. Figure 1.3 illustrates the IBM Personal Computer keyboard.

Figure 1.3   IBM Personal Computer Keyboard

Notice the shaded keys to the left and right of the keyboard. The keys at the left are labeled F1-F10. These extra keys are called **special-function keys**. A special-function key can be used in place of the WordStar coded command.

Computer operators who use WordStar only occasionally will find these special-function keys extremely helpful. However, word processing operators who use WordStar most of the workday will want to use the WordStar coded commands for their text editing, because once these commands are mastered an experienced operator can achieve great speed. This is because all of the WordStar coded commands can be entered by striking the Ctrl (control) key and a regular keyboard key at the same time. To strike the special-function keys, the computer operator's hands must leave the home-row position.

Appendix A gives suggestions for formatting disks. Appendix B gives additional information about the IBM, Apple, and TRS-80 keyboards. Consult your particular computer manual for more keyboard information.

Figure 1.4 illustrates some differences between a computer keyboard and a typewriter.

	Typewriter	**Computer**
Space bar	Inserts a space between characters	The space bar is a character key. If you space over another character key with the space bar, that character will be deleted and a space will be inserted.
Digit 1 and letter l (L lowercase)	Used interchangeably.	Lowercase letter L cannot be used for digit 1.
Shift key	Unlocks uppercase. Enters letters in uppercase when struck.	Does not unlock uppercase. Enters top portion of two-character keys. Strike Caps Lock key to return to lowercase.
Caps Lock key	Capitalizes and enters upper symbols of two-character keys.	Will not enter the upper symbols of two-character keys. To enter upper symbols, use the shift key.

Figure 1.4   Differences Between a Computer Keyboard and a Typewriter

WORDSTAR PAGE SETUP

When entering a letter, memorandum, manuscript, report, or table using WordStar, some basic decisions about how your document will look on a page have been preset for you. These preset format decisions are called **defaults** because a standard format is already on the computer by default. All of the defaults can be changed. You have complete control over the printed page. Let us examine these WordStar defaults.

Side margins	The left margin is preset at position 1. The right margin is preset at position 65. This means that the document will have a 65-space line. Printing will start 8 spaces from the left side of the page. The right margin will be **justified** (even). Because the right margin is justified, there may be more than one space between words.
Top margin	Text will print 3 lines (1/2 inch) from the top of the page.
Bottom margin	The bottom margin will be 8 lines or 1 1/3 inches between the last line of text and the bottom of the page.
Line spacing	Printout will be single spaced.
Tabs	Tabs are set every 5 spaces.
Headings	Page headings will print 2 lines above the text.
Footers	Footers such as footnotes will print 2 lines below the text at the bottom of the page.
Page length	The length of the page is 66 lines or a standard 8 1/2-inch by 11-inch page.
Page numbers	Each page will be numbered beginning with the number 1.
Pitch	The printout will be in pica or 10 characters per inch.
Printed lines	There will be 55 lines of text per page.
Page endings	WordStar will start a new page after 55 lines of text have been entered.

Figure 1.5   WordStar Defaults

LESSON 1 EXERCISE   Name _____ Date _____

The number in parenthesis at the end of each question refers to the learning objectives at the beginning of the lesson.

TRUE/FALSE

Each of the following statements is either true or false. Indicate your choice in the Answers column by circling T for a true statement or F for a false statement.

		Answers
1.	The elements of a word processing system are the (1) keyboard, (2) disk drives, (3) printer, (4) central processing unit, and (5) video display terminal. (Obj. 1)	1. T F
2.	A VDT stands for video display terminal. (Obj. 1)	2. T F
3.	Disk drives activate software programs. (Obj. 1)	3. T F
4.	Floppy disks come in a variety of sizes. (Obj. 1)	4. T F
5.	Hard copy stands for the material shown on the screen. (Obj. 1)	5. T F
6.	Word processing is a way to create, edit, store, and print text on a computer. (Obj. 2)	6. T F
7.	Word processors are not computers. (Obj. 2)	7. T F
8.	The computer keyboard and a typewriter keyboard are exactly the same. (Obj. 3)	8. T F
9.	WordStar needs only three special keys to execute its commands. (Obj. 3)	9. T F
10.	A special-function key can be used in place of a WordStar command. (Obj. 3)	10. T F
11.	The digit 1 and the lowercase letter l can be used interchangeably on the computer. (Obj. 4)	11. T F
12.	The shift key on a computer unlocks uppercase. (Obj. 4)	12. T F
13.	The space bar on a computer acts as a character key. (Obj. 4)	13. T F
14.	The preset WordStar format settings are called defaults. (Obj. 5)	14. T F
15.	The WordStar default line spacing is double. (Obj. 5)	15. T F
16.	The right margin will print out justified if not changed by the computer operator. (Obj. 5)	16. T F
17.	The computer operator must determine margin settings before a document can be printed. (Obj. 5)	17. T F
18.	Tabs are set every five spaces in the preset format. (Obj. 5)	18. T F
19.	There will be 66 lines of printed text on a standard sheet of paper. (Obj. 5)	19. T F
20.	Each page will be numbered automatically on the printout beginning with the number 1 unless changed by the computer operator. (Obj. 5)	20. T F

COMPLETION

Indicate the correct answer in the space provided.

1. List the five elements of a word processing system. (Obj. 1) ....

   1. a. _____
      b. _____
      c. _____
      d. _____
      e. _____

2. Give a more popular name for the video display terminal. (Obj. 1) ....

   2. _____

3. Give the name for the part of a word processor that activates software programs such as WordStar. (Obj. 1) ....

   3. _____

4. What looks like a 45 rpm phonograph record? (Obj. 1) ..

   4. _____

5. What produces the hard copy of words entered into the computer? (Obj. 1) ....

   5. _____

6. List four ways word processing helps produce documents. (Obj. 2) ....

   6. a. _____
      b. _____
      c. _____
      d. _____

7. List the four keys necessary to use WordStar. (Obj. 4) .

   7. a. _____
      b. _____
      c. _____
      d. _____

8. What key do you use to enter the upper symbols of two-character keys on a computer? (Obj. 4) ....

   8. _____

9. What is the preset format for WordStar called? (Obj. 5)

   9. _____

10. Unless changed by the operator, WordStar will default to what line space? (Obj. 5) ....

   10. _____

11. Unless changed by the operator, WordStar will default how many lines from the top of the page? (Obj. 5) ......

   11. _____

12. Unless changed by the operator, WordStar will default how many inches for the bottom margin? (Obj. 5) ......

   12. _____

13. Unless changed by the operator, WordStar will default to what type of spacing? (Obj. 5) ....

   13. _____

14. Unless changed by the operator, WordStar will default to how many spaces between tab stops? (Obj. 5) ....

   14. _____

15. How many characters will be printed per inch on the final printout? (Obj. 5) ....

   15. _____

16. Unless changed by the operator, WordStar will default to how many lines of text per page? (Obj. 5) ....

   16. _____

2. Getting into WordStar ———————

OBJECTIVES:

1. Power up the computer.

2. Getting into WordStar.

3. Changing from one disk drive to the other.

4. Exiting WordStar.

5. Power down the computer.

POWER UP THE COMPUTER

Power-up instructions for the IBM Personal Computer and IBM compatible computers, Apple II, TRS-80, and the Zenith computers are given in this section. If you are working on a computer other than the ones mentioned, consult your specific computer manual for power-up instructions.

Before powering up the computer, you should have a system master diskette that contains the operating system and WordStar. You should also have a formatted working diskette. (See Appendix A for instructions on formatting diskettes.)

Some computer manufacturers identify their disk drives with the numbers 1 and 2 and some identify the drives with the letters A and B. Disk Drive A is the same as Disk Drive 1 and Disk Drive B is the same as Disk Drive 2. Disk drives are sometimes situated side by side or with one drive on top of the other. Disk Drive A is usually the drive on the left for those that are side by side or the drive on the bottom for those with one drive on top of the other. Disk Drive B is the drive on the right for side-by-side configurations or the drive on the top for those with one drive on top of the other.

Power Up for IBM Computer

The power switch on the IBM Personal Computer is located on the right-hand side toward the back of the disk drives. A master WordStar diskette should be in Drive A and a formatted working diskette should be in Drive B before the power is turned on. Close the drive doors and turn on the power. A beep can be heard when the drives are turned on and a flashing light called a **cursor** will appear. Then a prompt is displayed asking for the time and date. After the time and date are entered, press the enter key. The enter key has an arrow pointing toward the keyboard. The prompt **A>** is then displayed on the screen.

Power Up for the Apple Computer
(Must Have a CP/M Card Installed)

The power switch is located in back of the keyboard on the left-hand side. The Apple II may use a variety of display units. Check your display for the power switch. A system master Word-Star diskette should be in Drive 1 and a formatted working diskette should be in Drive 2 before the power is turned on. Close the drive doors. If the disks are inserted after the power is turned on, hold down the Ctrl key and the Open Apple key (bottom row of keyboard) together while striking the Reset key. The message displayed may differ depending on the type of CP/M card installed in your Apple. If the Advanced Logic Systems CP/M card is used with CP/M version 3.0, some copyright information and **A>** is displayed.

Power Up for the TRS-80

Power on the main unit. Turn on the power switch on the video display terminal. Insert the system WordStar master diskette in Drive A and close the door. Insert the formatted working diskette in Drive B and close the door. Strike the Reset switch. The following prompt will appear: "Enter new date:" Key-in the current date. A message asking for a new time will appear. Enter the new time. (For example, 2:30 p.m. will be entered as 14:30.) Strike the ENTER key. The prompt **A>** is then displayed.

Power Up for the Zenith Computer

The power switch is located on the back of the keyboard on the left-hand side. The disk drives are turned on by a switch in the back of the drives on the right-hand side. A system master Word-Star diskette should be in Drive A and a formatted working diskette should be in Drive B. The prompt **H:** and a cursor will appear. Enter *B* (uppercase or lowercase) and press the RETURN key. The prompt **A>** is then displayed.

INSTRUCTIONS FOR GETTING STARTED

Complete the step-by-step instructions.

1. Power up your computer. Consult your computer manual for power-up instructions if you are not using a computer discussed earlier. Depending on your computer instructions, the disks are inserted either before you power up or after you power up.

2. Insert the disks. The system WordStar master diskette is in Drive A and the formatted working diskette is in Drive B. Figure 2.1 illustrates how a disk is inserted in the disk drive. Turning on your computer with the disk containing programs is called **booting** the system. After the system is booted, **A>** is displayed on the screen. The cursor position indicates where the next character will be displayed. The **A>** display means that you are in Disk Drive A.

3. If your computer does not boot, be sure that

   a. the system is plugged into an electrical outlet.
   b. there is a system master WordStar diskette in Drive A.
   c. all of the cable connections are attached.
   d. the disks are inserted in the disk drives properly.
   e. the disk drive doors are shut.

Figure 2.1   Inserting a Disk into the Disk Drive

Most computers are programmed to get into WordStar by keying in *WS* (for WordStar) at the **A>**. Your computer may have another code that should be entered. Consult with your instructor or the WordStar manual to determine what is keyed after **A>**.

You are now in the WordStar program. Your screen should look similar to Figure 2.2. Your opening menu format may be slightly different from the one shown here if your WordStar is not the 3.3 version (1983).

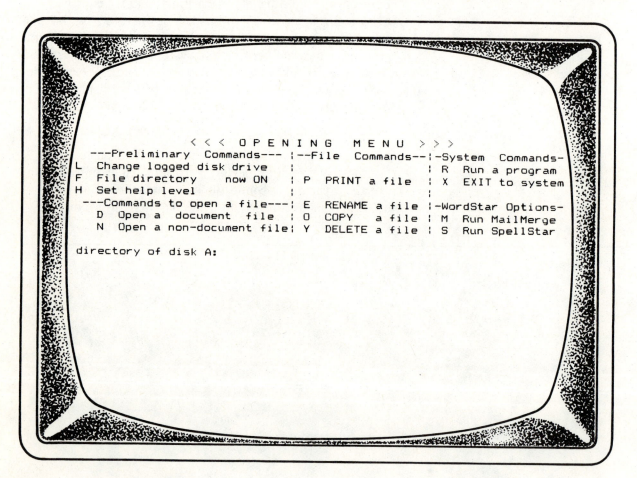

```
          < < < O P E N I N G   M E N U > > >
   ---Preliminary Commands--- ¦--File  Commands--¦-System  Commands-
L  Change logged disk drive   ¦                  ¦ R  Run a program
F  File directory    now ON   ¦ P  PRINT a file  ¦ X  EXIT to system
H  Set help level             ¦                  ¦
   ---Commands to open a file---¦ E  RENAME a file ¦-WordStar Options-
   D  Open a  document  file  ¦ O  COPY   a file  ¦ M  Run MailMerge
   N  Open a non-document file¦ Y  DELETE a file  ¦ S  Run SpellStar

directory of disk A:
```

Figure 2.2   Opening Menu

A list of options on a computer screen is called a **menu**. The computer menu is very much like a menu in a restaurant that gives the diner a list of choices. On the WordStar computer menu, you are given a list of choices also. This particular menu is called the **opening menu** because it is the first menu that appears when you are in WordStar. Sometimes this menu is referred to as **no-file** because at this point you are not in a file (document).

The directory of Disk Drive A is also displayed. The **directory** is a listing of all the document files on a disk.

Changing from One Disk Drive to Another

One of the options from the opening menu is to change from one disk drive to another. Of course, if you only have one disk drive, this option will not be used.

When the WordStar programs and the operating system programs are on one diskette, a lot of disk space is used. Consequently, the remaining disk space used for files (documents) is limited. Changing from the master disk to a disk without programs permits a larger area for document preparation.

To change from one disk drive to another, complete the following step-by-step instructions.

1. Key-in L at the cursor. L may be in uppercase or lowercase. The screen will appear as shown in Figure 2.3.

```
THE LOGGED DISK DRIVE IS NOW A:

NEW LOGGED DISK DRIVE (letter, colon, RETURN)?
```

Figure 2.3   Changing from Disk Drive A to Disk Drive B

---

2. Key-in B: (ENTER/RETURN). B may be in uppercase or lowercase. The screen shows the opening menu again plus the line, DIRECTORY OF DISK B. You are now working on Disk Drive B. If the computer does not show a directory of Drive B, be sure that a colon is entered after B:. To change from Drive B to Drive A, follow these steps:

   a. Key-in L. The screen will appear as shown in Figure 2.4.

```
THE LOGGED DISK DRIVE IS NOW B:

NEW LOGGED DISK DRIVE (letter, colon, RETURN)?
```

Figure 2.4   Changing from Disk Drive B to Disk Drive A

---

   b. Enter A: (ENTER/RETURN). The screen now shows the opening menu and the directory of Disk Drive A.

EXITING WORDSTAR

To exit the WordStar program and return to the operating system, enter X in uppercase or lowercase. The screen shows **A>**.

When the > is displayed preceded by A or B or any letter, you are in the operating system. You are no longer working in WordStar.

Power Down the Computer

On some computers, the disks should be removed before powering down. Disks are fragile and can be damaged easily. The shiny, exposed magnetic area of the disk must be kept clean or the computer may find the disk unreadable. Magnetic fields can erase material, so keep the disks away from electrical appliances. Complete the following step-by-step instructions to power down your computer.

1. Turn off all the power switches on the computer equipment.

2. Remove the disks from the disk drives and place the disks in their jackets.

LESSON 2 EXERCISE   Name _____ Date _____

TRUE/FALSE

Each of the following statements is either true or false. Indicate your choice in the Answers column by circling T for a true statement or F for a false statement.

Answers

1. All you need to boot-up the computer is to turn on the power. (Obj. 1) ....   1. **T**   **F**

2. A system WordStar master diskette should be in Drive A. (Obj. 1) ....   2. **T**   **F**

3. Powering up your computer with a disk containing programs is called booting the system. (Obj. 1)..   3. **T**   **F**

4. The cursor is a flashing light on the VDT where the next character will be displayed. (Obj. 1) ....   4. **T**   **F**

5. All computers get into WordStar by the command *WS*. (Obj. 2) ....   5. **T**   **F**

6. When the screen displays **A>** you are in Drive A. (Obj. 2).................   6. **T**   **F**

7. The first menu displayed after getting into WordStar is called the opening menu. (Obj. 2) ....   7. **T**   **F**

8. When the opening menu is displayed, you are in a document file. (Obj. 2) .   8. **T**   **F**

9. You can change disk drives from the opening menu. (Obj. 2)..............   9. **T**   **F**

10. The command to change disk drives is *L*. (Obj. 3) ....   10. **T**   **F**

11. When you change from one disk drive to another disk drive, the drive letter can be entered in uppercase or lowercase. (Obj. 3).........................   11. **T**   **F**

12. If **A>** is displayed on the screen, you are in WordStar. (Obj. 4) ....   12. **T**   **F**

COMPLETION

Indicate the correct answer in the space provided.

1. Name the two disks you need to start working on WordStar. (Obj. 1)...   1. a. _____
   b. _____

2. The system disk should be in which disk drive? (Obj. 1) ....   2. _____

3. The working disk should be in which disk drive? (Obj. 1) ....   3. _____

4. Turning on the computer with a disk containing programs is called? (Obj. 1) ....   4. _____

5. Give the command for getting into WordStar from the prompt **A>** on most computers. (Obj. 2) ....   5. _____

6. What is displayed after the system is booted? (Obj. 2)..   6. _____

7. The first menu display in WordStar is called the *?* (Obj. 2) . . . .

7. _____

8. A list of options on the computer screen is called *?* (Obj. 2) . . . .

8. _____

9. Since it is not in a document file, the opening menu may be called *?* (Obj. 2) . . . .

9. _____

10. The opening menu also displays the disk *?* (Obj. 2) . . . . .

10. _____

11. Give the opening menu command for changing from one disk drive to another. (Obj. 3) . . . .

11. _____

12. How do you change from disk drive A to disk drive B if the logged disk drive is A? (Obj. 3) . . . .

12. _____

13. When **A**> is displayed, you are in which disk drive? (Obj. 3) . . . .

13. _____

14. When **B**> is displayed, you are in which disk drive? (Obj. 3) . . . .

14. _____

15. Give the command for exiting WordStar from the opening menu. (Obj. 4) . . . .

15. _____

16. When you exit WordStar, what is displayed to tell you that you are in the operating system? (Obj. 4) . . . .

16. _____

17. The shiny, exposed magnetic area of the diskette must be kept clean or the diskette may become *?* (Obj. 5) . . . .

17. _____

18. What should you place the diskette in when you are not using it? (Obj. 5) . . . .

18. _____

19. What can erase material on a floppy disk? (Obj. 5) . . . . .

19. _____

COMPUTER EXERCISE

Directions: To complete this computer exercise, you should have a system WordStar diskette and a formatted working diskette. Follow the steps given to complete this exercise.

1. Power up your computer and disk drives. Consult your particular computer start-up instructions.

2. Boot your computer to display **A>**. Consult your particular computer start-up instructions.

3. Get into WordStar by entering *WS* (or appropriate word or letter) at the **A>**. The opening menu is displayed.

4. Change from Drive A to Drive B. From the opening menu, enter *L*. Key-in *B:* after the prompt "New logged disk (letter, colon, RETURN)?" The opening menu and the DIRECTORY OF DISK DRIVE B is displayed.

5. Change from Drive B to Drive A. Key-in *L* and answer *A:* to the prompt "New logged disk (letter, colon, RETURN)?" The opening menu and the DIRECTORY OF DISK A is displayed.

6. Exit WordStar from Drive A. Strike the *X* key. The prompt **A>** is displayed.

7. Power down the computer and remove the disks.

3. Creating and Saving a Document

OBJECTIVES:

1. Get into a document file.
2. Name files.
3. Describe the main menu.
4. Describe the status line.
5. Describe the ruler line.
6. Explain wordwrap.
7. Enter text.
8. Save the document.

GETTING INTO A DOCUMENT FILE

One of the options on the opening menu is to create a document. This option is found on the left-hand side of the opening menu as illustrated in Figure 3.1 under the heading "Commands to open a file."

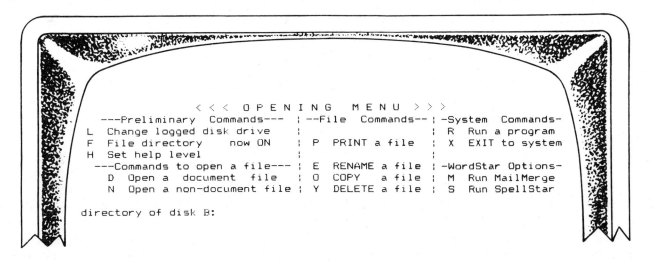

```
              < < <  O P E N I N G   M E N U  > > >
    ---Preliminary  Commands--- ¦ --File  Commands-- ¦ -System  Commands-
L  Change logged disk drive     ¦                    ¦ R  Run a program
F  File directory      now ON   ¦ P  PRINT a file    ¦ X  EXIT to system
H  Set help level               ¦                    ¦
   ---Commands to open a file--- ¦ E  RENAME a file  ¦ -WordStar Options-
   D  Open a  document  file     ¦ O  COPY    a file ¦ M  Run MailMerge
   N  Open a non-document file   ¦ Y  DELETE a file  ¦ S  Run SpellStar

directory of disk B:
```

Figure 3.1   Opening a Document File

Notice that the letter D is before the words "open a document file." Keying in *D* at the cursor from the opening menu will get you into a document file. Let us show how to create the first document now. You will first enter the letter *D*. The screen should appear as shown in Figure 3.2.

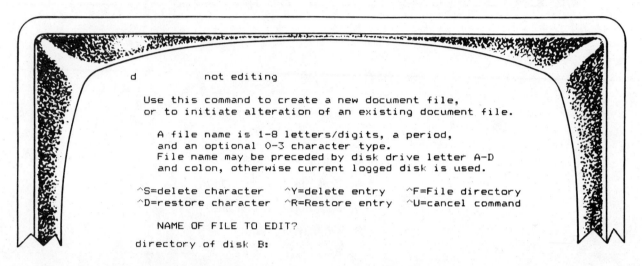

```
  d              not editing

      Use this command to create a new document file,
      or to initiate alteration of an existing document file.

         A file name is 1-8 letters/digits, a period,
         and an optional 0-3 character type.
         File name may be preceded by disk drive letter A-D
         and colon, otherwise current logged disk is used.

      ^S=delete character    ^Y=delete entry     ^F=File directory
      ^D=restore character   ^R=Restore entry    ^U=cancel command

         NAME OF FILE TO EDIT?

  directory of disk B:
```

Figure 3.2   Opening a Document File

Notice the prompt NAME OF FILE TO EDIT? at the bottom of Figure 3.2. WordStar uses the word *edit* to mean a new document or an old document; so when *D* is keyed-in from the opening menu, you can get into either a new file or a file that has already been created.

Also, notice the "^U = cancel command." The symbol ^ stands for the Ctrl (control) key. Strike the Ctrl key whenever you see this symbol. If you should ever strike a wrong key when entering a WordStar command or you do not want to complete a WordStar command, hold down the Ctrl key and strike the *U* (uppercase or lowercase). A prompt will be displayed asking you to strike the Esc (escape) key to cancel the command. You will find ^U very helpful when learning WordStar.

NAMING FILES

When WordStar asks "Name of File to Edit?" you must key-in the file name. For example, you may want to enter a file named LESSON3.DOC. To do this, enter LESSON3.DOC and strike the ENTER/RETURN key. The period plus DOC after LESSON3 describes the type of file. If the file were a letter instead of a document, the file name might be LESSON3.LTR. You could also name this file LESSON3 without any further identification. After the file name has been entered, the screen displays another type of menu called the *main menu* (shown in Figure 3.3). When the main menu is displayed, you are in a file ready to enter text or to change text.

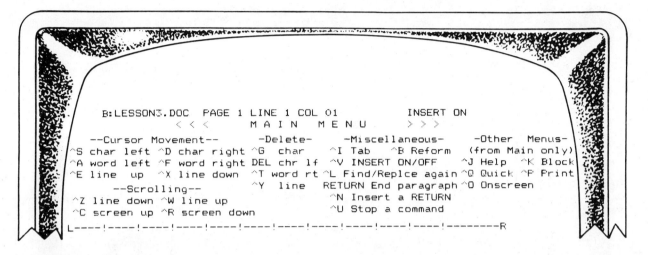

```
B:LESSON3.DOC  PAGE 1 LINE 1 COL 01              INSERT ON
             < < <      M A I N   M E N U      > > >
  --Cursor Movement--        -Delete-       -Miscellaneous-    -Other  Menus-
^S char left ^D char right ^G  char      ^I Tab    ^B Reform  (from Main only)
^A word left ^F word right DEL chr 1f  ^V INSERT ON/OFF      ^J Help  ^K Block
^E line  up  ^X line down  ^T word rt  ^L Find/Replce again ^Q Quick ^P Print
     --Scrolling--         ^Y  line    RETURN End paragraph ^O Onscreen
^Z line down ^W line up                ^N Insert a RETURN
^C screen up ^R screen down            ^U Stop a command
L----!----!----!----!----!----!----!----!----!----!----!-------R
```

Figure 3.3   The Main Menu

Certain rules must be followed when naming files:

1. File names cannot contain more than eight characters before a period.

2. There cannot be more than three characters after the period which separates the file name from the file type.

3. File names should not include spaces, question marks, or symbols.

4. Do not assign the same name to two documents.

A valid file name would be REPORT. An invalid file name would be MANUSCRIPT because there are more than eight characters in the name. Another invalid file name would be REPORT #1. This file name is invalid because it contains a space and a number sign.

MAIN MENU

The **main menu** (in Figure 3.3) is displayed when creating or editing documents. It contains information and options necessary for working with documents. The main menu gives important information about the document. It contains the following:

1. status line.

2. cursor movement information.

3. insert instructions.

4. delete instructions.

5. directions for moving through the document by screen.

6. instructions for getting into other menus.

7. ruler line.

Status Line

The status line is the first line of the main menu. Figure 3.4 illustrates the status line.

B:LESSON3.DOC   PAGE 1 LINE 1 COL 01   INSERT ON

Figure 3.4   The Status Line

The **B:** indicates that you are working from Disk Drive B. LESSON3.DOC is the name of the file you have selected. PAGE 1 indicates that you are working on Page 1. LINE 1 indicates that the cursor is on Line 1 of the document. COL 1 indicates the cursor is flashing on the first column or space within the margin setting. The column number will change as you key-in information and move across the screen. INSERT ON indicates that space will be made in the line when you insert any new words or letters; no material will be deleted when you correct errors.

Ruler Line

The ruler line is located at the bottom of the main menu. Figure 3.5 illustrates the ruler line.

L----!----!----!----!----!----!----!----!----!----!----!--------R

Figure 3.5   The Ruler Line

The L at the left of the ruler line indicates the left margin setting. The preset left margin is set at Column 1. The R at the right indicates the right margin setting. The preset right margin is at Column 65. The ! marks in the ruler line are the preset tab settings. Tabs are set at five-space intervals.

WORDWRAP

When keying-in text on a computer, the ENTER/RETURN key is only used to end a paragraph or to insert a required return within a paragraph. This is a major difference between creating documents on a typewriter and on a computer. As text is entered on a computer, the line automatically drops down when the right margin is reached. You do not have to listen for bells to return the text to the next line. The computer will do it for you. This feature is called **wordwrap.**

ENTERING TEXT

You will learn to enter text on the computer. Your first document will be created with the INSERT OFF. The WordStar command to turn INSERT OFF is $^\wedge V$ (uppercase or lowercase). If you make a mistake while entering data, backspace to the error and strike the correct character key. When INSERT is OFF, one character replaces the other. Do not be concerned if an error is made on a previous line. Do not correct it. Later you will learn how to correct errors on lines other than the cursor line.

As you enter text, you will notice that the right margin appears even or justified. WordStar justifies the right margin automatically. Right margin justification is one of the WordStar defaults and may be changed. Because the right margin is justified, some words will have more than one space between them.

Figure 3.6 illustrates how your screen will look after entering two paragraphs.

```
        You   are creating your first document on  the   computer.    If
you   make   a mistake while entering data,   backspace and key   over
your   mistake.    Remember,   you are keying with  INSERT/OFF   which
means if you make a mistake and backspace to correct it,   you lose
the character you key over.                                           <
                                                                     <

        On   a  word processor you do not have to press RETURN   until
you   want   to start a new paragraph or want the line to end   at   a
specific column.    Notice that when the end of the screen line   is
reached, the partial word that did not fit on that line moves down
to   the   next line.    This is called WORDWRAP and is   an   automatic
feature of WordStar.                                                 <
                                                                      .
```

Figure 3.6   Screen Display of Entered Text

If you entered the paragraphs in Figure 3.6, you would notice a number of things about the text displayed:

1. The right margin is even.

2. The text is single spaced.

3. A "less than" sign ($<$) appears beyond the right margin at the end of each paragraph. This graphic indicates a return was entered at the keyboard.

4. A dot (.) appears at the end of the document beyond the right margin. This graphic indicates the file end. There is no text beyond the dot (.). Sometimes at the beginning of the file you will notice a colon (:). This graphic indicates the file beginning. There is no text above the colon. The return graphic and the beginning and end of document graphics are called **flag characters**.

Sometimes text is entered with INSERT OFF and the screen does not display the text as you want it. For example:

1. If characters do not replace other characters when corrections are made, be sure INSERT ON is not displayed on the status line. If it is, turn it off by $^\wedge V$.

2. If wordwrap does not work, strike $^\wedge O$. A new menu called the **on screen menu** is displayed at the top of the screen. If this menu shows that wordwrap is turned off, turn it back on by striking the W key (uppercase or lowercase) and enter the text again.

3. If the text does not justify, strike $^\wedge O$. Look at the on screen menu displayed at the top of the screen. If the menu shows that justification is turned off, turn it back on by striking J (uppercase or lowercase).

SAVING THE DOCUMENT

All documents should be saved for later editing or for printing. After keying-in text, enter $^\wedge$**KD** (hold down the Ctrl key, strike K and then strike D) to save the document. The $^\wedge$KD save command may be entered anywhere within the document file. Think "keep document" as you enter the $^\wedge$KD save command.

The opening menu is again displayed after a document is saved with $^\wedge$KD. If you saved a document called LESSON3.DOC, the file name LESSON3.DOC will be listed on the directory following the opening menu as illustrated in Figure 3.7.

The command $^\wedge$KD saves the document and returns the opening menu to the screen. Two other save commands are helpful; they are the $^\wedge$**KS** command and the $^\wedge$**KX** command. The $^\wedge$KS saves the document, but does not exit the document. This is a valuable command when working in a very long document. Periodic saving with the $^\wedge$KS command stores all material entered and then returns you to the beginning of the file. The $^\wedge$KX command saves the document in edit and returns you to the operating system. To help you remember this command, think of exiting to the operating system.

If the directory does not show the file name LESSON3.DOC after saving the file with $^\wedge$KD, the file directory may be turned off. Strike F at the opening menu to display the file directory.

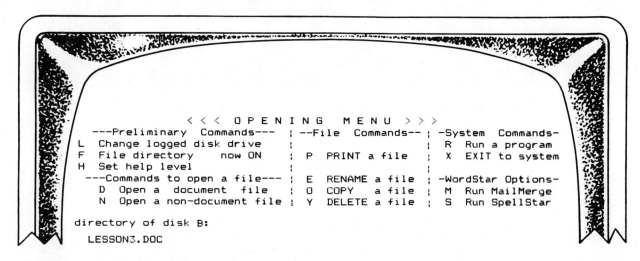

```
              < < <  O P E N I N G   M E N U  > > >
    ---Preliminary  Commands---  ¦ --File  Commands-- ¦ -System  Commands-
L   Change logged disk drive     ¦                    ¦  R  Run a program
F   File directory      now ON   ¦  P  PRINT a file   ¦  X  EXIT to system
H   Set help level               ¦                    ¦
    ---Commands to open a file--- ¦  E  RENAME a file  ¦ -WordStar Options-
    D  Open a  document  file     ¦  O  COPY   a file  ¦  M  Run MailMerge
    N  Open a non-document file   ¦  Y  DELETE a file  ¦  S  Run SpellStar

directory of disk B:
   LESSON3.DOC
```

Figure 3.7   The File Directory

LESSON 3 EXERCISE   Name _____ Date _____

TRUE/FALSE

Directions: Each of the following statements is either true or false. Indicate your choice in the Answers column by circling T for a true statement or F for a false statement.

1. Keying in *D* at the cursor from the opening menu will get you into a document file. (Obj. 1) ....   1. **T**   **F**

2. WordStar uses the word edit to mean a new document or an old document. (Obj. 1) ....   2. **T**   **F**

3. To create a new document, key in *D* at the opening menu. (Obj. 1) ....   3. **T**   **F**

4. To edit an old document, key in *D* at the opening menu. (Obj. 1) ....   4. **T**   **F**

5. The command ^*U* and *Esc* will cancel any WordStar command. (Obj. 1) ...   5. **T**   **F**

6. The letter commands used in the opening menu must be keyed in uppercase. (Obj. 1) ....   6. **T**   **F**

7. LESSON3 is a valid file name. (Obj. 2) ....   7. **T**   **F**

8. Lesson 3 is a valid file name. (Obj. 2) ....   8. **T**   **F**

9. LESSON #3 is a valid file name. (Obj. 2) ....   9. **T**   **F**

10. FILENAMES is a valid file name. (Obj. 2) ....   10. **T**   **F**

11. LESSON.LETTER is a valid file name. (Obj. 2) ....   11. **T**   **F**

12. After keying-in the letter D and the file name from the opening menu, the main menu is displayed. (Obj. 2) ....   12. **T**   **F**

13. The main menu indicates you are in a document file. (Obj. 2) ....   13. **T**   **F**

14. The status line is displayed in the opening menu. (Obj. 3) ....   14. **T**   **F**

15. The ruler line is displayed in the main menu. (Obj. 3) ....   15. **T**   **F**

16. The status line indicates the file name, the page number, and the line and column number of the cursor. (Obj. 4) ....   16. **T**   **F**

17. The ruler line displays a preset line of 65 spaces unless changed by the operator. (Obj. 5) ....   17. **T**   **F**

18. Preset tab settings are every 8 spaces on the ruler line unless changed by the operator. (Obj. 5) ....   18. **T**   **F**

19. The feature called wordwrap automatically starts a new line when the right margin is reached. (Obj. 6) ....   19. **T**   **F**

20. The insert may be turned off by the command ^*V*. (Obj. 7) ....   20. **T**   **F**

21. The preset right margin will be uneven. (Obj. 7) ....   21. **T**   **F**

22. The single dot (.) at the right side of the screen indicates the end of a document. (Obj. 7) ....   22. **T**   **F**

23. The colon (:) at the right side of the screen indicates the beginning of a document. (Obj. 7) ....   23. **T**   **F**

24. Documents must be saved for later editing after they arc keyed in. (Obj. 8) ....   24. **T**   **F**

25. The command to save a document and return to the opening menu is ^*KD*. (Obj. 8) ....   25. **T**   **F**

COMPLETION

Write in the Answers column the correct response to each of the following.

1. Give the command from the opening menu that gets into a document file. (Obj. 1)..................................   1. _____

2. Give the WordStar command to cancel a command. (Obj. 1) ....   2. _____

3. Indicate with a *yes* if the following file name is valid and a *no* if the file name is invalid. (Obj. 2) ....

   a. JOHNSON.LTR   3. a. _____

   b. ENGLEBERT   b. _____

   c. KOVAKS.LETTER   c. _____

   d. TEST #1   d. _____

4. What menu is displayed when a file is being created or edited? (Obj. 3) ....   4. _____

5. What part of the main menu displays the disk drive, the file name, the page number, and the line and column number? (Obj. 4)...   5. _____

6. If INSERT ON is displayed in the status line, can you correct errors by keying over the error? (Obj. 4)........   6. _____

7. What does the ruler line display? (Obj. 5) ....   7. a. _____
                                                              b. _____
                                                              c. _____

8. How many spaces apart are tabs set? (Obj. 5) ....   8. _____

9. The feature that permits the keyboarder to press the ENTER/RETURN key only when a paragraph is completed is called? (Obj. 6) ....   9. _____

10. What is displayed to the right of the screen to indicate a return? (Obj. 7) ....   10. _____

11. What is displayed to the right of the screen to indicate a document end? (Obj. 7) ....   11. _____

12. Is it possible to turn justification and wordwrap off? (Obj. 7) ....   12. _____

13. Give the command to save a document and return to the opening menu. (Obj. 8) ....   13. _____

14. Give the command to save entered text and remain in the document. (Obj. 8) ....   14. _____

15. Give the command to save a document and return to the operating system. (Obj. 8) ....   15. _____

16. Can the directory display be turned off? (Obj. 8) ....   16. _____

COMPUTER EXERCISE

Enter the following letter into a file on Disk Drive B. Call the file HOLLIS.LTR and save it on your working disk. Follow the steps given to create this letter.

1. Insert a system master WordStar diskette in Drive A and a formatted working disk in Drive B.

November 8, 19--

Ms. Betty Hollis
Publisher
BUSINESS OPPORTUNITIES
P. O. Box 2323
San Jose, CA 95153-4412

Dear Betty

Thank you for serving on the Secretarial Science's Advisory Committee for De Anza College. We look forward to seeing you December 2 at 2:30 p.m. Your formal invitation should arrive soon.

I am enclosing our degree requirements. In addition to the Secretarial Science Degree we also offer a Secretarial Certificate of Proficiency.

Enclosed is the list of members you requested. You will see that our advisory committee has an interesting cross section of the business community.

I am looking forward to seeing you at the meeting.

Sincerely

Frank Gray

Enclosure

Figure 3.8   Letter for Computer Exercise

2. Power up the computer. *Note:* Steps 1 and 2 may be reversed depending on your particular computer power-up instructions.

3. When the **A>** is displayed, enter *WS* (or appropriate word) to get into WordStar.

4. Enter *L* from the opening menu to change from Disk Drive A to Disk Drive B.

5. Enter the letter *D* and the name HOLLIS.LTR. (Do not place a period after LTR in the file name).

6. Turn INSERT OFF with the command ^*V*.

7. Enter the letter as it appears in Figure 3.8. Do not press the ENTER/RETURN key until the end of each paragraph. If you make a mistake on the same line as the cursor, backspace and enter the correct character. If you make a mistake on a line preceding the cursor, do not correct it. You will correct it in the next lesson.

8. Save the letter with the ^KD command.

9. Power down the computer.

10. Remove the disks and store them properly. *Note:* Steps 9 and 10 may be reversed depending on your particular computer power-down instructions.

4. Cursor Movements and Printing

OBJECTIVES:

1. Move the cursor through a document.
2. Scan a document by screen.
3. Scroll through a document.
4. Print a document file.

MOVING THE CURSOR THROUGH A DOCUMENT

The cursor can be moved around to various places within the document. Some computers have special-function keys designed to move the cursor. Some computers have arrow keys to move the cursor. In this lesson, use the WordStar commands for moving the cursor. It is recommended that you learn the WordStar cursor command movements even though your computer may have the function and arrow keys. Once the commands are mastered, editing becomes very fast because the fingers do not leave the home-row keys to execute commands.

Basically, the cursor movement commands are executed from the left side of the keyboard by the left hand along with the Ctrl key. Look closely at Figure 4.1 which shows the cursor keys at the left side of the keyboard.

Figure 4.1   The Cursor Keys

The upper keys point the cursor up the document, the lower keys point the cursor down the document, the left letters point the cursor to the left, and the right letters point the cursor to the right.

Notice that the letters E, S, D, X form a diamond. Think of this cursor diamond as you move the cursor up, down, left, and right. If you have access to a computer now, practice the cursor movement commands in the file you created in the previous lesson called HOLLIS.LTR. If you do not have a computer, study the following cursor movement commands. The computer exercise at the end of this lesson will give you further opportunity to move the cursor through a document.

When the computer has been powered up and the **A>** is displayed, you can get into a WordStar document in Drive B quickly without changing logged disk drives. To go directly to Drive B from the operating system prompt **A>**, enter *WS B:HOLLIS.LTR* and press ENTER/RETURN. B:HOLLIS.LTR should appear on the status line of the main menu. The cursor should be at the beginning of the document on line 1, column 1. If you do not get into the HOLLIS.LTR in Drive B after keying in *WS B:HOLLIS.LTR* at the **A>**, check to make sure that you left a space after entering *WS*.

The cursor will move down one line if you strike $^\wedge X$ (uppercase or lowercase). Remember that the $^\wedge$ symbol stands for the Ctrl key. You must hold down the Ctrl key while striking the X. If the cursor does not move down one line, you did not hold the Ctrl key completely down while striking X. When this happens, an X appears on the screen. Ignore any characters that may appear on your screen as a result of these cursor movement exercises. You will learn how to delete these characters in another lesson.

The cursor moves up one line when you strike $^\wedge E$. The cursor moves to the right, character by character, when you strike $^\wedge D$. The cursor moves to the left, character by character, when you strike $^\wedge S$. Notice that the up ($^\wedge E$), down ($^\wedge X$), right ($^\wedge D$), and left ($^\wedge S$) cursor movements form the cursor diamond as shown in Figure 4.2.

Figure 4.2   The Cursor Diamond

The cursor moves to the right, word by word, when you strike $\wedge F$. The cursor will move left, word by word, when you strike $\wedge A$. The cursor diamond may be widened by the $\wedge A$ (word left) and $\wedge F$ (word right) commands. Figure 4.3 illustrates the expanded cursor diamond.

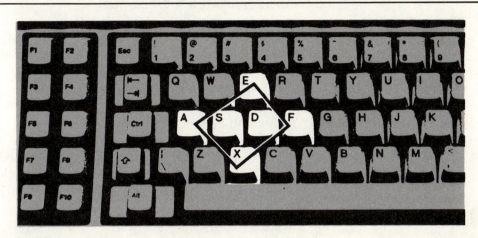

Figure 4.3   The Expanded Cursor Diamond

To move the cursor directly to the end of a line, strike the $\wedge QD$. Strike $\wedge QS$ to move the cursor directly to the beginning of a line. Think of the letter Q in the commands to mean *quick*. The $\wedge QD$ and $\wedge QS$ move the cursor to the end and the beginning of the line quickly. Strike the $\wedge QR$ to get to the beginning of the entire document. To move rapidly to the end of the document, strike $\wedge QC$. A summary of the cursor movement commands is listed in Figure 4.4.

```
Down by line            ^X      Right by word        ^F
Up by line              ^E      Left by word         ^A

Right by character      ^D      Line End             ^QD
Left by character       ^S      Line Beginning       ^QS

End of file             ^QC     Beginning of file    ^QR
```

Figure 4.4   The Cursor Movement Commands

Scrolling by Screen

A document can be viewed screen by screen. The following commands permit you to read a document from the screen without moving the cursor.

Strike $\wedge C$ to scroll the text up, screen by screen to view the end of the document. Remember the bottom cursor keys point to the end of the document. The text is being scrolled up by screen to reach the document's end. Strike the letter ^R to scroll toward the beginning of the document, screen by screen. The top cursor keys point the cursor to the beginning of the document. The text is being scrolled down by screen to reach the document's beginning.

Scrolling Through a Document

To scroll to the end of a document, strike the letter ^Z. (You will notice that the cursor does not move when using the scroll commands.) Strike ^W to reach the beginning of the document. The document can be scanned from the beginning to the end with one command. Strike the letters ^QZ and the document will scroll continuously to the end of the file.

When the command to scroll is given, a prompt "Type 1 - 9 to vary speed" is displayed. The lower the number, the faster the scrolling speed. If you key-in 2 at the prompt, the scroll will be fast. If you key-in 8 at the prompt, the speed will be slow as the document is scrolled to the end. The scroll may be stopped at any point by striking the space bar. Strike the letters ^QW to scroll continuously to the beginning of the document. The scrolling speed can be increased by entering a low number (from 1 to 9) and can be decreased by entering a high number (from 1 to 9) at the prompt. A summary of the scroll commands is listed in Figure 4.5.

```
To Get To Document End            To Get To Document Beginning

Text scrolls by screen    ^C       Text scrolls by screen    ^R
Text scrolls by line      ^Z       Text scrolls by line      ^W
Continuous scroll         ^QZ      Continuous scroll         ^QW
(strike (1-9 to vary speed)        (strike 1-9 to vary speed)
```

Figure 4.5   A Summary of Scroll Commands

PRINT A DOCUMENT FILE

The print command is executed from the opening menu. But before the file can be printed, it must be saved. You will recall that the command to save is ^KD. Power up the printer and position the paper properly. The paper should be at the top of the paper bail. Strike the letter P. The screen shows "Name of File To Print?" Enter the file name and strike the Esc key. The document file will begin to print. If the file does not print, you may have struck the ENTER/RETURN key instead of the Esc key. If so, a number of questions will appear on the screen. Press the ENTER/RETURN key after each question.

LESSON 4 EXERCISE

Name _____ Date _____

TRUE/FALSE

Each of the following statements is either true or false. Indicate your choice in the Answers column by circling T for a true statement or F for a false statement.

1. Some computers have special-function keys and arrow keys that will move the cursor through a document. (Obj. 1) ....   1. **T**   **F**

2. The cursor movement commands are executed with a Ctrl key and keys on the right side of the keyboard. (Obj. 1) ....   2. **T**   **F**

3. A WordStar command will not execute if the Ctrl key is not held down firmly along with another key or keys. (Obj. 1) ....   3. **T**   **F**

4. The command to move the cursor to the end of the line quickly is $\wedge D$. (Obj. 1) ....   4. **T**   **F**

5. If the $\wedge C$ command is given to scroll by screen, the document will advance down. (Obj. 3) ....   5. **T**   **F**

6. If the document is scrolling down continuously, the beginning of the document will eventually come to the screen. (Obj. 3) ....   6. **T**   **F**

7. Scrolling speed can be regulated by entering a number from 1 to 9. (Obj. 3) ....   7. **T**   **F**

8. Scrolling can be stopped by striking the space bar. (Obj. 3) ....   8. **T**   **F**

9. The print command is given from the opening menu. (Obj. 4)..............   9. **T**   **F**

10. The Ctrl key must be pressed before the command to print is executed. (Obj. 4) ....   10. **T**   **F**

COMPLETION

Indicate the correct WordStar command for each function.

1. Move the cursor down by line. (Obj. 2) .... 1. _____

2. Move the cursor up by line. (Obj. 2) .... 2. _____

3. Move the cursor right one character. (Obj. 2) .... 3. _____

4. Move the cursor left one character. (Obj. 2) .... 4. _____

5. Move the cursor by word to the right. (Obj. 2) .... 5. _____

6. Move the cursor by word to the left. (Obj. 2) .... 6. _____

7. Move the cursor to the end of a line quickly. (Obj. 2)... 7. _____

8. Move the cursor to the beginning of a line quickly. (Obj. 2) .... 8. _____

9. Move the cursor to the beginning of the document. (Obj. 2) .... 9. _____

10. Move the cursor to the end of the document. (Obj. 2)...   10. _____

11. From which side of the keyboard are the cursor movement commands executed? (Obj. 1) ....   11. _____

12. Which keys in the cursor diamond point the cursor toward the beginning of the document? (Obj. 1) ....   12. _____

13. Which keys in the cursor diamond point the cursor toward the end of the document? (Obj. 1) ....   13. _____

14. After you power up the computer, at the **A>** you must key-in what command to go directly to Drive B and a file called HOLLIS.LTR without changing logged disk drives? (Obj. 1) ....   14. _____

15. The command to move the cursor down by a line is *?* (Obj. 1) ....   15. _____

16. The command to move the cursor up by a line is *?* (Obj. 1) ....   16. _____

17. The command to move the cursor to the right by a character is *?* (Obj. 1) ....   17. _____

18. The command to move the cursor to the left by a character is *?* (Obj. 1).......................................   18. _____

19. The command to move the cursor to the right by a word is *?* (Obj. 1)...   19. _____

20. The command to move the cursor to the left by a word is *?* (Obj. 1)...   20. _____

21. The command to move the cursor to the end of the line quickly is *?* (Obj. 1) ....   21. _____

22. The command to move the cursor to the beginning of the line quickly is *?* (Obj. 1).................................   22. _____

23. The command to move the cursor to the beginning of a document quickly is *?* (Obj. 1) ....   23. _____

24. The command to move the cursor to the end of a document quickly is *?* (Obj. 1) ....   24. _____

25. What permits the operator to view the document without moving the cursor *?* (Obj. 2) ....   25. _____

26. The command to scroll by screen to the end of the document is *?* (Obj. 2) ....   26. _____

27. The command to scroll by screen toward the beginning of a document is *?* (Obj. 2)..............................   27. _____

28. The command to scroll by line to reach the end of a document is *?* (Obj. 3) ....   28. _____

29. The command to scroll by line to reach the beginning of a document is *?* (Obj. 3).................................   29. _____

30. To increase the scrolling speed when using the continuous scroll command, do you key-in a high or low number from 1-9? (Obj. 3) ....   30. _____

31. From which menu is the print command executed? (Obj. 4) ....   31. _____

32. The command from the opening menu to print a document is *?* (Obj. 4) ....   32. _____

COMPUTER EXERCISE

Directions: Perform the following activities in the file called HOLLIS.LTR that you created in the computer exercise in Lesson 3.

1. Scroll document to the beginning.

2. Move the cursor to the letter D in Dear.

3. Move the cursor, character by character, to the y in Betty.

4. Move the cursor down to the beginning of the second paragraph to I.

5. Move the cursor, word by word, to the end of the line.

6. Move the cursor, word by word, to the beginning of the line.

7. Move the cursor quickly to the end of the line.

8. Move the cursor quickly to the beginning of the line.

9. Scroll the document to the beginning.

10. Scroll the document to the end.

11. Scroll down, screen by screen, to the beginning of the document.

12. Scroll up, screen by screen, to the end of the document.

13. Move to the beginning of the document quickly.

14. Move to the end of the document quickly.

15. Save and print the file HOLLIS.LTR.

5. Inserting and Deleting Text

OBJECTIVES:

1. Insert text with INSERT ON.

2. Insert a blank line.

3. Delete a character at left.

4. Delete a line to the left of the cursor.

5. Delete a character at the cursor.

6. Delete a word.

7. Delete a line to the right of the cursor.

8. Delete an entire line.

9. Reformat text after insertions and deletions.

INSERTING TEXT WITH INSERT ON

When the WordStar program is started on the computer, certain preset features such as line length, line spacing, and tabs have already been established for you. Another preset feature is INSERT ON. The words INSERT ON appear on the right side of the status line of the main menu when editing a document. INSERT ON means that no material will be lost when text is inserted. If you go back in a document and insert a word before previously entered text, the text after the insert will move to the right.

The insert mode can be changed by the command ^V. To turn INSERT OFF, strike $^\wedge V$ (uppercase or lowercase). To turn INSERT ON back on, strike $^\wedge V$. This is called a **toggle command** because the same command is used to turn INSERT ON off and then back on again.

Look at the sentences in Figure 5.1. The first entry is the sentence as it was originally keyed-in. The second entry shows the word *job* inserted before the word *market* with INSERT ON. The third entry shows the word *job* inserted before the word *market* with INSERT OFF. Notice that when insert is on, no text is lost; when insert is off, one character replaces another.

```
Many forecasts indicate a strong market during the next decade.

Edit with INSERT ON:

Many forecasts indicate a strong job market during the next decade.

Edit with INSERT OFF ^V:

Many forecasts indicate a strong jobket during the next decade.
```

Figure 5.1   Inserting Text with INSERT ON and INSERT OFF

The ENTER/RETURN key will insert blank lines, but sometimes you may want to enter a blank line without the cursor moving down. The command $^\wedge$N will insert a blank line without moving the cursor. Any text beyond the cursor will move down.

Striking the Del (delete) key will delete a character to the left of the cursor. The $^\wedge$QDel ($^\wedge$Q and Del keys) command will delete an entire line to the left of the cursor. The text to the right of the cursor will move to the beginning of the line. The $^\wedge$G command deletes the character at the cursor. The $^\wedge$T command will delete a word to the right of the cursor. The cursor should be on the first character of the word to be deleted. Strike $^\wedge QY$ to delete a line to the right of the cursor. The line to the left of the cursor will remain. Strike $^\wedge Y$ to delete an entire line. Figure 5.2 shows a summary of all the deletion commands.

```
Character at left       Del        Line left of cursor     ^QDel
Character at cursor      ^G        Line right of cursor     ^Qy
Delete word              ^T        Delete line              ^Y
```

Figure 5.2   A Summary Of Deletion Commands

Reformatting Text After Insertions and Deletions

After text has been changed, the format of the paragraph is changed. WordStar will reformat or restore the paragraph to the settings on the ruler line with the command $^\wedge$B. The cursor must be at the beginning of the paragraph that is to be reformatted. The reformatting process continues until the first hard return is reached. A **hard return** is a return keyed-in by the operator. The < graphic on the far right side of the screen indicates a hard return. You must reformat each paragraph separately with the ^B command because reformatting stops at the end of each paragraph. WordStar will also reformat an entire document all at once without stopping at a hard return. This command will be introduced later.

When text is reformatted with the ^B command, it may be necessary to make some hyphenation decisions. When WordStar sees a word that is too long to fit on a line, the reformatting will stop and a message will be displayed in the upper left side of the screen as shown in Figure 5.3.

```
TO HYPHENATE, PRESS -  Before pressing -, you may
    move cursor:  ^S=cursor left, ^D=cursor right
If hyphenation not desired, type ^B
```

Figure 5.3   The Hyphenation Help Display

If you wish to hyphenate a word, move the cursor by using the ^S or ^D commands to the proper hyphenation place and strike the hyphen key. Reformatting will continue. If you do not wish to hyphenate, strike ^B and the paragraph will continue to reformat.

LESSON 5 EXERCISE

Name _____ Date _____

TRUE/FALSE

Each of the following statements is either true or false. Indicate your choice in the Answers column by circling T for a true statement or F for a false statement.

1. The *insert* is *on* when the WordStar program is started on the computer. (Obj. 1) ....

    1. T   F

2. The words INSERT ON appear in the opening menu when the WordStar program is started on the computer. (Obj. 1) ....

    2. T   F

3. No text will be lost when material is inserted with INSERT ON. (Obj. 1)..

    3. T   F

4. The insert mode can be changed by the command $\wedge$V. (Obj. 1).............

    4. T   F

5. The $\wedge$V command must be entered in uppercase. (Obj. 1)..................

    5. T   F

6. The $\wedge$V command is called a toggle command. (Obj. 1) ....

    6. T   F

7. To insert a blank line and move the cursor down, key-in $\wedge$N. (Obj. 2) .....

    7. T   F

8. The ENTER/RETURN key will do the same thing as the $\wedge$N command. (Obj. 2) ....

    8. T   F

9. To delete a character at the left of the cursor, strike the Del key. (Obj. 3)

    9. T   F

10. To delete a line to the left of the cursor, strike $\wedge$QDel. (Obj. 4)............

    10. T   F

11. To delete a character at the cursor, strike $\wedge$G. (Obj. 5)....................

    11. T   F

12. To delete a word, strike $\wedge$QY. (Obj. 6) ....

    12. T   F

13. To delete a line to the right of the cursor, strike $\wedge$QY. (Obj. 7)............

    13. T   F

14. To delete an entire line, strike $\wedge$T. (Obj. 8) ....

    14. T   F

15. WordStar will reformat paragraphs after an edit without any operator command. (Obj. 9) ....

    15. T   F

16. WordStar reformats paragraphs to the settings on the ruler line. (Obj. 9) .

    16. T   F

17. The command to reformat a paragraph is $\wedge$B. (Obj. 9) ....

    17. T   F

18. The cursor must be at the first letter of a paragraph to reformat the entire paragraph. (Obj. 9) ....

    18. T   F

19. Reformatting will stop when the computer sees the first hard return. (Obj. 9) ....

    19. T   F

20. If hyphenation is not desired, strike $\wedge$B to continue the reformatting process. (Obj. 9) ....

    20. T   F

COMPLETION

Give the command for the following functions and indicate the correct answer in the space provided.

1. Turn INSERT ON or INSERT OFF. (Obj. 1) ....   1. _____

2. Insert a blank line. (Obj. 2) ....   2. _____

3. Delete a character at left. (Obj. 3) ....   3. _____

4. Delete a line to the left of the cursor. (Obj. 4) ....   4. _____

5. Delete a character at the cursor. (Obj. 5)...............   5. _____

6. Delete a word. (Obj. 6)...............................   6. _____

7. Delete a line to the right of the cursor. (Obj. 7) ....   7. _____

8. Delete an entire line. (Obj. 8)..........................   8. _____

9. Reformat a paragraph after corrections. (Obj. 9) ....   9. _____

10. Command no hyphenation after the *hyphen help* is displayed. (Obj. 9)...   10. _____

COMPUTER EXERCISE ONE

Directions: Create a file called LESSON5.EX1. Key-in the sentence shown in Figure 5.4. Do not strike ENTER/RETURN after the period. The cursor should remain on the entered line. Make the insertions and deletions as instructed. Insert should be on. If it is not, strike $\wedge V$ to turn it on. If you get into a WordStar command by mistake, strike $\wedge U$ and *Esc*.

Many forecasts indicate a strong market during the next decade.

Figure 5.4   Computer Exercise One

After you key-in the sentence in Figure 5.4, follow these steps to correct the sentence:

1. Move the cursor to the *m* in market.

2. Enter the word *job* and a space.

3. Insert a blank line after moving the cursor to the beginning of the line. Enter another blank line following this line.

4. Move the cursor down two lines to the *m* in market.

5. Delete the word *job*, character by character.

6. Move the cursor to the *i* at the beginning of the word *indicate*.

7. Delete the line to the left of the cursor.

8. Delete the word *indicate*, character by character.

9. Move the cursor to the word *strong*.

10. Delete the word *strong*.

11. Move the cursor to the word *during*.

12. Delete the line to the right of the cursor. The only words left on the line should be *a market*.

13. Delete the entire line.

14. Your screen should be blank. The line has been completely deleted.

COMPUTER EXERCISE TWO

Directions: Enter the following text in a file called LESSON5.EX2. Turn off the right margin justification with ^OJ. Remember, let wordwrap work for you. Do not press the ENTER/RETURN key until you reach the end of the paragraphs. Print Computer Exercise Two. *Note:* If wordwrap does not work, strike ^O to view the on-screen menu. Wordwrap should be turned on. If it is off, strike W to turn it on. If the hyphen does not print in the hyphenated word, *nongoods-producing*, strike ^O to view the on-screen menu. The soft-hyphen display should be OFF to print the hyphen. Strike *E* to turn the soft-hyphen display to off.

MEMO TO ALL WORD PROCESSING OPERATORS

Many forecasts on where the jobs will be during the next decade indicate that there will be many more jobs than people to fill them. Reports show that the population growth of eligible workers will not satisfy the tremendous increase of the growing job market.

Estimates are that the growing job market will average 1.6 million new jobs per year through 1990. Even more startling is the prediction that the nongoods-producing segments of the economy will make up almost 80 percent of all employment. One out of every five workers will be in the clerical field in the year 1990.

Figure 5.5   Computer Exercise Two

COMPUTER EXERCISE THREE

Directions: Make the following corrections in the Computer Exercise Two file named LESSON5.EX2. Print the edited memo.

MEMO TO ALL WORD PROCESSING OPERATORS

Many forecasts on ~~where the~~ jobs ~~will be during~~ *for* the next decade indicate
that there will be many more jobs than people to fill them. Reports show
that the population growth of eligible workers will not satisfy the
tremendous increase of the growing job market.

Estimates are that the growing job market will average 1.6 million new jobs
per year through 1990. ~~Even more startling is the prediction that the~~
~~nongoods-producing segments of the economy will make up almost 80 percent~~
~~of all employment.~~ One out of every five workers will be in the clerical
field in the year 1990.

A shift from blue-collar jobs to white-collar jobs will occur.

Figure 5.6   Computer Exercise Three

6. WordStar Horizontal Page Setup and Help Levels

OBJECTIVES:

1. Describe the horizontal page setup.

2. Change the left margin on the main menu ruler line.

3. Change the right margin on the main menu ruler line.

4. Explain horizontal scrolling.

5. Describe the preset tab settings.

6. Explain the tab command.

7. Set help levels.

THE HORIZONTAL PAGE SETUP

The standard paper width is 8 1/2 inches. WordStar's preset character width is 10 characters per horizontal (across) inch; Word-star's preset line length is 65 characters. Therefore, the preset line length is 6 1/2 inches long (65 characters in the line length divided by 10 characters per inch).

When the paper is positioned in the printer properly, Word-Star will start printing eight characters from the left edge of the paper (or almost one inch). The term, **page offset**, refers to the space between the left edge of the paper and the start of printed text. The default value, then, for page offset is the dot command *.PO 8*. A **dot command** is a dot (.) and two letters that are embedded in a document to change a default. Of course, you do not enter this command since it is a default. If you would like to change the number of spaces in the left margin when using the preset line length of 65, key-in the dot command *.PO* and the number of spaces you want. As with all dot commands, it is keyed-in at column 1. For example, if you do not want to change the preset line length and want the left margin to print four spaces from the left edge of the paper, key-in *.PO 4*. (Another way to change the page offset is to change the left margin setting. This is discussed later in this lesson.)

The preset character width of 10 horizontal spaces to an inch can be illustrated by the dot command *.CW 12*. Again, you would not need to enter this because *.CW 12* is the character-width default. Character width is calculated in 120th of an inch. See page 254. To print out 12 characters per inch, you must enter the dot command *.CW 10* (10/120) at column 1 at the beginning of the document. The horizontal page setup and the default values are illustrated in Figure 6.1.

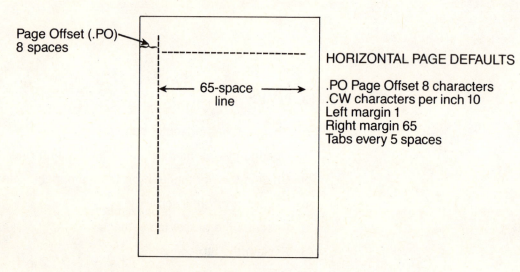

Page Offset (.PO)
8 spaces

65-space
line

HORIZONTAL PAGE DEFAULTS

.PO Page Offset 8 characters
.CW characters per inch 10
Left margin 1
Right margin 65
Tabs every 5 spaces

Figure 6.1   The Horizontal Page Setup and Defaults

CHANGING MARGINS ON THE MAIN MENU RULER LINE

The left margin can be changed from column 1 of the main menu ruler line by striking ^O and the *L* key. When ^OL is keyed-in, your screen will show the prompt as illustrated in Figure 6.2.

```
LEFT MARGIN COLUMN NUMBER (ESCAPE for cursor column)?_
```

Figure 6.2   Setting a New Left Margin

Enter the column number and press ENTER/RETURN. The left margin will change on the main menu ruler line to reflect the new setting. If you strike the Esc key, the left margin will change to reflect the column number where the cursor was when you keyed-in

^OL. So if the cursor is at column 5 and you key-in ^*OL* and *Esc*, the left margin will be set at column 5.

The right margin can be changed from column 65 by striking ^*O* and the letter *R*. When ^OR is entered, a prompt is displayed as illustrated in Figure 6.3. Enter the new column number and an ENTER/RETURN. If you strike the Esc key, the right margin will reflect the column number where the cursor was when you keyed-in ^OR.

```
RIGHT MARGIN COLUMN NUMBER (ESCAPE for cursor column)?_
```

Figure 6.3   Setting a New Right Margin

HORIZONTAL SCROLLING

A total of 80 characters can be displayed across a computer screen. But you may want to set a right margin beyond column 80 to print on paper wider than 8 1/2 inches. Enter the column number after the ^OR command and strike ENTER/RETURN. As text is entered with this new right margin setting, the symbol + will appear on the right side of the screen. This + symbol means that text is beyond column 80. Using the cursor control movements ^*QD* (line end quickly) or ^*D* (character right) will move you through column 80 after the text has been entered. The column number on the status line will reflect the wide right margin setting as the cursor moves beyond column 80. To return the cursor to the left side of the screen, press ^*QS* (line beginning quickly) or ^*S* (character left).

PRESET TAB SETTINGS

The preset ruler line on the main menu shows the ! symbol every 5 spaces. Changing these settings will be discussed in a later lesson. Tabs can be inserted on the screen by striking the Tab key or ^*I*. There is no tab graphic that displays when the Tab key or ^I is struck. But the text will be indented when these keys are struck and the screen will reflect this indention.

When you print a WordStar document file, the print will look exactly like the screen display. This is an important feature, making the task of formatting documents much easier before the final printing.

HELP LEVELS

You probably have noticed that WordStar features many types of menus that help the word processing operator enter the correct command. WordStar contains over 120 single commands, making it one of the most sophisticated word processing software packages on the market. Because of the WordStar menus, you do not have to consult manuals to find the correct command for your formatting and printing needs. (A thorough explanation of all the menus is in a later lesson.)

The menus, the status line, and the ruler line all take up space on the screen. You have the option of changing the amount of on-screen help, giving you more room for text. The help level is preset at level 3. Level 3 gives the most on-screen help. Level 2 omits the main menu display, leaving only the status line and the ruler line. However, menus can be brought to the screen by striking the Ctrl key and the menu letter. Level 1 omits access to any menu. Level 0 omits all explanation of any commands.

The help level can be changed two ways. One way is by striking *H* from the opening menu before you create or edit a file. Another way is to enter $\wedge JH$ from the main menu when you are in a document file. Either way, the screen will display text and a question as illustrated in Figure 6.4. Enter 2, 1, or 0 to the question. Only the status line and the ruler line will be displayed at the top of the screen.

```
HELP LEVELS
    3   all menus and explanations displayed
    2   main editing menu (1-control-char commands) suppressed
    1   prefix menus (2-character commands) also suppressed
    0   command explanations (including this) also suppressed

CURRENT HELP LEVEL IS 3

ENTER Space OR NEW HELP LEVEL (0, 1, 2, OR 3):
```

Figure 6.4   The Help Level Command Display

LESSON 6 EXERCISE

Name _____ Date _____

TRUE/FALSE

Each of the following statements is either true or false. Indicate your choice in the Answers column by circling T for a true statement or F for a false statement.

Answers

1. WordStar's preset character width is 12 characters per inch. (Obj. 1) ......   1. T F

2. WordStar's preset line length is 65 characters. (Obj. 1) ....   2. T F

3. Page offset refers to the space between the left edge of the paper and the beginning of text. (Obj. 1) ....   3. T F

4. The default for page offset is 8 characters. (Obj. 1) ....   4. T F

5. To change the left margin to 10 without changing the preset line length, key-in *.PO 10*. (Obj. 1) ....   5. T F

6. To change the character width from 10 to 12, key-in *.CW 12*. (Obj. 1) .....   6. T F

7. Tabs are set every 10 spaces on the main menu ruler line. (Obj. 1) ....   7. T F

8. The left margin can be changed on the main menu ruler line by the command ^OR. (Obj. 2) ....   8. T F

9. The left margin can be changed by striking the Esc key at the command ^OL prompt. (Obj. 2) ....   9. T F

10. The right margin can be changed by the command ^OR. (Obj. 3) ....   10. T F

11. A total of 85 characters can be displayed on most computer screens. (Obj. 4)   11. T F

12. The symbol < is displayed when text moves beyond column 80. (Obj. 4) ..   12. T F

13. The cursor movement commands ^QD and ^D will move the cursor to the left side of the screen. (Obj. 4) ....   13. T F

14. The tabs cannot be changed. (Obj. 5) ....   14. T F

15. A tab graphic will display when the *Tab* key or ^I is struck. (Obj. 6) ......   15. T F

16. The printout will look exactly like the entered text on the screen. (Obj. 6)   16. T F

17. The default help level is 0. (Obj. 7) ....   17. T F

18. Only the status line and the ruler line will be displayed at help level 3. (Obj. 7) ....   18. T F

19. The menus can be displayed on the screen with the ^ and prefix menu letter at help level 2. (Obj. 7) ....   19. T F

20. The help level can be changed from the main menu only. (Obj. 7) ....   20. T F

21. The help level can be changed by keying-in *H* from the opening menu. (Obj. 7) ....   21. T F

22. The help level can be changed by keying-in ^*JH* from the main menu. (Obj. 7) ....   22. T F

COMPLETION

Indicate the correct answer in the space provided.

1. Give the measurements of a standard sheet of paper. (Obj. 1) ....   1. _____

2. Give the preset character width in characters per horizontal inch. (Obj. 1) ....   2. _____

3. What is the preset line length? (Obj. 1) ....   3. _____

4. How many characters are in the default for the page offset? (Obj. 1) ....   4. _____

5. The .PO dot command stands for *?* (Obj. 1) ....   5. _____

6. The left margin can be changed by the page offset dot command or by changing the left margin on the ruler line in which menu? (Obj. 1) ....   6. _____

7. The default for the printed character width is *?* (Obj. 1)   7. _____

8. If the dot command .CW 12 is entered, how many characters per inch will the printout show? (Obj. 1) ....   8. _____

9. The left margin is preset at *?* (Obj. 1) ....   9. _____

10. The right margin is preset at *?* (Obj. 1) ....   10. _____

11. The command to change the left margin on the main menu ruler line is *?* (Obj. 2) ....   11. _____

12. The command to change the right margin on the main menu ruler line is *?* (Obj. 3) ....   12. _____

13. Which key can be used to place the left or right margin at the cursor position? (Objs. 2, 3) ....   13. _____

14. How many total characters can be displayed horizontally on the screen? (Obj. 4) ....   14. _____

15. What symbol will appear on the far right side of the screen as text is entered with the right margin set beyond 80? (Obj. 4) ....   15. _____

16. What two cursor commands will move the cursor beyond column 80 when margins are set for wide documents? (Obj. 4) ....   16. a. _____
    b. _____

17. What two cursor commands will move the cursor back to the left side of the screen when scrolling through wide documents? (Obj. 4) ....   17. a. _____
    b. _____

18. How many spaces apart are the preset tabs set? (Obj. 5)   18. _____

19. The help level can be changed from the opening menu by entering the command *?* (Obj. 7) ....   19. _____

20. The help level is preset at *?* (Obj. 7) ....   20. _____

COMPUTER EXERCISE

Directions: Key-in the paragraph shown in Figure 6.5. Name the file MARGINS. Set the left margin at 10 and the right margin at 55. Key-in the paragraph again, this time with the left margin set at 5 and the right margin set at 60. Key-in the paragraph a third time. Set the left margin at 1 and the right margin at 100. Delete the third paragraph you keyed-in since some printers may be unable to print with a right margin of 100. Set the help level at 2. Print the document called MARGINS.

```
WordStar has two other options that are valuable to any word

processing system; they are MailMerge and SpellStar.  The SpellStar program

finds spelling and typing errors.  This can save you countless hours of

proofreading.  The MailMerge option enables you to merge data from two or

more files at print time.  Any work that requires merging data from

multiple sources into a single file can be performed through MailMerge.
```

Figure 6.5   Text for Computer Exercise

7. WordStar Vertical Page Setup and Pagination _____

OBJECTIVES:

1. Describe the vertical page layout.

2. Describe the page break default.

3. Change the page break default.

4. Describe page number default.

5. Omit page numbering.

VERTICAL PAGE LAYOUT

The most commonly used paper size is 8 1/2 inches wide by 11 inches long. Most printers will print 6 vertical (up and down) lines to an inch; therefore, a full sheet of standard-size paper will have a total of 66 lines from top to bottom (ll inches long multiplied by 6 lines per inch).

WordStar automatically sets the paper length at 66 lines. This default (preset) value can be shown in a dot command .PL 66. As explained in Lesson 6, a dot command is a dot (.) and two letters that are embedded in a document to change a default. It is not necessary to key-in the dot command *.PL 66* because the paper length of 66 lines is a default. But if you ever print on paper that is shorter or longer than 66 lines or 11 inches, you can embed the dot command .PL and key-in the paper length. For example, if your paper is 11 7/10 inches long (the standard-length paper in Britain) you would embed a dot command to change the paper length default. The dot command would be .PL 70 (ll 7/10 inches long times 6 lines per inch). The letters PL in the command stand for paper length. It is necessary to use the dot command .PL for nonstandard-length paper in order for the printer to advance a page properly. You will want to change the preset paper length when printing envelopes. Since a business envelope is 4 inches long, key-in *.PL 24* (4 inches long X 6 lines to an inch) and the envelope will advance to print the next envelope in the printer.

Dot commands must always be keyed-in at column 1. If they do not start at column 1, they print out. Dot commands should be followed by a hard return.

WordStar automatically sets a margin top of three lines. This means that the print will start on the fourth line. If you want to change the margin top, the dot command is .MT and the appropriate number of lines. MT stands for margin top. For example, if you want a margin top of six lines instead of three, embed the dot command .MT 6 at column one at the beginning of your file.

WordStar automatically sets a margin bottom of eight lines. This means that the printer will advance to a new page when eight lines remain at the bottom of the page. If you want to change this eight-line margin-bottom default, embed the dot command .MB and the appropriate number of lines. MB stands for margin bottom. For example, if you want a margin bottom of ten, embed .MB 10 and an ENTER/RETURN at column 1 at the file beginning. Because the margin top is preset at 3 lines and the margin bottom is preset at 8 lines, there will be 55 lines of text printed on a page (the 66 line page length minus a total of 11 lines for the top and bottom margins).

Figure 7.1 illustrates the default vertical page layout for paper length, margin top, and margin bottom and also gives the dot commands to change these vertical page defaults.

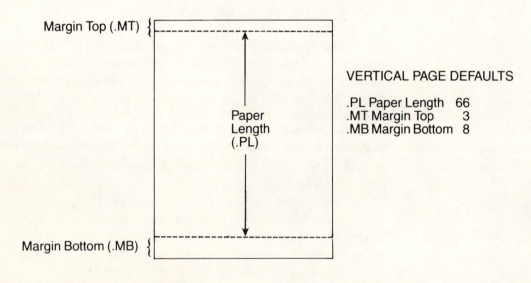

VERTICAL PAGE DEFAULTS

.PL Paper Length   66
.MT Margin Top   3
.MB Margin Bottom   8

Figure 7.1   The Vertical Page Defaults

PRESET PAGE BREAKS

WordStar automatically starts a new page after 55 lines of text have been entered. You do not have to worry about where to start a new page. The page break appears on your screen as illustrated in Figure 7.2.

--P

Figure 7.2   The Page Break Display

The page break display shows a line of hyphens with the letter P at the end of the line. This display will not print. It is shown in your file to indicate where the page will break during printing. If the page break display does not appear on your screen, it may be turned off. You can turn it back on with the command ^OP. To determine if the display has been turned off, look at the on-screen menu by striking ^O. Figure 7.3 shows the on-screen menu.

```
                    < < <  O N S C R E E N   M E N U  > > >
-Margins & Tabs-  : -Line  Functions- :  --More Toggles-- :  -Other  Menus-
L Set left margin :C Center text       :J Justify   now OFF : (from Main only)
R Set right margin:S Set line spacing  :V Vari-Tabs now ON  :^J Help  ^K Block
X Release margins :                    :H Hyph-help now OFF :^Q Quick ^P Print
I Set  N Clear tab:   ---Toggles---    :E Soft hyph now OFF :^O Onscreen
G Paragraph tab   :W Wrd wrap now ON   :D Prnt disp now ON  :Space Bar returns
F Ruler from line :T Rlr line now ON   :F Pge break now ON  :you to Main Menu.
```

Figure 7.3   The On-Screen Menu

If the page break display is turned OFF, turn it back on by striking the letter P (uppercase or lowercase). If the page break display is already on, exit the on-screen menu by striking the space bar. The ^OP command turns the page break display on and off and is therefore a *toggle* command.

Changing the Default Page Breaks

When keying-in a manuscript, you will want to follow the guideline of always placing at least two lines of text in a paragraph at the beginning and end of each page. When keying-in tables, you will want to keep the table on one page if possible.

WordStar permits you to change the preset page advance. You can change the place where a new page will start with the dot command .PA (uppercase or lowercase) and an ENTER/RETURN. This command is entered at column 1 above the line you wish to print on a new page. PA stands for page advance. Figure 7.4 illustrates the screen display after the .PA page advance command is keyed-in. (If this display prints on your printout, the dot command was not keyed-in at column 1.)

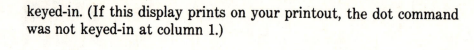

Figure 7.4   The Page Advance Dot Command Display

Page Number Default and Omitting Page Numbers

A page number beginning with the numeral 1 prints out automatically at the bottom and center of each page by default. The numbers increase by one as the pages are printed.

When printing letters and memorandums, you will not want to have the page numbers printed. Page numbering can be canceled by using the dot command .OP (uppercase or lowercase) and an ENTER/RETURN at column 1 at the beginning of your document file. OP stands for omit page numbering.

The page numbering default can be turned back on again with the dot command .PN and an ENTER/RETURN at column one in the file. This command may be be entered anywhere in the document to reinstate the page numbering after it has been turned off.

LESSON 7 EXERCISE   Name _____ Date _____

TRUE/FALSE

Each of the following statements is either true or false. Indicate your choice in the Answers column by circling T for a true statement or F for a false statement.

Answers

1. A standard sheet of paper is 11 inches long. (Obj. 1) .... 1.   T   F
2. Most printers will print eight vertical lines to an inch. (Obj. 1) .... 2.   T   F
3. The WordStar default is 66 lines for paper length. (Obj. 1) .... 3.   T   F
4. A dot command is used to change a default. (Obj. 1) .... 4.   T   F
5. .PL is the dot command to change the paper length. (Obj. 1) .... 5.   T   F
6. Dot commands may be entered at any column number. (Obj. 1)............ 6.   T   F
7. The command to change the paper length for paper that is 5 1/2 inches long would be .PL 33. (Obj. 1) .... 7.   T   F
8. The paper length should be changed if paper is shorter or longer than 11 inches. (Obj. 1)... 8.   T   F
9. WordStar has a preset margin top of eight lines. (Obj. 1) .... 9.   T   F
10. WordStar has a preset margin bottom of eight lines. (Obj. 1) .... 10. T   F
11. .TM is the dot command to change the margin top. (Obj. 1)............... 11. T   F
12. .MB is the dot command to change the margin bottom. (Obj. 1) .... 12. T   F
13. The page break display will print. (Obj. 2).................................. 13. T   F
14. The page break display must be keyed-in by the operator. (Obj. 2) .... 14. T   F
15. The page break display may be turned on and off by the ^OP toggle command. (Obj. 2) .... 15. T   F
16. The on screen menu will indicate if the page display is turned off. (Obj. 2) 16. T   F
17. The operator cannot change the place where a page will break. (Obj. 3)... 17. T   F
18. The command .PA and an ENTER/RETURN will start a new page. (Obj. 3) 18. T   F
19. The command .PA will print if it is keyed-in at column 5. (Obj. 3)......... 19. T   F
20. The page numbers print automatically at the top of each page. (Obj. 4) ... 20. T   F
21. The command .OP and an ENTER/RETURN will omit page numbering. (Obj. 5) .... 21. T   F
22. The page numbering can be turned back on with the command .OP keyed-in at column 1. (Obj. 5)... 22. T   F

COMPLETION

Indicate the correct answer in the space provided.

1. The most commonly used paper size is *?* (Obj. 1)........   1. _____

2. How many vertical lines to an inch will most printers print? (Obj. 1)...........................   2. _____

3. WordStar automatically sets the paper length at how many lines? (Obj. 1) ....   3. _____

4. To change the paper length for the printout, you must key-in what command in addition to the paper length (in lines) at column 1 at the beginning of the document? (Obj. 1) ....   4. _____

5. A dot command must always be keyed-in at which column? (Obj. 1) ....   5. _____

6. How many lines are preset for the top margin? (Obj. 1)   6. _____

7. How many lines are preset for the bottom margin? (Obj. 1) ....   7. _____

8. To change the top margin to begin text on line 7, what dot command should be keyed-in at column 1? (Obj. 1) .   8. _____

9. To change the bottom margin to leave ten lines at the bottom of a page, what dot command should be keyed-in at column 1? (Obj. 1) ....   9. _____

10. WordStar automatically starts a new page after how many lines of text have been entered? (Obj. 2) ....   10. _____

11. What two things indicate a page break display on a line of the screen?...........................   11. a. _____
    b. _____

12. If the page break does not display, what must you strike to turn on the display? (Obj. 2)........................   12. _____

13. Which menu shows whether the page break display is turned off or on? (Obj. 2)...........................   13. _____

14. After viewing the on-screen menu with the ^O command, you can exit the menu by striking *?* (Obj. 2).....   14. _____

15. The dot command to start a required new page is *?* (Obj. 3) ....   15. _____

16. The dot command to omit page numbering is *?* (Obj. 5)   16. _____

17. Where will the page number print on the page? (Obj. 5)   17. _____

18. What dot command must you key-in to turn the page numbering back on if it has been turned off? (Obj. 5) ..   18. _____

COMPUTER EXERCISE ONE

Directions: Key-in the report in Figure 7.5. Name the document LESSON7.EX1. Do not make any changes in the preset format. To reset any WordStar defaults that may have been changed, enter WordStar from the operating system. If you are now in WordStar, strike *X* from the opening menu to get into the operating system. Then enter WS B:LESSON7.EX1 at the **A>** or WS LESSON7.EX1 at the **B>**. Triple space after the heading. Double space between paragraphs. Use help level 2 to get maximum screen display. Print out the document.

WORD PROCESSING AND TODAY'S SECRETARY

Word processing is much more than a method for producing documents efficiently on a computer. It is an important career objective which offers challenge and opportunity to those who qualify.

Large word processing centers have opened in most major corporations replacing typing pools. The secretary's job has changed significantly due to the computer revolution. Word processing terminals are replacing typewriters forcing office support people to retrain for their changing role within the company.

A typing speed of at least 45 words per minute is required for most word processing students. Industry will require a typing speed of at least 65 words per minute for word processing operators.

Excellent business English, spelling, proofreading, and machine transcription skills are also essential for the career word processor. These important skills are taught in many vocational centers around the country.

Many vocational training centers have waiting lists of people who desire word processing training. Computer training is in great demand. Office support personnel who continue to keep up with the dynamic office automation explosion have many new job opportunities. Some of the new job titles that have opened up in the word processing field are:

word processing trainee

word processing specialist

word processing trainer

word processing supervisor

proofreader

There are many different kinds of word processors in industry today. WordStar is among the most commonly used word processing packages for microcomputers in industry. But there are also computers that will only do word processing tasks. These computers are called dedicated word processors because they only perform word processing tasks.

Whether you are preparing for a word processing career or preparing for a career in or out of the office environment, computer knowledge is essential.

Figure 7.5   Computer Exercise One

COMPUTER EXERCISE TWO

Directions: Make the changes (shown in Figure 7.6) in the file called LESSON7.EX1 you created in Computer Exercise One. Omit the page numbering. Insert the page breaks where required. Omit the right margin justification. Reformat each paragraph after corrections after moving the cursor to the first letter in each paragraph. Do not hyphenate.

WORD PROCESSING AND TODAY'S SECRETARY

Word processing is ~~much~~ more than a method for producing documents ~~efficiently~~ on a computer. It is an important career objective which offers challenge and opportunity to those who qualify.

Large word processing centers have opened in ~~most~~ *all* major corporations replacing typing pools. The secretary's job has changed significantly due to the computer revolution. Word processing terminals are replacing typewriters forcing office support people to retrain for their changing role within the company.

A typing speed of at least 45 words per minute is required for most word processing students. Industry will require a typing speed of at least 65 words per minute for word processing operators.
——— *new page*

Excellent business English, spelling, proofreading, and machine transcription skills are also essential for the career word processor. These important skills are taught in many vocational centers around the country. *No ¶*

No ¶ Many vocational training centers have waiting lists of people who desire word processing training. Computer training is in great demand. Office support personnel who continue to keep up with the dynamic office automation explosion have many new job opportunities. Some of the new job titles that have opened up in the word processing field are:

word processing trainee

word processing specialist

word processing trainer

word processing supervisor

proofreader
——— *new page*

There are many different kinds of word processors in industry today. WordStar is among the most commonly used word processing packages for microcomputers in industry. But there are also computers that will only do word processing tasks. These computers are called dedicated word processors because they only perform word processing tasks. *Some common dedicated word processors in industry are:*

~~Whether you are preparing for a word processing career or preparing~~ ℓ ~~for a career in or out of the office environment, computer knowledge is~~ ℓ ~~essential.~~ ℓ

the Wang Word Processor

NBI

VYDEC

IBM Office System 6

Figure 7.6   Computer Exercise Two

8. Margins ─────────────────────────────

OBJECTIVES:

1. Change margins from the main menu ruler line.

2. Explain how to change the even right margin to an uneven right margin.

3. Describe how to release margins.

4. Explain the nonprinting ruler line.

5. Change margins from the nonprinting ruler line.

6. Change margins from existing text.

7. Change the margin top.

8. Change the margin bottom.

CHANGING MARGINS FROM THE MAIN MENU RULER LINE

Lesson 6 explained in detail how to change the left and the right margins from the main menu. Remember, the margins are preset at columns 1 and 65. These settings will give you margins of about one inch on the right and left side of a standard sheet of paper if you print out in the default of ten character widths to an inch.

The left margin is changed by the command ^OL. When the ^OL command is entered, a prompt appears asking for the column number of the new left margin. Key-in the column number plus an ENTER/RETURN. The ruler line will reflect the new left margin setting.

The right margin is changed by entering the command ^OR. A prompt will be displayed asking for the column number of the new right margin. Key-in the new right margin column number and an ENTER/RETURN. The ruler line will reflect the new right margin setting.

The left and right margins can also be changed by striking the Esc key at the ^OL and ^OR prompt commands. The margins will change to reflect the column number where the cursor was at the time the ^OL or ^OR command was entered.

Uneven and Even Right Margins

WordStar will print an even right margin. This is called **right margin justification**. The problem with printing with the justification turned on is that the printout has extra spaces between words to make the right margin even.

Justification should be turned off when creating business letters and tables. When justification is turned off, the right margin will be ragged (uneven). The command to turn off a justified right margin is ^OJ. It is a toggle command and is used to toggle the justification on and off. You can check whether justification is on or off by viewing the on-screen menu with the ^O command when editing a document. If, after viewing the on-screen menu you do not wish to change the mode, strike the space bar to remove the on-screen menu display. If you wish to change the justification mode, strike *J* while the on-screen menu is displayed.

Releasing Margins

The margin release command is useful when text needs to be inserted to the left or right of margin settings. Keying beyond the right margin is done by using the ^OX command. After striking ^*OX*, the words MAR REL will appear on the status line as illustrated in Figure 8.1. You can continue to key data beyond the right margin until you press the ENTER/RETURN key.

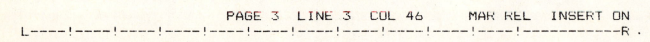

Figure 8.1   The Margin Release Display

The left margin cannot be released beyond column 1. But if the left margin is changed to column 10, for example, you can key-in data to the left of column 10 by using the ^OX command. Figure 8.2 illustrates how the status line appears when the margin release is on and the left margin is set at 10.

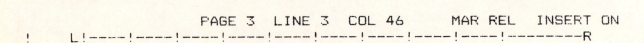

Figure 8.2   The Ruler Line for Left Margin Release

Notice that the tab graphic ! appears to the left of the L at position 5 in Figure 8.2. This indicates that the margin release is on and the cursor can be moved to the left of the margin setting (10). After the text is inserted beyond the left margin and the set left margin is reached (in this case column 10), the ruler line returns to the normal display (omitting the ! beyond 10). Notice also that the drive and document file name is omitted on the status line when margin release is on.

Paragraphs do not reformat properly when some lines have been entered outside of the margin settings with the margin release. This is because reformatting always matches the ruler line margin and tab settings. So after the ^B command, any line that needs to be outside of the margins will have to be entered again. The ^OX margin release command is canceled by entering ^OX again or by pressing the ENTER/RETURN key.

THE NONPRINTING RULER LINE

You can create a ruler line similar to the one below the status line anywhere in your document. When keying-in a nonprinting ruler line, you are creating an alternate ruler line. A nonprinting ruler line is displayed on the screen showing the margin and tab settings, but as the name implies the ruler line will not print out.

Alternate ruler lines are helpful when typing tables or other text within a document that has an unusual format. It is extremely helpful to see the format changes on your screen. You will recall that the main menu ruler line will reflect the margins and tabs set by default (if entering WordStar from the operating system) or will reflect the margins and tabs set on a previous document (if entering a document from the opening menu). Therefore, you do not know exactly where the margins and tabs might have been set in a document. A nonprinting ruler line will show the document formats and will never change unless changed by the operator.

A nonprinting ruler line command is entered by keying-in two dots (..), ^P, and ENTER/RETURN. The screen will look like Figure 8.3 after the command is given.

..   –

Figure 8.3   The Nonprinting Ruler Line Display

Notice the hyphen (-) at the far right in Figure 8.3. This is a flag character indicating that the next typed line will not print. The two dots (..) must be keyed-in at column 1 or the alternate ruler line will print. The ruler line itself is a series of hyphens (-) beginning at the column where you want your left margin to begin and ending at the column where you want your right margin to end.

Setting Margins on the Nonprinting Ruler Line

To set a left margin of 10, for example, and a right margin of 55, begin the line of hyphens at column 10 and end the line of hyphens at column 55. Your nonprinting ruler line will now look like Figure 8.4.

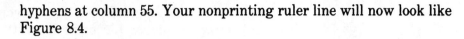

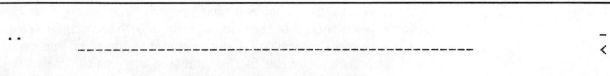

Figure 8.4   The Nonprinting Ruler Line and Hyphen Display

If you have set a left margin other than 1 on the main menu ruler line, you will be unable to key-in the dot command at column 1. To move the cursor to column 1, enter the margin release command ^OX and move the cursor to column 1. Then key-in the dot command (..^P ENTER/RETURN).

After the hyphens have been entered beginning and ending at the proper margin column numbers, enter the command ^OF. The cursor must be on the line of hyphens when the ^OF command is entered. This command activates the margin settings. You will notice that the main menu ruler line will now change to reflect the margins on the nonprinting ruler line. Press an ENTER/RETURN to move the cursor out of the nonprinting ruler line. All text entered after this nonprinting ruler line will have margins of 10 and 55.

Changing Margins from Existing Text

When editing a document, you may want to duplicate a margin setting used in keying-in a certain portion of the text. A quick and easy way to reset those margins is to position the cursor at the same place in the text as the margin you want to match and then enter the command ^OF. The main menu ruler line will automatically reflect the left and right margin settings of the previously entered text.

Changing the Margin Top

WordStar presets the margin top at three lines. This means that the print will start on the fourth line from the top of the paper. The margin top default is changed by the dot command .MT. If you wanted the print to start two inches from the top of the paper, enter the command .MT 12 at column 1 at the beginning of your document file and the print will start on the thirteenth line from the top of the paper. (Remember, there are 6 vertical lines to an inch by default; therefore, two inches is 12 vertical lines.)

Changing the Margin Bottom

WordStar presets the margin bottom at eight lines. A new page will begin when the computer reads eight lines remaining at the bottom of a page. The margin bottom default is changed by the dot command .MB and the number of lines wanted at the bottom of a page. If you wanted a margin bottom of two inches, enter .MB 12 at column 1 at the beginning of the document file. Figure 8.5 summarizes the margin commands.

```
Left Margin                      ^OL
Right Margin                     ^OR
Right Margin Justify Toggle      ^OJ
Margin Release                   ^OX

Margins From Existing Text       ^OF
Margin Top                       .MT
Margin Bottom                    .MB


Nonprinting Ruler Line

    ..(entered at column 1) ^P ENTER/RETURN                  -
    ----------------------------------------------------      <
        (start hyphens at new left margin)
        (stop hyphens at new right margin)
        ^OF
```

Figure 8.5   The Margin Commands

LESSON 8 EXERCISE   Name _____ Date _____

TRUE/FALSE

Each of the following statements is either true or false. Indicate your choice in the Answers column by circling T for a true statement or F for a false statement.

Answers

1. The preset margin settings will print out a 2-inch left and right margin. (Obj. 1) ....   1. **T**   **F**

2. The left margin is changed by the command ^OL. (Obj. 1)...............   2. **T**   **F**

3. The right margin is changed by the command ^OX. (Obj. 1)..............   3. **T**   **F**

4. Business letters and tables should be printed with justified right margins. (Obj. 2) ....   4. **T**   **F**

5. The command to turn off justification is ^OJ. (Obj. 2) ....   5. **T**   **F**

6. The on-screen menu can be exited by striking the space bar. (Obj. 2) ......   6. **T**   **F**

7. The margin release is used to key-in text beyond the left or the right margin. (Obj. 3)..   7. **T**   **F**

8. The left margin can be released beyond column 1. (Obj. 3) ....   8. **T**   **F**

9. .OX is the margin release command. (Obj. 3) ....   9. **T**   **F**

10. The words MAR REL are displayed on the status line when the margin release is activated. (Obj. 3) ....   10. **T**   **F**

11. The main menu ruler line will not change when the margin release command is entered and the left margin is set at 10. (Obj. 3)........................   11. **T**   **F**

12. Paragraphs do not reformat properly with the ^B command when text has been entered beyond the margins using the margin release. (Obj. 3).......   12. **T**   **F**

13. The margin release is canceled by striking the Esc key. (Obj. 3) ....   13. **T**   **F**

14. The nonprinting ruler line will print if the dot command is entered at column 2. (Obj. 4) ....   14. **T**   **F**

15. Nonprinting ruler lines go back to the default when entering WordStar again from the operating system. (Obj. 4) ....   15. **T**   **F**

16. The nonprinting ruler line command is ..^P ENTER/RETURN and a line of hyphens. (Obj. 4) ....   16. **T**   **F**

17. The margins are not set on the nonprinting ruler line until ^OF is entered with the cursor on the hyphen line. (Obj. 5) ....   17. **T**   **F**

18. The command to change margins to match existing text is ^OF. (Obj. 6) .   18. **T**   **F**

19. The top margin is preset to print six lines from the top of the page. (Obj. 7)   19. **T**   **F**

20. The bottom margin is preset to leave two inches at the bottom of the page. (Obj. 8) ....   20. **T**   **F**

COMPLETION

Indicate the correct answer in the space provided.

1. How many inches will the preset margin leave at the right and left side of a standard sheet of paper? (Obj. 1)

2. What command must be entered to change the left margin? (Obj. 1) ....

3. What command must be entered to change the right margin? (Obj. 1) ....

4. What key must be struck after the ^OL or ^OR to set margins at the cursor position? (Obj. 1) ....

5. What is the term for an even right margin? (Obj. 2) ...

6. Should justification be turned on or turned off when creating business letters and tables? (Obj. 2)..............

7. What command toggles the justification on and off? (Obj. 2) ....

8. Which menu shows if justification is turned on or off? (Obj. 2) ....

9. To exit from the on-screen menu if no changes need to be made, you strike the ? (Obj. 2) ....

10. What command allows you to key beyond the right margin? (Obj. 3) ....

11. What will appear on the status line after you strike the command ^OX? (Obj. 3) ....

12. What two commands will cancel the margin release? (Obj. 3) ....

13. Can the left margin be released beyond column 1? (Obj. 3) ....

14. What graphic appears to the left of the left margin setting of 10 when the margin release is turned on? (Obj. 3)

15. What will display margins on the screen and tab settings, but will not print? (Obj. 4)......................

16. The dot command that instructs the printer not to print the next line is ? (Obj. 4)...............................

17. The flag character that appears on the right side of the screen indicating the next line will not print is called? (Obj. 4) ....

18. To set a left margin of 10 on a nonprinting ruler line, enter a line of hyphens beginning at which column? (Obj. 5) ....

1. _____

2. _____

3. _____

4. _____

5. _____

6. _____

7. _____

8. _____

9. _____

10. _____

11. _____

12. a. _____
    b. _____

13. _____

14. _____

15. _____

16. _____

17. _____

18. _____

19. After the hyphens have been entered on the nonprinting ruler line, what command activates the margin settings? (Obj. 5) ....

19. _____

20. The command to change margins to match existing text is called? (Obj. 6) ....

20. _____

21. To start the print 13 lines from the top of the paper, enter which command? (Obj. 7)........................

21. _____

22. To leave ten lines at the bottom of a page, enter which command? (Obj. 8)....................................

22. _____

COMPUTER EXERCISE

Directions: Key-in the paragraphs in Figure 8.6 at the margin settings as indicated. Do not indent the paragraph. Name the file LESSON8.EX. Set a margin top of two inches (12 lines). Set a margin bottom of two inches (12 lines). Margins for the first and third paragraphs should be 10 and 55. Margins for the second paragraph should be 5 and 60 set from a nonprinting ruler line. Turn justification off for paragraphs 1 and 2. Turn it back on for paragraph 3. Do not hyphenate when reformatting. Save the file. Print the file named LESSON8.EX.

The development of software for personal computers during the past few years has been very exciting. Time Magazine (April 16, 1984) reports software sales have increased from $260 million in 1980 to $1.5 billion projected sales by the end of this year (1984). There are over 1,000 companies making software.

Time Magazine also reports that although no one really knows for sure just how many software programs are available on the market today, an estimated 8,000 to 40,000 programs actually exist. In fact, a mini-industry has grown up to keep track of the titles.

Software developers may become millionaires at age 20 and has-beens at the age of 30. Software producer Michael Gates of Microsoft has a personal fortune of an estimated $100 million. These superstars of the microcomputer industry are wooed by hardware companies to produce software for their machines. Software publisher Fred Gibbons says "Control of the personal-computer industry is shifting from the hardware manufacturer to the software supplier."

Figure 8.6   Text for Computer Exercise

9. Tabulation

OBJECTIVES:

1. Explain tabulation.
2. Describe preset tab positions.
3. Setting tabs on the main menu ruler line.
4. Clearing tabs on the main menu ruler line.
5. Resetting the tab default.
6. Setting tabs on the nonprinting ruler line.
7. Clearing tabs on the nonprinting ruler line.
8. Explain the variable tab default.

TABULATION DEFINED

A **tabulation** is an indention from the left margin using the tab key or the ^I WordStar command. Tab indentions are used to indent the first line of a paragraph and to line up columns of numbers or text. One way to indent text from the left margin is to use the space bar, spacing to the column where the indention starts. A more efficient way is to tab or ^I to the point of indention. A tab must be set at the point you want text to be indented.

TABS ON THE MAIN MENU RULER LINE

WordStar has preset tabs every five spaces on the ruler line. This means that the tab stop is actually at the sixth column on the ruler line, leaving five spaces between tab stops as illustrated in Figure 9.1.

```
L  -  -  -  -  !  -  -  -  -  !  -  -  -  -  !  -  -  -  -  !
1  2  3  4  5  6  7  8  9  10 11 12 13 14 15 16 17 18 19 20 21
```

Figure 9.1   Preset Tab Stops

73

The graphic symbol for a tab stop is the exclamation point !. Tab stops can be entered anywhere on the ruler line. To set a tab stop at column position 33, enter the command ^OI. A prompt appears on your screen as shown in Figure 9.2.

```
SET TAB AT COLUMN (ESCAPE for cursor column)?_
```

Figure 9.2   The Tab Set Prompt

Key-in 33 at the cursor and an ENTER/RETURN. The ruler line will now display a ! at position 33. A tab has been set at position 33. Notice that the prompt also instructs you to strike the Esc key to set a tab stop at the cursor column. This means that if you strike the Esc key at the prompt, a tab stop will be set at the column number where the cursor was positioned before you entered the ^OI command. All tab stops can be cleared at once, or each tab stop can be cleared individually. To clear all the tabs at once, first enter the ^ON command. A prompt appears on your screen as shown in Figure 9.3. Strike *A* (uppercase or lowercase) to clear all the tabs on the ruler line.

```
CLEAR TAB AT COL (ESCAPE for cursor col; A for all)?_
```

Figure 9.3   The Tab Clear Prompt

To clear an individual tab stop, enter the ^ON command and the column number where the tab is set. For example, to clear a tab stop at column position 20, enter the command ^ON and the tab clear prompt in Figure 9.3 will appear on your screen. Key-in *20* and an ENTER/RETURN. The ! graphic will disappear at position 20 on the ruler line. If the Esc key is struck at the prompt, the tab at the column position where the cursor was before the ^ON command was entered will clear. (*Note:* If you enter a wrong command, enter the command ^U and strike Esc to cancel it.)

RESETTING THE TAB DEFAULT

The last margin and tab settings used in a file will remain in effect even though that particular file has been saved and another file has been entered on the screen. For example, if all tabs were cleared in File A, all tabs will be cleared on the ruler line when entering File B. It is important, then, to check the ruler line when entering a different file to make sure that it reflects the format you want.

To reset the tab default (tab stops every 5 spaces) and the margin default (left 1, right 65), you must exit the WordStar program by striking *X* from the opening menu and log on to WordStar again from **B>**. A quick and more efficient method to exit WordStar while in a file is to enter ^*KX* instead of ^*KD* to save the document. This command saves the file; but instead of returning to the opening menu, you will return to the operating system and **B>** will be displayed. Then log on to WordStar again by entering *WS*. Now all the WordStar defaults are in effect again.

TABS ON THE NONPRINTING RULER LINE

Lesson 8 explained how to enter a nonprinting ruler line anywhere in a document. The command is ..^P ENTER/RETURN keyed-in at column 1 and a line of hyphens beginning and ending at the left and right margin column settings. An example of how your screen looks when a nonprinting ruler line with a left margin of 10 and a right margin of 55 is entered is shown in Figure 9.4.

Figure 9.4   The Nonprinting Ruler Line with Margins at 10 and 55

To set a tab on the nonprinting ruler line, position the cursor on the hyphen line at the column number you want the tab stop. Turn insert off (^V). Enter !. Then enter the command ^OF to activate the new setting. For example, to set a tab stop at position 20, move the cursor to position 20 on the hyphen line with insert off. Strike the ! key. A tab is now set at column position 20. Insert should be off. If it is not, the hyphen line will increase by one column when the ! is inserted, thus changing your right margin setting. A nonprinting ruler line with margins set at 10 and 55 and a tab stop at 20 will now appear as illustrated in Figure 9.5. Do not forget to enter ^OF to activate the new setting.

Figure 9.5   Tab Set on a Nonprinting Ruler Line

To clear a tab on a nonprinting ruler line, position the cursor at the ! on the hyphen line and, with insert off, enter a hyphen. The !

is replaced with a hyphen (-). Then enter the ^OF command to activate the new ruler line setting.

THE VARIABLE TAB MODE

The **variable tab** mode should always be on when doing word processing. To check if the variable tab is on, look at the on-screen menu by entering ^O. If the variable tab says off, strike *V* (uppercase or lowercase) to turn the variable tab on. Use the space bar to exit the ^O menu.

When the variable tab is in the off mode, the ruler line continues to show the tab stops, but the tab stops will not work. When the variable tab is in the off mode, the tab positions are set every 8 places and will act like the tab used by the CP/M operating system. This tab mode is used by program developers. You, as a word processor, will not need to use this feature. So, if you set tab stops and they do not work, check the variable tab mode; it must be turned on.

Name _____ Date _____

TRUE/FALSE

Each of the following statements is either true or false. Indicate your choice in the Answers column by circling T for a true statement or F for a false statement.

Answers

1. A tabulation is made by using the tab key or the ^I command. (Obj. 1) ...   1. **T**   **F**

2. WordStar presets tabs every 8 spaces. (Obj. 2) ....   2. **T**   **F**

3. The graphic symbol for a tab stop is !. (Obj. 2) ....   3. **T**   **F**

4. ^ON is the command to set a tab stop. (Obj. 3) ....   4. **T**   **F**

5. Tabs can be set by keying-in the column number after ^OI is entered or by striking the Esc key. (Obj. 3) ....   5. **T**   **F**

6. Striking the Esc key after the ^OI command will cancel the tab stop command. (Obj. 3) ....   6. **T**   **F**

7. Each tab stop must be cleared individually. (Obj. 4) ....   7. **T**   **F**

8. ^ON is the command to clear tabs. (Obj. 4) ....   8. **T**   **F**

9. If the letter A is entered after the ^ON command, all the tab stops will be cleared. (Obj. 4) ....   9. **T**   **F**

10. If the letter A is entered after the ^ON command, it must be in uppercase. (Obj. 4) ....   10. **T**   **F**

11. To clear a tab at the cursor position, strike the Esc key after the ^OI command. (Obj. 4) ....   11. **T**   **F**

12. To clear a tab at position 20, enter *20* after the ^ON command. (Obj. 4) ..   12. **T**   **F**

13. After saving a file with ^KD, the margin and tabs return to the WordStar default. (Obj. 5) ....   13. **T**   **F**

14. If ^KX is entered to save a file, the operating system prompt will be displayed. (Obj. 5) ....   14. **T**   **F**

15. The best way to reset the defaults is to exit WordStar. (Obj. 5) ....   15. **T**   **F**

16. The tab graphic on a nonprinting ruler line is !. (Obj. 6) ....   16. **T**   **F**

17. Insert should be on when entering a tab on the nonprinting ruler line. (Obj. 6) ....   17. **T**   **F**

18. You must enter ^OF after setting the tab graphic on the nonprinting ruler line or the tab will not work. (Obj. 6) ....   18. **T**   **F**

19. Tabs are cleared on the nonprinting ruler line by keying-in a hyphen at the tab graphic with insert off. (Obj. 7) ....   19. **T   F**

20. If the variable tab mode is off, the tab settings will not work correctly. (Obj. 8) ....   20. **T   F**

21. Programmers and software developers will turn the variable tab mode off. (Obj. 8) ....   21. **T   F**

22. The ^O menu displays the variable tab mode. (Obj. 8) ....   22. **T   F**

COMPLETION

Indicate the correct answer in the space provided.

1. List the three ways you can indent text using WordStar. (Obj. 1) ....
 1. a. _____
 b. _____
 c. _____

2. Preset tabs are set how many spaces apart? (Obj. 2)....
 2. _____

3. The graphic for a tab is *?* (Obj. 2)......................
 3. _____

4. The command to set tabs on the main menu ruler line is *?* (Obj. 3) ....
 4. _____

5. To set a tab at column 27 on the main menu ruler line, what must be keyed-in after the ^OI command? (Obj. 3)
 5. _____

6. To set a tab at the cursor position after the ^OI command, which key must be struck? (Obj. 3) ....
 6. _____

7. The first command entered to clear tabs on the main menu ruler line is *?* (Obj. 4) ....
 7. _____

8. What letter must be entered at the ^ON prompt to clear all the tabs set on the main menu ruler line? (Obj. 4) ..
 8. _____

9. What must be entered to clear a tab at column 17 after the ^ON prompt appears? (Obj. 4) ....
 9. _____

10. What key must be struck after the ^ON prompt to clear a tab at the cursor position? (Obj. 4) ....
 10. _____

11. When entering files, to be sure the format is correct for the document, it is important to check the *?* (Obj. 5) ...
 11. _____

12. Exiting to the operating system will reset all the *?* (Obj. 5) ....
 12. _____

13. To exit WordStar when saving a document file, key-in the command *?* (Obj. 5).................................
 13. _____

14. What WordStar command must be given to activate the nonprinting ruler line settings? (Obj. 6)................
 14. _____

15. When entering tab stops on the nonprinting ruler line, insert should be *?* (Obj. 6) ....
 15. _____

16. The tab symbol on a nonprinting ruler line is *?* (Obj. 6)
 16. _____

17. To clear a tab on the nonprinting ruler line, position the cursor at the tab graphic and strike *?* (Obj. 7) ....
 17. _____

18. What command must be given after each change on the nonprinting ruler line to activate the new settings? (Obj. 7) ....
 18. _____

19. When entering text, the variable tab mode should be *?* (Obj. 8) ....
 19. _____

20. You can check whether the variable tab mode is on or off by viewing which menu? (Obj. 8).......................
 20. _____

COMPUTER EXERCISE

Directions: Create a file named TAB.EX9 by entering the text in Figure 9.6. Do not enter the instructions that are in parentheses. Clear all the tabs from the main menu ruler line. Set new tabs at 20 and 30 on the main menu ruler line and key-in the information in Figure 9.6 at these columns. Create a nonprinting ruler line after MISSOURI. Set the left margin at 10 and the right margin at 60. Set tab stops at column numbers 30 and 40. *Note:* Do not press the ENTER/RETURN key after each line. Instead, strike the ^I key and the cursor will go directly to the first tab stop on the next line. Save the file. Print the file named TAB.EX9. Exit to the operating system to reset the defaults.

TABULATIONS WITH STOPS SET ON MAIN MENU RULER LINE

```
        AL      Alabama
        AK      Alaska
        AZ      Arizona
        AR      Arkansas
        CA      California
        CO      Colorado
        CT      Connecticut
        DE      Delaware
        FL      Florida
        GA      Georgia
        HI      Hawaii
        ID      Idaho
        IL      Illinois
        IN      Indiana
        IA      Iowa
        KS      Kansas
        KY      Kentucky
        LA      Louisiana
        ME      Maine
        MD      Maryland
        MA      Massachusetts
        MI      Michigan
        MN      Minnesota
        MS      Mississippi
        MO      Missouri          (Insert four returns here.)
```

TABULATIONS WITH STOPS SET ON NONPRINTING RULER LINE

```
        MT      Montana
        NE      Nebraska
        NV      Nevada
        NH      New Hampshire
        NJ      New Jersey
        NM      New Mexico
        NY      New York
        NC      North Carolina
        ND      North Dakota
        OH      Ohio
        OK      Oklahoma
        OR      Oregon
        PA      Pennsylvania
        RI      Rhode Island
        SC      South Carolina
```

Figure 9.6   Text for Computer Exercise

10. Decimal Tabs and Paragraph Tabs

OBJECTIVES:

1. Define decimal tabs.

2. Set decimal tabs on the main menu ruler line.

3. Clear decimal tabs on the main menu ruler line.

4. Set decimal tabs on the nonprinting ruler line.

5. Clear decimal tabs from the nonprinting ruler line.

6. Define paragraph tabs.

7. Indent text with paragraph tabs.

8. Cancel the paragraph tabs.

9. Reformat text with paragraph tabs.

DECIMAL TABS

A **decimal tab** (dec tab) is an indent command that moves text to the left of a tab setting until a decimal point is entered or the ENTER/RETURN or space bar is struck. A decimal tab setting is useful for aligning a column of numbers with decimal points. The decimal points will be aligned automatically with a decimal tab command as illustrated in Figure 10.1.

```
      1.1                    2.2                    3.3
     11.11                  22.22                  33.33
    111.111                222.222                333.333
   1111.1111              2222.2222              3333.3333
```

Figure 10.1 Decimal Points Aligned With Decimal Tab Command

Decimal tabs are also useful when text should be aligned to the left of a tab setting as illustrated in Figure 10.2.

```
              Aligning
                 Text
                Using
              Decimal
                 Tabs
```

Figure 10.2   Text Aligned With Decimal Tab Command

Setting Decimal Tabs on the Main Menu Ruler Line

Decimal tabs are set on the main menu ruler line with the same command used to set regular tabs on the main menu ruler line. In Figure 10.1 a decimal tab was set at column 6, column 31, and column 56. To set a decimal tab at column 6 on the main menu ruler line, enter the command ^OI. The screen appears as illustrated in Figure 10.3.

```
For decimal tab stop enter "#" and decimal point column
```

Figure 10.3   The Decimal Tab Prompt

Key-in the pound symbol (#), 6, and an ENTER/RETURN. A pound symbol will appear at position 6 on the ruler line. If a tab was previously set at column 6, the tab graphic (!) will be replaced by the decimal tab graphic (#).

If you want to set a decimal tab at the cursor position, enter the ^OI command, the pound symbol, and strike the Esc key. The dec tab symbol (#) will appear at the column number where the cursor was before entering the ^OI command.

When entering columns of numbers at a dec tab, tab over to the column number that has the dec tab display. A prompt that says "decimal" will appear on the status line. Enter the numbers. The cursor will stay at the dec tab setting and the numbers will move to the left of the cursor until a decimal point is entered. A decimal point, a space, another tab, or an ENTER/RETURN cancels the "decimal" prompt on the status line and permits the cursor to move to another position.

Clearing Decimal Tabs on the Main Menu Ruler Line

The command to clear a decimal tab from the main menu ruler line is the same as that for clearing a regular tab from the main menu ruler line. To clear a dec tab at column 6, enter ^ON. A prompt appears on the screen as shown in Figure 10.4. Enter 6 and an ENTER/RETURN. The decimal tab graphic (#) will be replaced by a hyphen (-) on the ruler line.

```
CLEAR TAB AT COL (ESCAPE for cursor col; A for all)?_
```

Figure 10.4   The Tab Clear Prompt

Setting and Clearing Decimal Tabs on a Nonprinting Ruler Line

To set decimal tabs at positions 30 and 40 on a nonprinting ruler line that has a left margin of 10 and a right margin of 55, position the cursor at position 30 in the hyphen line. Turn insert off (^V). Strike the # key. Position the cursor at position 40. Strike the # key. Then enter ^OF to activate the new ruler line settings. If you are creating the nonprinting ruler line and you know where the decimal tab needs to be, you can enter it when you key-in the hyphen line. Decimal tabs set at columns 30 and 40 on a nonprinting ruler line with margins of 10 and 55 are illustrated in Figure 10.5.

```
..                                                                              –
        ----------------------#---------#--------------                         <
```

Figure 10.5   Decimal Tab Settings on a Nonprinting Ruler Line

To clear a decimal tab setting from a nonprinting ruler line, position the cursor at the # graphic on the hyphen line and with insert off, strike the hyphen key. The dec tab graphic (#) will be replaced with a hyphen (-).

THE PARAGRAPH TAB

A **paragraph tab** is an indention from the left margin that remains in effect until an ENTER/RETURN cancels the indention. It is a temporary left margin setting. When an ENTER/RETURN is struck, the left margin returns to its original setting. The paragraph tab is useful when entering outlines or other text that needs a temporary left margin setting. The second paragraph in Figure 10.6 illustrates text entered with a paragraph tab command.

```
MicroPro's WordStar word processing package has
features  that make this sophisticated program very
easy to learn.  One of these features is
        new,  easier-to-understand MENUS.  Special
        HELP menus save time when seeking quick
        reference to a command.  The menus can be
        viewed  on the screen with a simple  command.
        These  menus  are the MAIN  MENU,  the  BLOCK
        MENU,  the ONSCREEN MENU,  the PRINT MENU and
        the HELP MENU.
WordStar has two other options that are valuable to
any  word  processing system.  These  options  are
SpellStar and MailMerge.
```

Figure 10.6   Text with Paragraph Tab

Indenting Text with Paragraph Tab

The paragraph tab command is ^OG. When ^OG is entered, text will indent to the first tab setting on the ruler line. If ^OG is entered twice, text will indent to the second tab setting on the ruler line. If ^OG is entered three times, text indents to the third tab setting, and so forth. The indention continues until an ENTER/ RETURN is struck, and then the left margin returns to the original setting.

Look closely at Figure 10.6. The first paragraph was entered with justification on and wordwrap working. At the end of the first paragraph, one return was entered followed by *^OG*. The ruler line highlights up to the first tab setting which is the preset tab at column 6. The second paragraph was entered as usual with wordwrap working until an ENTER/RETURN was struck after MENU. The ENTER/RETURN cancels the paragraph tab, and the third paragraph was entered with the left margin at the original 1 position.

Figure 10.7 illustrates how the ruler line looks when *^OG* has been entered once. The ruler line is highlighted up to column 6 on the preset tab settings. When text is entered with the ruler line shown, all text will be indented at column 6.

Figure 10.7   Ruler Line with Paragraph Tab Command

Canceling the Paragraph Tab Command and Reformatting Text

To cancel the paragraph tab (^OG), strike the ENTER/ RETURN key. The ruler line will return to the original left margin setting. The paragraph tab can also be canceled by moving the cursor to text entered before the ^OG command was given.

If a paragraph must be reformatted after insertions or deletions, and that paragraph was entered with a temporary left margin set with an ^OG command, the ruler line must reflect the ^OG setting or the paragraph will not reformat properly. Instead, the indented paragraph will reformat to the original left margin setting. So, be sure that the ruler line reflects the format you want before you reformat with ^B.

LESSON 10 EXERCISE   Name _____   Date _____

TRUE/FALSE

Each of the following statements is either true or false. Indicate your choice in the Answers column by circling a T for a true statement or an F for a false statement.

1. A decimal tab is an indent command that moves text to the right of a tab setting until a decimal point is entered or the ENTER/RETURN or space bar is struck. (Obj. 1) ....   1. **T**   **F**

2. The decimal point will be aligned automatically with a decimal tab command. (Obj. 1) ....   2. **T**   **F**

3. A decimal tab is useful for aligning text to the left of a tab setting. (Obj. 1)   3. **T**   **F**

4. To set a tab on the main menu ruler line, enter the command ^OI. (Obj. 2)   4. **T**   **F**

5. The exclamation mark, !, is the symbol for a decimal tab. (Obj. 2) ....   5. **T**   **F**

6. To set a decimal tab at position 6 on the main menu ruler line, enter # and 6 after the ^OI prompt. (Obj. 2) ....   6. **T**   **F**

7. To set a decimal tab at the cursor position, enter the command ^OI, the # symbol, and strike the Esc key. (Obj. 2) ....   7. **T**   **F**

8. The status line will change when the cursor is at a decimal tab. (Obj. 2) ..   8. **T**   **F**

9. The decimal tab is deactivated by an ENTER/RETURN, a decimal point, a space, or another tab. (Obj. 2) ....   9. **T**   **F**

10. The command ^ON will clear a decimal tab on the main menu ruler line. (Obj. 3) ....   10. **T**   **F**

11. To clear a decimal tab at position 6, enter the command ^OI and key-in # and 6 at the prompt. (Obj. 3) ....   11. **T**   **F**

12. When a decimal tab is cleared, a hyphen replaces the # symbol on the ruler line. (Obj. 3) ....   12. **T**   **F**

13. Insert should be on when inserting a decimal tab on the nonprinting ruler line. (Obj. 4) ....   13. **T**   **F**

14. The command ^OF must be entered from the nonprinting ruler line to activate the settings. (Obj. 4) ....   14. **T**   **F**

15. A decimal tab is cleared from the nonprinting ruler line by positioning the cursor at the # graphic on the hyphen line, and with insert off, striking the hyphen key. (Obj. 5) ....   15. **T**   **F**

16. The left margin must be reset whenever a paragraph tab is canceled. (Obj. 6)   16. **T**   **F**

17. ^OG is the command to paragraph tab. (Obj. 7) ....   17. **T**   **F**

18. To set a temporary left margin at the third tab stop, enter ^OG twice. (Obj. 7) ....   18. **T**   **F**

19. The paragraph tab is canceled by an ENTER/RETURN or by moving the cursor to text entered before the ^OG command was given. (Obj. 8)....... 19. **T   F**

20. The ruler line must reflect the format you want before text can be reformatted properly. (Obj. 9) .... 20. **T   F**

COMPLETION

Indicate the correct answer in the space provided.

1. A decimal tab is an indent command that moves the text in which direction of the tab setting until a decimal point, ENTER/RETURN, or space bar is struck? (Obj. 1)

   1. _____

2. When using the dec tab command, decimal points will be automatically *?* (Obj. 1)..................................

   2. _____

3. What command aligns text to the left of a tab? (Obj. 1)

   3. _____

4. What command must be entered first to set a decimal tab at column 22? (Obj. 2) ....

   4. _____

5. After the decimal tab is entered at column 22, you must enter which symbol before the number 22 and an ENTER/RETURN? (Obj. 2) ....

   5. _____

6. What graphic will appear on the ruler line after a dec tab has been set? (Obj. 2)................................

   6. _____

7. After tabbing to a dec tab, what prompt will appear on the status line? (Obj. 2)..................................

   7. _____

8. What two responses must be entered after the ^OI command is entered for a dec tab to be set at the cursor position? (Obj. 2)...

   8. a. _____
      b. _____

9. A decimal point, a space, another tab, or an ENTER/RETURN will cancel the decimal prompt on which line? (Obj. 2) ....

   9. _____

10. What command clears a decimal tab from the main menu ruler line? (Obj. 3) ....

   10. _____

11. Should insert be on or off when entering dec tabs on a nonprinting ruler line? (Obj. 4) ....

   11. _____

12. To enter a decimal tab at position 25 on a nonprinting ruler line, position the cursor at column 25, and with the insert off, strike *?* (Obj. 4)..............................

   12. _____

13. What command must be entered before the settings on a nonprinting ruler line can take effect? (Obj. 4) ....

   13. _____

14. To clear a decimal tab setting on a nonprinting ruler line, position the cursor at the decimal tab setting in the hyphen line, and with insert off, enter a *?* (Obj. 5) . . . .   14. _____

15. A paragraph tab is really a temporary *?* (Obj. 6) . . . .   15. _____

16. The left margin returns to its original setting when which key is struck? (Obj. 6) . . . .   16. _____

17. What is the command for a paragraph tab? (Obj. 7) . . . .   17. _____

18. If the ^OG command is given four consecutive times, the indention will occur at the fourth *?* (Obj. 7) . . . .   18. _____

19. When *^OG* is entered, the ruler line will highlight to which tab stop? (Obj. 7) . . . .   19. _____

20. The paragraph tab can be canceled by entering an ENTER/RETURN or by moving the *?* (Obj. 8) . . . .   20. _____

21. When reformatting text entered with a paragraph tab, what must reflect the ^OG indention? (Obj. 9) . . . .   21. _____

COMPUTER EXERCISE ONE

Directions: Enter the memorandum in Figure 10.8 and name the file LESSON10.EX1. Clear all tabs. Set a decimal tab at column 16 in the main menu ruler line to align the memorandum headings and the left column. Set a tab at column 20 to use as a temporary left margin. Double space between items. Justify the right margin. Use the preset margins. Omit page numbering. Save the file. Print out the file named LESSON10.EX1.

```
          TO:      All Word Processing Personnel

          FROM:    Communications Center

          DATE:    December 1, 19--

          SUBJECT: Punctuation Rules


Please use the following punctuation rules for commas when transcribing all
correspondence.

          Rule:     Use  a comma before conjunctions that join independent
                    clauses.

          Example:  The meeting is at 10 o'clock,  and all personnel  will
                    attend.   The operator  completed the  call, but I did
                    not talk to Frank.

          Rule:     Use a comma to separate words and phrases in a series.

          Example:  Our  division is responsible for letters,  memos,  and
                    reports  entered  on  the  computer terminals.    The
                    secretaries in  the office,  the managers in the plant,
                    and the salespeople in the  field must all submit their
                    word processing material through this office.

          Rule:     Use a comma to separate  introductory dependent clauses
                    from the rest of the sentence.

          Example:  When  this project  is completed,  I will return to the
                    home office.

          Rule:     Use a comma to set off nonrestrictive clauses.

          Example:  Carol Conners, who was my secretary for many years, was
                    promoted to Personnel Manager.

          Rule:     Use a comma before "Inc." in a company name.

          Example:  The  contract  will go to  the lowest bidder  which  was
                    Graham and Sons, Inc.

          Rule:     Use a comma to set off words of a direct address.

          Example:  It is my  pleasure,   Mr. Smith, to introduce to you the
                    next President of the United States of America.

          Rule:     Use a comma before "Jr." and "Sr." in a person's name.
```

Figure 10.8   Computer Exercise One

COMPUTER EXERCISE TWO

Directions: Create the following table shown in Figure 10.9 and name the file LESSON10.EX2. Set left margin at 1, right margin at 75. Clear tabs on the main menu ruler line. Set tabs on the main menu ruler line at 27, 39, 50, and 62 for the table headings. Set decimal tabs at 31, 43, 55, and 67 on a nonprinting ruler line for the column figures. *Note:* Key-in the headings first. Then create a nonprinting ruler line, set dec tabs, then enter the rest of the table. Turn justification off. Print page number 1. Save the file. Print the file named LESSON10.EX2.

FINANCIAL FIGURES FOR THE WEEK

STOCKS	THIS WEEK	LAST WEEK	LAST MONTH	LAST YEAR
Standard & Poor's 500				
stock index	153.65	150.29	160.52	162.77
Price earnings ratio	10.09	10.71	11.42	13.05
Divided yield	4.82%	4.92%	4.50%	4.33%
Dow Jones ind. avg.	1124.89	1101.24	1176.30	1194.90
Lipper growth mutual				
fund index	196.65	190.39	205.04	86.8
Average daily NYSE	1665	1453	1749	1445
MONEY MARKETS				
Federal funds	10.65%	10.51%	11.06%	8.95%
Prime rate	12.50%	12.50%	12.50%	10.50%
Commercial paper	10.60%	10.50%	10.20%	8.63%
New treasury bills				
3-month	9.76%	9.89%	10.05%	8.80%
New treasury bills				
6-month	10.48%	10.66%	10.31%	8.94%
Eurodollar rate				
3-month	11.63%	11.59%	10.99%	9.41%
Certificates of deposit	11.05%	11.25%	11.13%	9.35%

Figure 10.9   Computer Exercise Two

11. The Rest of the On-Screen Menu Features _____

OBJECTIVES:

1. Center a line.
2. Define line spacing default.
3. Change the line spacing.
4. Explain the soft hyphen display.
5. Explain how to delete the ruler line.
6. Describe the print control display.
7. Describe the hyphen help display.
8. Describe the status line when page break display is off.

CENTERING A LINE AND LINE SPACING

A line can be centered by entering the command ^OC anywhere on the line that is to be centered. For example, to center the title "WordStar Commands," first key-in the title name. Position the cursor anywhere in the line and enter the command ^OC. The title "WordStar Commands," will move to the center of the margin settings.

WordStar automatically displays text on the screen and prints out in single spacing. This single-spaced line default can be changed by the ^OS command which is the command to change line spacing. When ^OS is entered, a prompt appears on the screen as illustrated in Figure 11.1.

```
ENTER space OR NEW LINE SPACING (1-9) _
```

Figure 11.1   The New Line Spacing Prompt

If double spacing is required for a document, enter *2* after the ^OS prompt and an ENTER/RETURN. The right side of the status line will reflect the new line spacing as illustrated in Figure 11.2. Line spacing can be changed from 2 (1 line between text) up to 9 (8 lines between text).

```
B:LESSON11.TXT    PAGE 2  LINE 4  COL 42           LINE SPACING 2
```

Figure 11.2   The Status Line When Using Double Spacing

SOFT HYPHEN DISPLAY

When the soft hyphen display is in its default mode (off), all hyphens except a hyphen entered at the end of a line are considered required or hard. The end-of-line hyphen is considered a *soft* hyphen.

A **soft hyphen** is a hyphen that is entered at the end of a line in response to the hyphenation prompt that appears on the screen when you reformat a paragraph. You will recall that if the computer sees a word that is too long to fit within the set right margin when reformatting a paragraph, a prompt appears on the screen as shown in Figure 11.3.

```
TO HYPHENATE, PRESS -   Before pressing -, you may
    move the cursor:  ^S=cursor left, ^D=cursor right
If hyphenation not desired, type ^B
```

Figure 11.3   The Hyphenation Help Display

You can either hyphenate the word or continue the reformatting without hyphenating the word. If a hyphen is inserted, the computer reads it as a soft hyphen, one that can be dropped if the word should fall in the middle of a line after another reformatting command. The end-of-line hyphen will be highlighted (if your VDT supports this feature).

A soft hyphen, then, is one entered at the end of the line in a hyphenation decision and one that is highlighted when the hyphen display is in the default mode. If the hyphenated word at the end of a line should reformat to another position in a line, the soft hyphen display will stay on the screen in highlighted video, but the hyphen will not print.

If the soft hyphen display ($^\wedge$OE) is turned on, all hyphens are considered soft. The only hyphens that will print when $^\wedge$OE is turned on will be the hyphens at the end of a line. When the soft hyphen display is on and you enter a hyphen, the screen will display the hyphen very quickly and then it will disappear from the screen. The hyphen entered at the end of a line will be the only hyphen that will be displayed and it will be highlighted. You cannot enter any required hyphens when $^\wedge$OE is on. The $^\wedge$OE (soft hyphen) display is the only toggle command that has a default in the off mode.

RULER LINE DISPLAY

The default mode for the ruler line display is on. Deleting the ruler line display will give an extra line for text. Of course, if you delete the ruler line display, you will also want to set your help display below 3 to give maximum room for text to be displayed on your video screen. The command to delete the ruler line is $^\wedge$OT.

PRINT CONTROL DISPLAY

The default for the print control display is on. The print control display is the on-screen display of some commands entered with the control key ($^\wedge$) and another letter. For example, $^\wedge$PS is the command to underscore a word. When entering this command with the $^\wedge$OD (print display) default on, $^\wedge$S will show on the screen. If you change the $^\wedge$OD display mode to off, the $^\wedge$S will be deleted from the screen, but the underscore command will still be in effect.

The print control display mode should be off when viewing the screen to determine how the text will print. Control characters take up room on the screen even though they do not print, and this display distorts the way the printout will look. By turning off the print control display, the screen will reflect exactly how the printout will look.

A soft hyphen displayed in a line will be removed with the print control display in the off mode. However, the soft hyphen inserted at the end of the line will still display. Again, it is helpful to have soft hyphens that have been reformatted to the middle of a line removed from the screen to show exactly how the printout will look.

HYPHEN HELP

When reformatting paragraphs with $^\wedge B$, the reformatting stops at the end of a line for a hyphenation decision when a word is too long to fit within the margin setting. If you do not wish to make hyphenation decisions, you can turn the hyphenation help from the default on mode to the off mode by entering $^\wedge OH$. When the hyphen help is turned off, the word that will not fit in the right margin will drop automatically down to the next line. This may cause a lot of blank space between words if justification is on, or it may cause extremely ragged margins if justification is turned off.

PAGE BREAK DISPLAY

WordStar automatically generates a new page after 55 lines of text have been entered. The page break display appears as shown in Figure 11.4.

- P

Figure 11.4   The Page Break Display

This display may be turned off by the toggle command ^OP. When this display is turned off, the status line also changes. The letters FC replace the page number on the status line, and the letters FL replace the line number on the status line. F (file) C (characters) stands for the number of characters from the beginning of a file up to the cursor position. F (file) L (lines) stands for the number of lines from the beginning of a file to the cursor position. The cursor must be at the end of the file to determine all the characters and all the lines in an entire file. Figure 11.5 illustrates how the status line looks when the page break display is turned off. The illustration shows that there are 7,718 characters from the file beginning to the cursor position in the file called LESSON11.TXT and that there are 260 lines from the file beginning to the cursor position.

B:LESSON11.TXT   FC=7718 FL=260 COL 40   INSERT ON

Figure 11.5   Status Line When Page Break Display is Off

LESSON 11 EXERCISE   Name _____ Date _____

TRUE/FALSE

Each of the following statements is either true or false. Indicate your choice in the Answers column by circling T for a true statement or F for a false statement.

1. The cursor must be at the end of a line when entering the center command. (Obj. 1) ....   1. T   F

2. The WordStar default for line spacing is 2. (Obj. 2) ....   2. T   F

3. A vertical line space can be entered up to 9. (Obj. 3) ....   3. T   F

4. The status line is unchanged when a new line spacing is entered. (Obj. 3) .   4. T   F

5. When the soft hyphen display is in the default mode, all hyphens except a hyphen entered at the end of a line are considered hard or required. (Obj. 4)   5. T   F

6. The soft hyphen display mode is the only toggle command that has a default of off. (Obj. 4) ....   6. T   F

7. Hyphens entered at the end of a line in response to a hyphenation prompt are considered soft hyphens. (Obj. 4) ....   7. T   F

8. The end-of-line hyphens are highlighted. (Obj. 4) ....   8. T   F

9. A soft hyphen located in the middle of a sentence will not print. (Obj. 4) .   9. T   F

10. If the hyphen display is turned on, all hyphens are considered soft. (Obj. 4)   10. T   F

11. Hyphens typed in the middle of a line will not display if the hyphen display is turned on. (Obj. 4) ....   11. T   F

12. The ruler line cannot be deleted from the screen. (Obj. 5) ....   12. T   F

13. ^OS is the command to delete the ruler line. (Obj. 5) ....   13. T   F

14. The print control display should be turned off to see how text with control commands will print. (Obj. 6) ....   14. T   F

15. The hyphenation help display should be turned off if you do not want to hyphenate when reformatting. (Obj. 7) ....   15. T   F

16. The status line will change when the page break display is turned off. (Obj. 8) ....   16. T   F

17. The command ^OP will turn off the page break display. (Obj. 8) ....   17. T   F

18. The letters FC will replace the page number on the status line when the page break display is turned off. (Obj. 8) ....   18. T   F

19. The letters FL will replace the line number on the status line when the page break display is turned off. (Obj. 8) ....   19. T   F

20. The cursor can be anywhere in a file when determining the total number of characters entered in the file. (Obj. 8) ....   20. T   F

21. The letters FC stand for file characters and refer to the number of characters entered from the file beginning to the cursor position. (Obj. 8) .... **21. T   F**

22. The letters FL stand for file lines and refer to the number of lines entered from the file beginning to the cursor position. (Obj. 8) .... **22. T   F**

COMPLETION

Indicate the correct answer in the space provided.

1. A line can be centered by entering the WordStar command *?* (Obj. 1) .... 1. _____

2. The line spacing default is for *?* (Obj. 2) .... 2. _____

3. To change the line spacing in a document, enter the command *?* (Obj. 3) .... 3. _____

4. The highest number that can be entered for line spacing is *?* (Obj. 3) .... 4. _____

5. If you entered the command ^OS 2 ENTER/RETURN, the status line will read *?* (Obj. 3)...................... 5. _____

6. The default for the soft hyphen display is *?* (Obj. 4).... 6. _____

7. The end-of-line hyphenation entered to divide a word too long to fit within the right margin is called a *?* (Obj. 4) 7. _____

8. Will soft hyphens print in the middle of a line? (Obj. 4) 8. _____

9. A hard hyphen is the same as a *?* (Obj. 4) .... 9. _____

10. If ^OE is on, only the end-of-line hyphens will print and all hyphens are considered to be *?* (Obj. 4) .... 10. _____

11. The ^OE display is the only toggle command with a default mode of *?* (Obj. 4) .... 11. _____

12. The ruler line display may be deleted by the command *?* (Obj. 5) .... 12. _____

13. At what level should you set the help display to get maximum screen for text? (Obj. 5) .... 13. _____

14. The print control display should be in what mode for a soft hyphen displayed in the middle of the line to be removed from the screen? (Obj. 6)...................... 14. _____

15. Should the print control display be turned on or off to determine how the file will print? (Obj. 6) .... 15. _____

16. If no hyphenation decisions are wanted when reformatting paragraphs, you can turn the hyphenation help display off with the command *?* (Obj. 7) .... 16. _____

17. When the page break display is turned off, what will re-place the page number and what will replace the line number on the status line? (Obj. 8).....................

17. a. _____

b. _____

18. To determine the total number of characters in a file, you should turn the page break display off and position the cursor where in the file? (Obj. 8)...................

18. _____

19. WordStar automatically generates a new page when how many lines of text have been entered? (Obj. 8) ....

19. _____

20. To turn off the page break display, enter the command *?* (Obj. 8) ....

20. _____

COMPUTER EXERCISE

Directions: Follow the step-by-step instructions.

1. Reset all the defaults by entering WordStar from the operating system.

2. Create a new file named LESSON11.EX.

3. Center the heading "WORD PROCESSING PRIORI-TIES" in Figure 11.6 on line 1. (See p. 100 for Figure 11.6.)

4. Key-in the paragraph in Figure 11.6 using double spacing.

5. Press the ENTER/RETURN two times.

6. Turn on the soft hyphen display.

7. Key-in the same paragraph again with the soft hyphen display in the on mode. With the soft hyphen display on, the hyphenated words will be highlighted even though they are required hyphens.

8. Press ENTER/RETURN until the page break displays on the screen.

9. Change the right margin setting to 63.

10. Position the cursor on the first letter of the second para-graph you entered.

11. Reformat the paragraph with the following hyphenation decisions: a. Divide document (as docu-ment) at each place it occurs in the second and third lines. b. Divide paragraph (as para-graph) in the fourth line. c. Divide delegate (as dele-gate) in the fifth line. Now both hard and soft hyphens are highlighted because the soft hyphen display is on. Notice that each mid-line hyphenated word causes the line in which it occurs to extend one space beyond the right margin.

12. Set the help level at 2. The main menu disappears, leaving only the ruler line and the status line.

13. Turn off the ruler line display.

14. Turn off the print control display. The only hyphenated words in the second paragraph are at the end of the line. The printout should look exactly like the screen display. Because the soft hyphen display was turned on when this paragraph was entered, only end-of-line hyphenations will print.

15. Turn off hyphen help.

16. Reset the right margin to 65.

17. Position the cursor at the first character in the paragraph and reformat the paragraph. The paragraph reformats without stopping for any hyphenation decisions because the hyphen help is turned off. All hyphens have been eliminated from the screen.

18. Turn off the page break display. Go to the end of the file. The page break display will not appear on the screen. Notice that the status line has changed to reflect the number of characters (FC) in this file up to the cursor position and the number of lines (FL) in this file up to the cursor position.

19. Save the file.

20. Print the file named LESSON11.EX.

21. Return to the operating system to reset all the defaults. Strike *X* from the opening menu to exit to the operating system.

```
                    WORD PROCESSING PRIORITIES

     Decide  what work should and should not be done on the  word

processor.  Reserve busy equipment for large documents, documents

that require a lot of changes, large mailings, and documents that

use  same  phrases  or  paragraphs  (boiler-plate  paragraphs).

Eliminate short or one-time letters and memos.  Delegate  simple

and short documents to ordinary typewriters.
```

Figure 11.6   Text for Computer Exercise

12. Review of the On-Screen Menu Features

OBJECTIVES:

1. Define the on-screen menu.

2. Describe how to view the on-screen menu.

3. Describe how to get out of the on-screen menu.

4. Give the on-screen menu commands and defaults.

5. Explain how to reset the defaults.

THE ON-SCREEN MENU

The on-screen menu (^O) is a listing of text-editing format commands that control the screen display. The ^O menu commands cause the screen to display text exactly the way it will print. This on-screen formatting feature makes WordStar a superior word processing program. Many other programs require embedded commands within the text to instruct the printer to do specific formatting. With such word processing programs, you cannot be certain about the document format until the file has been printed. This translates into wasted time and resources. When working with WordStar, your document prints out exactly as you see it on the screen. Figure 12.1 shows the ^O menu.

```
              < < < O N S C R E E N   M E N U > > >
-Margins & Tabs- ¦ -Line  Functions- ¦ --More Toggles-- ¦ -Other  Menus-
L Set left margin ¦C Center text      ¦J Justify   now OFF ¦ (from Main only)
R Set right margin¦S Set line spacing ¦V Vari-Tabs now ON ¦^J Help   ^K Block
X Release margins ¦                   ¦H Hyph-help now OFF ¦^Q Quick  ^P Print
I Set  N Clear tab¦    ---Toggles---  ¦E Soft hyph now OFF ¦^O Onscreen
G Paragraph tab   ¦W Wrd wrap now ON  ¦D Prnt disp now ON ¦Space Bar returns
F Ruler from line ¦T Rlr line now ON  ¦P Pge break now ON ¦you to Main Menu.
```

Figure 12.1   The On-Screen Menu

VIEWING AND EXITING THE ON-SCREEN MENU

The ^O menu is displayed on the screen by holding down the Ctrl (control) key and striking the letter O (uppercase or lowercase). The help level (^JH) must be at 3 or 2 in order for the menu to display. If the help level is set at 1 or 0, the ^O menu cannot be viewed.

The ^O menu is exited by striking another letter or by striking the space bar. An on-screen command can be entered slowly by entering ^O (which displays the ^O menu) and then striking the letter for the format command. An on-screen command can also be entered quickly so that the ^O menu does not display at all. For example, to change the right margin justification, you can enter *^OJ*, and the ^O menu will not display at all. Or you can enter *^O* to see the on-screen menu, look at the menu displayed on the screen, and then enter the J. If you decide not to enter any command after viewing the ^O menu, press the space bar to exit the menu.

ON-SCREEN COMMANDS AND DEFAULTS

Figure 12.2 illustrates the on-screen commands, their features, and their defaults. When the defaults are changed, the change remains in effect even when the document is saved and

^O Command	Feature	Default
L	Sets left margin.	Column 1
R	Sets right margin.	Column 65
X	Releases margins.	------
N	Clears tabs.	------
I	Sets tabs.	Every 5 spaces
G	Indents left margin.	At tab stops
F	Sets margins from text and sets margins and tabs from non-printing ruler line.	------
C	Centers a line.	------
S	Sets line spacing.	Single space
W	Wordwrap.	ON
T	Ruler line display.	ON
J	Right margin justification.	ON
V	Variable tab to set tabs other than preset positions.	ON
H	Asks for hyphenations.	ON
E	Soft hyphen display.	OFF
D	Print control display.	ON
P	Page break display.	ON

Figure 12.2   The On-Screen Commands, Features, and Defaults

another file is being edited. For example, if you turn the right margin justification off when editing a document, the right margin will also be ragged when editing all subsequent files.

RESETTING THE DEFAULTS

There are three ways to reset any change made in a default. One way is to enter the command again, as in toggle commands. For example, if justification was turned off by entering ^OJ, enter ^OJ again to toggle justification back on. The second way to reset a default is to reenter the command and specific formatting instructions, as in margin settings. For example, to reset a changed left margin back to column 1, enter ^OL and 1 and an ENTER/ RETURN. The third way to reset defaults is to leave WordStar by striking X from the opening menu and get into WordStar again by entering WS at the **B**>. This third method, of course, will reset all the defaults.

Name _____ Date _____

TRUE/FALSE

Each of the following statements is either true or false. Indicate your choice in the Answers column by circling T for a true statement or F for a false statement.

1. It is necessary to print a file to know how the printout will look. (Obj. 1) .   1. **T** **F**

2. The ^O menu is a listing of text-editing format commands that control the screen display. (Obj. 1) ....   2. **T** **F**

3. The help level can be set at any level to view the ^O menu. (Obj. 2) ......   3. **T** **F**

4. The ^O menu can be viewed by entering the ^O command. (Obj. 2) ....   4. **T** **F**

5. If you enter the ^O menu by mistake, strike the space bar to exit the menu. (Obj. 3) ....   5. **T** **F**

6. The ^O menu will leave the screen after ^O plus another letter is struck. (Obj. 3) ....   6. **T** **F**

7. One way to reset a changed default is to enter the command again. (Obj. 5)   7. **T** **F**

8. One way to reset a changed default is to reenter the command and specific formatting instructions. (Obj. 5) ....   8. **T** **F**

COMPLETION

Indicate the correct answer in the space provided.

1. The on-screen menu commands cause the screen to display text exactly the way it will ? (Obj. 1) ....   1. _____

2. What type of text-editing commands controlling the screen display are listed on the on-screen menu? (Obj. 1)   2. _____

3. To view the on-screen menu, enter the command ? (Obj. 2) ....   3. _____

4. The on-screen menu cannot be displayed if the help level is set on which two levels? (Obj. 2).....................   4. a. _____
                                                                                                                         b. _____

5. The on-screen menu can be exited by striking another letter or striking the ? (Obj. 3)........................   5. _____

6. If the left margin is set at 10 in a file and the file is saved and a new file is created, the left margin in the new file will be set at ? (Obj. 4) ....   6. _____

7. The command to set a new left margin is ? (Obj. 4) ....   7. _____

8. The command to set a new right margin is ? (Obj. 4) ..   8. _____

9. The command to release margins is ? (Obj. 4) ....   9. _____

10. The command to set a new tab is *?* (Obj. 4).............   10. _____

11. The command to clear a tab is *?* (Obj. 4)...............   11. _____

12. The command to set a temporary left margin indention is *?* (Obj. 4)...................................   12. _____

13. The command to set margins from existing text or to set margins and tabs from a nonprinting ruler line is *?* (Obj. 4) ....   13. _____

14. The command to center a line is *?* (Obj. 4).............   14. _____

15. The command to set a new line space is *?* (Obj. 4)......   15. _____

16. To turn wordwrap off, enter the command *?* (Obj. 4)...   16. _____

17. To turn the ruler line display off, enter the command *?* (Obj. 4) ....   17. _____

18. To turn off the right margin justification, enter the command *?* (Obj. 4) ....   18. _____

19. To set a tab, the variable tab toggle command must be *?* (Obj. 4) ....   19. _____

20. To turn off hyphenation help, enter the command *?* (Obj. 4) ....   20. _____

21. To turn on the soft hyphen display, enter the command *?* (Obj. 4) ....   21. _____

22. To turn the print control display off, enter the command *?* (Obj. 4)...................................   22. _____

23. To turn the page break display off, enter the command *?* (Obj. 4) ....   23. _____

24. When the same command is entered to turn a feature on and then to turn it off, the command is called a *?* (Obj. 5)   24. _____

25. All defaults are reset when exiting WordStar from the opening menu by striking *?* (Obj. 5)...................   25. _____

COMPUTER EXERCISE

Directions: Follow the step-by-step instructions to complete the computer exercise.

1. You will create the memorandum shown in Figure 12.3. Name the file LESSON12.EX.

2. Set the line spacing for double space.

3. Set the left margin at 5 and the right margin at 60.

4. Clear all tabs from the ruler line.

5. Set tabs at column positions 11, 15, 29, and 41.

6. Indent paragraphs to tab position 11.

7. Set a decimal tab at position 10 to align the memorandum headings at the beginning of the memorandum.

8. Use the paragraph indention to set the temporary left margin at position 11 in the itemized list under the "Basic Word Division Rules" heading, and center this heading above the itemized list.

9. Use the margin release key when making the solid line below the memorandum headings. The line should extend from column 1 to column 70.

10. Do not enter the material in parentheses. The text in parentheses gives you instructions for preparing this document.

11. If you get the wrong command, use the ^U and Esc to cancel it.

12. Save the memorandum.

13. Print out the memorandum.

```
(Tab over to decimal tab setting 10.   Space twice after colon.)
· TO:   ALL WORD PROCESSING OPERATORS

FROM:   COMMUNICATIONS CENTER

DATE:   DECEMBER 1, 19--

SUBJECT:   WORD DIVISION
   (Use margin release to enter line from column 1 to 70.)
----------------------------------------------------------------------

(Tab over to column 11 for paragraph indention.)

        In an effort to continually improve the quality of

our document production, please follow the word division

rules outlined in this memo.
```

(Fig. 12.3, continued on p. 108)

When WordStar asks for a hyphenation, try to
divide the word at a point that will not interrupt the
reader's comprehension of the word. Try to avoid too
many hyphenated words in a paragraph. It may be
necessary to skip some hyphenation decisions in order to
keep word divisions at a minimum.
(Center the next line.)

                    Basic Word Division Rules
(Use column 11 for a temporary left margin.)

1.   Divide words only between syllables. Never divide
      a one-letter syllable at the beginning or end of a
      word. For example, the word amount should not be
      divided as a-mount. The word piano should not be
      divided as pian-o.

2.   One syllable words should not be divided.

3.   At least three characters, including the hyphen,
      must be left at the end of a line or carried to
      the beginning of the next line. One of the
      characters may be a punctuation mark or a hyphen.

      The following words are divided correctly.
(Tab over to columns 15, 29, and 41.)

          ad-journed   turn-ing   un-avoidable

4.   Do not divide abbreviations.   For example, do not
      divide the following abbreviations:

          UNESCO   Ph.D.   ASCAP

          NAACP   SPCA   YMCA

5.   Do not divide contractions. For example, do not
      divide the following contractions:

          doesn't   don't   wouldn't

6.   Divide compound words between the words. For
      example, divide the following compound words:
          home-owner   time-table   micro-computer

Figure 12.3   Text for Computer Exercise

13. Reformatting Text ──────────

OBJECTIVES:

1. Define text reformatting.
2. Explain how to get reformatting help and how to reformat a paragraph.
3. Explain how to reformat text with temporary margins.
4. Explain how to reformat without hyphenation help.
5. Explain how to reformat text around illustrations.
6. Explain how to reformat an entire document at once.

REFORMATTING TEXT

When additions and deletions are made in a paragraph, the text format may appear very strange on the screen. For example, sometimes a line will run only part way to the right margin; sometimes a word or phrase will be separated from the rest of a line in an unusual way; sometimes a plus (+) will appear on the right side of the screen at the end of a line. Because WordStar prints out the exact format displayed on the screen, it is necessary to reformat paragraphs after edits.

Text reformatting is the reshaping of text to match margin, line spacing, and right margin justification settings. The reformatting process begins from the line where the cursor is positioned and stops at the first hard return. You will recall that a hard return is one that has been entered by the computer operator. A return graphic ($<$) appears on the right side of the screen to indicate a hard return.

REFORMATTING A PARAGRAPH

WordStar will display on-screen help for reformatting paragraphs. Enter the command ^JB. The screen will then display information about paragraph reformatting.

The command to reformat a paragraph is entered by holding down the Ctrl key and then striking the B key at the same time. Three things will happen when text is reformatted:

1. The text will conform to the left and right margins on the ruler line, beginning at the line where the cursor is positioned and ending at the first hard return.

2. The text will conform to whatever the line spacing is on the status line.

3. The text will conform to either right margin justification or be ragged right depending on whether the justification default is on or off.

REFORMATTING WITH TEMPORARY LEFT MARGINS

When reformatting text that has been indented from the left margin temporarily, the ruler line must reflect the indention or the text will not reformat properly. To reformat text entered at a temporary left margin, be sure the ruler line reflects the temporary left margin setting. The command for left margin indentions, or paragraph tabs, is ^OG. The command ^OG causes the ruler line to indent to the first tab setting. A second ^OG command causes the ruler line to indent to the second tab setting, and so on. An ENTER/ RETURN will cancel the paragraph tab, so be sure to check the ruler line before reformatting temporary left margins.

REFORMATTING WITHOUT HYPHENATION

If you do not want the reformatting process to stop for hyphenation decisions, turn off the hyphen help by entering the command ^OH. The paragraph will reformat without stopping until the first return is reached.

REFORMATTING AROUND ILLUSTRATIONS

If your page layout requires that an illustration be inserted to the right of the text, follow these steps:

1. First enter the text with the default margins of 1 and 65 and make sure the justification is turned on.

2. After the text is entered, set the right margin at 30 (or appropriate number column to allow for the illustration) by entering the command ^OR 30 and ENTER/RETURN.

3. Position the cursor at the beginning of the text.

4. Enter ^B. The text will reformat to the new margin of 30, leaving a wide right margin to insert the illustration.

Figure 13.1 illustrates a paragraph entered with standard margins. Figure 13.2 illustrates the paragraph in Figure 13.1 after the right margin has been changed to 30 and the command ^B has been entered with the cursor on the first line of the paragraph. An illustration can be inserted on the right side of the text after the paragraph is reformatted.

```
The disk drives use a floppy disk (as shown in the figure at  the
right) to  store material.   A floppy disk looks like a  45  rpm
phonograph  record.    Disks used can be 5 1/4 inches or 8 inches,
depending on the disk drive.
```

**Figure 13.1   Text Entered with Margins and Justification at
                    Default**

```
The  disk drives use a  floppy
disk  (as shown in the  figure
at  the  right)  to    store
material.  A floppy disk looks
like  a  45  rpm  phonograph
record.   Disks  used can be 5
1/4  inches  or  8   inches,
depending on the disk drive.
```

Figure 13.2   Text Reformatted with Right Margin at 30

Of course, the text could have been entered from the beginning with the right margin at 30. The same procedure would be followed if you wanted an illustration on the left of the text; the left margin would be set at 30 with the command ^OL, and then the paragraph would be reformatted.

Suppose you would like to have an illustration with text surrounding it. Figure 13.3 illustrates text reformatted for this purpose.

```
The disk drives use a floppy disk (as shown in the figure at  the
right) to store  material.    A
floppy  disk  looks like a  45       (PLACE ILLUSTRATION HERE)
rpm phonograph record.   Disks
used  can  be  5 1/4 inches or  8 inches,  depending on  the  disk
drive.
```

Figure 13.3   Text Surrounding an Illustration

These steps should be followed to reformat the text in Figure 13.1 so that it will appear as shown in Figure 13.3:

1. Position the cursor on the line where the indention is to begin. In Figure 13.1, the cursor should be placed on line 2.

2. Change the right margin using ^OR. The margin should be changed to 30 to achieve the result in Figure 13.3.

3. Enter the command ^B. All the text in Figure 13.1 beginning at line 2 will conform to the new right margin setting of 30.

4. Position the cursor on the line that will fall after the illustration. To achieve the results in Figure 13.3, the cursor was positioned on the fifth line of text.

5. Reset the right margin to the original setting. In Figure 13.3, the right margin was reset at 65.

6. Enter the reformat command ^B.

REFORMATTING AN ENTIRE DOCUMENT AT ONCE

WordStar has a command that means "repeat the next command at the rate set by the operator until stopped by the operator." This "repeat next command" feature is entered by striking the Ctrl key, the Q (uppercase or lowercase) key twice, and the reformat command ^B (^QQ^B). This feature can be used to reformat all paragraphs in a document to the end of the file without stopping at hard returns. If the cursor is at the beginning of the file, the entire file will conform to the margin, line, and justification settings.

When the command ^QQ^B is entered, a prompt appears in the upper left-hand corner of the screen. Figure 13.4 illustrates the ^QQ^B prompt.

TYPE 1 - 9 TO VARY SPEED.   SPACE TO STOP

Figure 13.4   ^QQ^B Repeat Command Prompt

The repeat command speed rate can be changed by entering any number between 1 and 9. The lower the number, the higher the speed; the higher the number, the slower the speed. The default speed is 3. For practical purposes, you might want to enter a speed of 1 to reformat an entire document more quickly. The command to do this would be ^QQ^B1.

The repeat command (^QQ) can be used with other commands such as the ^C command. This command moves the text up by screen toward the end of a document. If you enter ^QQ^C, the text will move up by screen continually at the speed of 3 (the default) until the operator stops the command by striking the space bar. The ^R command can also be used with the ^QQ feature (^QQ^R). This command will cause the text to move down by screen toward the beginning of a document until stopped by the operator.

LESSON 13 EXERCISE

Name _____ Date _____

TRUE/FALSE

Each of the following statements is either true or false. Indicate your choice in the Answers column by circling T for a true statement or F for a false statement.

Answers

1. Text reformatting is the reshaping of text to match margin, line spacing, and right margin justification settings. (Obj. 1) ....   1. **T F**

2. When additions and deletions are made to text, WordStar automatically reformats the text. (Obj. 1) ....   2. **T F**

3. The reformatting process stops at the first hard return. (Obj. 1)..........   3. **T F**

4. The command to reformat a paragraph is ^B. (Obj. 2) ....   4. **T F**

5. When a paragraph is reformatted, the paragraph will conform to the margin, line spacing, and justification settings. (Obj. 2) ....   5. **T F**

6. The ruler line must reflect the temporary left margin setting before reformatting indented text. (Obj. 3) ....   6. **T F**

7. The command for a paragraph tab or a temporary left margin is ^OL. (Obj. 3) ....   7. **T F**

8. When ^OG is entered, the ruler line will indent to the first tab setting. (Obj. 3) ....   8. **T F**

9. WordStar will display information about reformatting paragraphs when the command ^JB is entered. (Obj. 2) ....   9. **T F**

10. Hyphenation help can be turned off by entering the command ^OH. (Obj. 4) ....   10. **T F**

11. Text can be reformatted around an illustration by first entering the text at the margin defaults of 1 and 65. (Obj. 5) ....   11. **T F**

12. To leave a wide right margin for an illustration, enter the command ^OL 30. (Obj. 5) ....   12. **T F**

13. To reformat text around an illustration, the original margins must be reentered on the ruler line to align text below the illustration. (Obj. 5) ....   13. **T F**

14. The command to reformat an entire document at once is ^QQ^B. (Obj. 6) ....   14. **T F**

15. The speed of the reformatting process can be varied when using the repeat command feature. (Obj. 6)...   15. **T F**

16. The repeat reformatting process can be stopped by striking the space bar. (Obj. 6) ....   16. **T F**

17. If you enter 9 after the repeat command prompt, the reformatting process will go quickly. (Obj. 6)...   17. **T F**

18. The repeat command should be used with the ^B command only. (Obj. 6) .   18. **T F**

19. The default speed for the repeat command is 3. (Obj. 6) ....   19. **T F**

COMPLETION

Indicate the correct answer in the space provided.

1. After deletions and additions are made in a file, the text will need to be *?* (Obj. 1)..............................   1. _____

2. When you reformat text, the text will conform to *?* (Obj. 1)..   2. a. _____
   b. _____
   c. _____

3. A return that has been entered by the operator is called *?* (Obj. 1) ....   3. _____

4. The command to reformat a paragraph is *?* (Obj. 2) ....   4. _____

5. The temporary left margin or paragraph tab command is *?* (Obj. 3)..   5. _____

6. What must reflect the temporary left margin indention, if the paragraph is to reformat properly? (Obj. 3) ......   6. _____

7. If the command ^OG is entered four times, a temporary left margin will be set at the *?* (Obj. 3) ....   7. _____

8. What will cancel the temporary left margin setting? (Obj. 3) ....   8. _____

9. The screen will display reformatting help if the operator enters the command *?* (Obj. 2) ....   9. _____

10. To turn off hyphenation help, enter the command *?* (Obj. 4) ....   10. _____

11. To make space for an illustration to the right of text, which margin must be reset? (Obj. 5) ....   11. _____

12. One way to surround an illustration with text is to first enter the text at the original margin settings, and then *?* (Obj. 5) ....   12. _____

13. The repeat command is *?* (Obj. 6) ....   13. _____

14. To reformat an entire document without stopping at hard returns, enter the command *?* (Obj. 6).............   14. _____

15. To display text by screen until the end of the document is reached, enter the command *?* (Obj. 6)...............   15. _____

16. To display text by screen until the beginning of the document is reached, enter the command *?* (Obj. 6) ....   16. _____

17. The default for the repeat command speed is *?* (Obj. 6) ....   17. _____

18. To enter the repeat reformat command at the highest speed, enter the command *?* (Obj. 6) ....   18. _____

19. To enter the repeat reformat command at the slowest speed, enter the command *?* (Obj. 6) ....   19. _____

20. To stop the repeat command, strike the *?* (Obj. 6) ......   20. _____

COMPUTER EXERCISE ONE

Directions: Follow these step-by-step instructions to complete Computer Exercise One:

1. Create a file and name it LESSON13.EX1.

2. Enter the text in Figure 13.5. Do not key-in the text in parentheses.

3. Use the standard default margins.

4. Set the help level at 2.

5. Omit the page number.

6. Turn off the justification.

7. Double space your copy.

8. Center the title.

9. Triple space after the title.

10. Indent the numbered text to the first default tab. (The numbers should begin at column one.)

11. Save your file.

12. Print out the file named LESSON13.EX1.

A SAMPLE BRIDGE HAND

1.   The following bridge hand was dealt at a recent bridge tournament in San Francisco.

2.   Look at the illustration below and see if you can figure out the key play that makes the contract for the East.

3.   Bridge expert Alfred Sheinwold gives an analysis of the hand and describes how to win or defeat the contract in the text below.

South takes the second spade with the king and leads the queen of diamonds to dummy's king. East takes the ace of diamonds and then must make the key play.

If East makes a passive return, such as the jack of clubs, South wins in dummy and cashes a high diamond to discard the queen of spades. Then, since there is no danger of a spade ruff, South can afford to try a heart finesse.

(Fig. 13.5, continued on p. 116)

West can do no damage when he takes the queen of hearts.   South
returns to dummy with a club to repeat the heart finesse.   When East
takes the ace of diamonds, his key play is to return his low trump.
If South finesses, West wins and gives East a spade ruff to defeat the
contract.   If South doesn't finesse, the defenders get two natural
~~mp tricks.

Directions: Follow these step~~~
Computer Exercise Two:

1. Make a copy of the file named LESSON13.EX1 you made in Computer Exercise One. To do this, follow these steps:

   a. Enter the letter O (uppercase or lowercase) from the opening menu.

   b. The screen shows the prompt NAME OF FILE TO COPY FROM? Enter LESSON13.EX1.

   c. The screen shows the prompt NAME OF FILE TO COPY TO? Enter LESSON13.EX2. You now have two copies of the same file. One copy is named LESSON13.EX1 and the other copy is named LESSON13.EX2.

2. Edit the file named LESSON13.EX2.

3. Turn the justification on.

4. Change the line spacing to single space.

5. Turn off hyphen help.

6. Enter $\wedge JB$ and read the information displayed on the screen about reformatting paragraphs.

7. Reformat the numbered items, making sure the ruler line is indented to reflect the temporary left margin. The cursor should be at column 6 before each reformat. Stop reformatting after the third numbered item in the text.

8. Reformat the rest of the text with the repeat format command.

9. Reformat the text to make room for an illustration that will be inserted at the left of the text. The illustration will be two inches long and two inches wide.

10. Save the document.

11. Print the file named LESSON13.EX2.

14. Finding Text

OBJECTIVES:

1. Explain the find or search concept.
2. Define a string.
3. Describe the find command.
4. Introduce the find options.
5. Explain how to find a string from the cursor to the file beginning.
6. Explain how to find whole words.
7. Explain how to find words in uppercase or lowercase.
8. Explain how to find a specific occurrence of text.
9. Describe how to combine the find options.
10. Explain how to return the cursor after the find command.
11. Define place markers.
12. Describe the place marker command.
13. Explain how to find text with place markers.

THE FIND OR SEARCH CONCEPT

One of the most important parts of any word processing program is the ability to find and display designated text quickly within a document. When documents are produced using a typewriter, you have to visually scan the document from beginning to end to find a specific word or words. This can be time consuming and frustrating if the document is long. WordStar will go directly to the character, word, or group of words you specify. After specific text has been found, you can delete it, add to it, correct it, or just read it.

In addition to using the find command to search for text to edit, this command can be used to advance the cursor to a particular page number. A key word or phrase on a page can be identified in the command to locate the page quickly.

DEFINITION OF A STRING

To find text within a document, you must, of course, know what you want to find. Text identified in the find command is called a **string**. A string may be just one character (such as a letter, a return, or a space), a string may be one word, or a string may be a group of words. The maximum length of a string is 30 characters.

FIND COMMAND

The command to find a string is ^QF (quickly find). When ^QF is entered, the screen displays the prompt illustrated in Figure 14.1.

```
^S=delete character    ^Y=delete entry    ^F=File directory
^D=restore character   ^R=Restore entry   ^U=cancel command

   FIND?
```

Figure 14.1   The Find Command Prompt

Enter the string you wish to find and press ENTER/ RETURN. For example, if you want to find the string "word," enter *word* and press ENTER/RETURN. The screen will display the prompt illustrated in Figure 14.2.

```
^S=delete character    ^Y=delete entry    ^F=File directory
^D=restore character   ^R=Restore entry   ^U=cancel command

   FIND? word    OPTIONS? (? FOR INFO)
```

Figure 14.2   Find Prompt After Identifying String

Press ENTER/RETURN at the "OPTIONS? (? FOR INFO)." The find command begins by searching for "word" from the cursor position to the end of the file. The cursor will stop at the end of the first occurrence of the string you designated as "word."

Four things should be noted here about entering the ^QF command, identifying a string, and pressing the ENTER/RETURN after the option prompt:

1. Only the exact string entered at the prompt will be found. So, "Word" with a capital *W* will not be found.

2. The search will begin at the cursor position. So if the ^QF

command was entered in the middle of the document, the search will start from the middle of the document.

3. The search will stop at the first occurrence of the string.

4. The search will stop at any word containing the string. For example, the search for "word" will stop at "sword," "words," "wording," "swordfish," "swordsmanship," and so on.

If the computer cannot find "word," the screen displays the prompt illustrated in Figure 14.3. The cursor will be at the end of the file when this prompt displays. Strike the Esc key.

```
FIND? word    OPTIONS? (? FOR INFO)


*** NOT FOUND: "word" *** Press ESCAPE Key
```

Figure 14.3   Prompt When String is not Found

To continue searching for the next occurrence of a designated string, enter $\land L$. For example, to find the next occurrence of the string "word," enter $\land L$ and the cursor will stop when the next "word" is found. If there are no more occurrences of "word," the screen will display the prompt shown in Figure 14.3.

FIND OPTIONS

You have four options with the find command:

1. You may search for a string from the cursor position to the beginning of the file. You will recall that by striking the ENTER/RETURN key after the "OPTIONS? (? FOR INFO)" prompt, the search begins from the cursor position to the end of the file.

2. You may search for a complete word. You will recall that by striking the ENTER/RETURN key after the "OPTIONS? (? FOR INFO)" prompt, the cursor will stop at text that contains the string (sword, swordsmanship, and so on).

3. You may search for a string in uppercase or lowercase. Again, you will recall that striking ENTER/RETURN after the "OPTIONS? (? FOR INFO)" prompt will cause the computer to search for the string exactly as it was entered, so "Word" with a capital W will not be found if "word" is identified as the string.

4. You may search for a specific occurrence of a string. You may want to find only the third occurrence of a string and skip the first two.

FIND OPTION FROM CURSOR TO FILE BEGINNING

To search for a string from the cursor position to the beginning of the file, enter *B* and press ENTER/RETURN at the "OPTIONS? (? FOR INFO)" prompt as illustrated in Figure 14.4. Strike ^*L* to find the next string.

```
FIND?  word    OPTIONS? (? FOR INFO) B
```

Figure 14.4   Search From Cursor Position To File Beginning

FIND A COMPLETE WORD OPTION

To search for a complete word to avoid the cursor stopping at a string within a string, enter *W* and press ENTER/RETURN at the "OPTIONS? (? FOR INFO)" prompt as illustrated in Figure 14.5.

```
FIND?  word    OPTIONS? (? FOR INFO) W
```

Figure 14.5   Search for a Complete Word

FINDING WORDS IN UPPERCASE AND LOWERCASE

To find a word regardless of whether it begins with a capital letter or a lowercase letter, enter *U* and press ENTER/RETURN after the "OPTIONS? (? FOR INFO)" prompt as illustrated in Figure 14.6.

```
FIND?  word   OPTIONS? (? FOR INFO) U
```

Figure 14.6   Search in Uppercase and Lowercase

FINDING A SPECIFIC OCCURRENCE

To find a specific occurrence of a string, such as its second or fifth occurrence, enter the number of the occurrence. The cursor will skip the previous times the string was entered and stop at the number entered in the option prompt. For example, to find the third occurrence of "word," enter 3 and press ENTER/RETURN after the "OPTIONS? (? FOR INFO)" prompt as illustrated in Figure 14.7. The cursor will skip the first two times "word" was entered and stop at the third occurrence of "word."

```
FIND?  word   OPTIONS? (? FOR INFO) 3
```

Figure 14.7   Finding a Specific Occurrence of Text

COMBINING THE FIND OPTIONS

All four options can be combined to apply the find command to your particular specifications. For example, to search from the cursor to the file beginning for the fifth occurrence of the complete word of the string "word" regardless of uppercase or lowercase, enter BWU5 and press ENTER/RETURN at the "OPTIONS? (? FOR INFO)" prompt. All options or a combination of the find options can be chosen. The options may be entered in any order.

It is possible to duplicate the last find command and its options by entering $^\wedge QF$ and then $^\wedge R$ to answer the FIND? prompt. The last string you entered in the find command will display on the screen. You can make any changes in the previous string you entered and the find command will display on the screen. You can make any changes in the previous string, or you can leave it as it is. Then press ENTER/RETURN to get the "OPTIONS? (? FOR INFO)" prompt. If you want the same options as last time, enter $^\wedge R$ and press ENTER/RETURN. The search will begin. The cursor will return to its original position after you are finished with the find command if you enter $^\wedge QV$.

PLACE MARKERS

When editing a file, you may want to look at text before or after the material you are now editing, and then return to your original position quickly without scrolling through the file searching for the position you left. When creating a file, you may want to identify text that you know will need revisions and further editing.

A place marker identifies a specific section of a file. You can return to that specific section quickly without reading through your document.

PLACE MARKER COMMAND

A total of ten place markers can be entered in a file. To mark text for quick access, hold down the Ctrl key and strike the letter K (uppercase or lowercase) and any number from 0 to 9. To mark text in a file that contains one place marker (^K0) already, key-in the command ^K1 at the beginning of the text you want to mark. The screen will display <1>. This display will not print. To cancel the place marker, enter the command ^K1 again.

Saving a file with ^KD cancels all place markers; however, saving a file with ^KS will keep the place markers because with ^KS you are still in the edit mode.

FINDING TEXT WITH PLACE MARKERS

To find text that has been marked, hold the Ctrl key and strike the letter Q (uppercase or lowercase) and the number of the marker. To find text that has been marked ^K5, enter ^Q5. If the place marker cannot be found, the screen displays the message as illustrated in Figure 14.8. (Figure 14.9 illustrates a summary of the commands to find text.)

```
*** ERROR E5:   THAT PLACE MARKER NOT SET *** Press ESCAPE Key
```

Figure 14.8   Display When Place Marker is not Found

Applications	Command	Prompt	Command
Find text from cursor position to file end.	^QF	FIND? (*enter string*)	ENTER/RETURN
		OPTIONS? (? FOR IN-FO)	ENTER/RETURN
	^L (*to continue search*)		
Find text from cursor position to file beginning.	^QF	FIND? (*enter string*)	ENTER/RETURN
		OPTIONS? (? FOR IN-FO) *B*	ENTER/RETURN
	^L (*to continue search*)		
Find a complete word.	^QF	FIND? (*enter string*)	ENTER/RETURN
		OPTIONS? (? FOR IN-FO) *W*	ENTER/RETURN
	^L (*to continue search*)		
Find text regard-less of uppercase or lowercase.	^QF	FIND? (*enter string*)	ENTER/RETURN
		OPTIONS? (? FOR IN-FO) *U*	ENTER/RETURN
	^L (*to continue search*)		
Set place marker.	^K (*and marker number from 0-9*)		
Find place mark-er.	^Q (*and marker number from 0-9*)		
Return cursor to original position after find com-mand.	^QV		
Repeat the last find command.	^QF^R		

Figure 14.9   Summary of Find and Place Marker Commands

Name _____ Date _____

TRUE/FALSE

Each of the following statements is either true or false. Indicate your choice in the Answers column by circling T for a true statement or F for a false statement.

Answers

1. WordStar will go directly to any character, word, or group of words specified. (Obj. 1) ....   1.   **T**   **F**

2. Text identified in the find command is called a string. (Obj. 2) ....   2.   **T**   **F**

3. A string can be a return. (Obj. 2) ....   3.   **T**   **F**

4. A string can be any length. (Obj. 2)...   4.   **T**   **F**

5. The find command is ^F. (Obj. 3) ....   5.   **T**   **F**

6. When an ENTER/RETURN is struck after the FIND? prompt, the search begins. (Obj. 3) ....   6.   **T**   **F**

7. Only the exact string entered at the FIND? prompt will be found unless some options are chosen. (Obj. 3)...   7.   **T**   **F**

8. The search always starts from the beginning of the file. (Obj. 3) ....   8.   **T**   **F**

9. If WordStar is looking for "and" with no options, the cursor will stop at "stand," "band," "standing," and "brand." (Obj. 3) ....   9.   **T**   **F**

10. Esc must be entered after the ***NOT FOUND*** prompt. (Obj. 3) ......   10.   **T**   **F**

11. WordStar searches for every occurrence of a string throughout the file without any further commands from the operator. (Obj. 3) ....   11.   **T**   **F**

12. The command to search from the cursor position to the file beginning is B at the OPTIONS? prompt. (Obj. 5) ....   12.   **T**   **F**

13. The command to search for a complete word is W at the OPTIONS? prompt. (Obj. 6) ....   13.   **T**   **F**

14. The command to search for a word in uppercase or lowercase is U at the OPTIONS? prompt. (Obj. 7) ....   14.   **T**   **F**

15. To search for the ninth occurrence of a string, enter 9 at the OPTIONS? prompt. (Obj. 8) ....   15.   **T**   **F**

16. When combining options, *B* must always be entered before *U*. (Obj. 9) ....   16.   **T**   **F**

17. To search backwards through a file for the word "computer," enter *BW*. (Obj. 9) ....   17.   **T**   **F**

18. To search for "Computer," beginning with a capital *C*, enter *W* and *U* at the OPTIONS? prompt. (Obj. 9) ....   18.   **T**   **F**

19. To duplicate the last command at the FIND? prompt, enter ^*R*. (Obj. 9) ..   19.   **T**   **F**

20. To duplicate the last command at the OPTIONS? prompt, enter ^*R*. (Obj. 9) ....   20.   **T**   **F**

21. The command to return the cursor to the original position before the find command is ^R. (Obj. 10) ....   21.   **T**   **F**

22. A place marker identifies a section of text. (Obj. 11).....................   22.   **T**   **F**

23. Place markers are saved when entering ^KD. (Obj. 12) ....   23.   **T**   **F**

24. Place markers are canceled by entering the place marker command again. (Obj. 12) ....   24.   **T**   **F**

25. To move the cursor to a place marker labeled ^K4, key-in ^Q4. (Obj. 13) ..   25.   **T**   **F**

COMPLETION

Indicate the correct answer in the space provided.

1. What is the name of the command that allows you to go directly to a specific page in the document? (Obj. 1)....   1. _____

2. Text identified in the find command is called a *?* (Obj. 2) ....   2. _____

3. How many characters are the maximum for a string? (Obj. 2) ....   3. _____

4. The find command is *?* (Obj. 3)........................   4. _____

5. When the find command is executed with no options, the cursor will stop at the beginning or end of the first occurrence of the string? (Obj. 3).....................   5. _____

6. When the find command is executed, the search will start from the *?* (Obj. 3)...   6. _____

7. Which key must you strike when the ***NOT FOUND*** is displayed? (Obj. 3) ....   7. _____

8. What must you enter at the OPTIONS? prompt to search from the cursor position to the file beginning? (Obj. 5).   8. _____

9. What must you enter at the OPTIONS? prompt to search for a complete word? (Obj. 6) ....   9. _____

10. What must you enter at the OPTIONS? prompt to search for a string in uppercase or lowercase? (Obj. 7).........   10. _____

11. What must you enter at the OPTIONS? prompt to find the seventh occurrence of a string? (Obj. 8).............   11. _____

12. What must you enter at the OPTIONS? prompt to find the third occurrence of a complete word in uppercase only? (Obj. 9) ....   12. _____

13. To return the cursor to its original position after a find command, enter *?* (Obj. 10)..............................   13. _____

14. What identifies a specific section of a file? (Obj. 11) ...   14. _____

15. To set a place marker, what must you enter along with a number at the beginning of the text you want to mark? (Obj. 12) ....   15. _____

16. How many place markers can a file contain? (Obj. 12) .   16. _____

17. To find text that has been identified with ^K8, enter *?* (Obj. 13) ....   17. _____

18. What key must be struck if the place marker is not set? (Obj. 13) ....   18. _____

COMPUTER EXERCISE

Directions: Follow the step-by-step instructions given to complete the computer exercise.

1. The file you previously named LESSON7.EX1 will be used for this computer exercise. If you did not create the file named LESSON7.EX1, do so now by following the directions for Computer Exercises One and Two in Lesson 7 on pages 61 and 62; then continue with this exercise. If you did create a file named LESSON7.EX1, continue with step 2 of these directions.

2. Copy the file named LESSON7.EX1 to a new file named LESSON14.EX. To do this, follow these instructions:

   a. Strike the letter O from the opening menu. A prompt is then displayed: NAME OF FILE TO COPY FROM?

   b. Enter LESSON7.EX1 and press ENTER/RETURN. A prompt is displayed: NAME OF FILE TO COPY TO?

   c. Enter LESSON14.EX. The file directory will now show two files containing the same information.

3. You will edit the file named LESSON14.EX. If you enter a wrong command as you work through the rest of these instructions, strike the ^U and the Esc key. Enter the appropriate options.

4. Position the cursor at the beginning of the file.

5. Find "word." (Enter *word* and press ENTER/RETURN at the FIND? prompt.)

6. Edit "word" so that it appears in all capital letters throughout the document. Continue this process until ***NOT FOUND*** is displayed.

7. Strike Esc when the ***NOT FOUND*** prompt is displayed. Your cursor should be at the end of the file.

8. Now find "WORD" and change "WORD" to "text".

9. Strike Esc at the ***NOT FOUND*** prompt. The cursor should be at the beginning of the text.

10. Find "process" each time it occurs regardless of whether it is uppercase or lowercase. Do not make any changes. Strike ^L to continue the search until the ***NOT

FOUND*** message is displayed. Strike the Esc key. The cursor should be at the end of the file.

11. Find the sixth occurrence of "text." Because the cursor is at the end of the file, enter *B* as well as *6* at the OPTIONS? prompt. Also key-in *W* at the OPTIONS? so that the complete word will be found, and key-in in *U* so that every "text," whether it is uppercase or lowercase, will be searched.

12. Repeat the last find command. Enter ^*R* after FIND? The last find command was to find "text." Press the ENTER/ RETURN key. Enter ^*R* after the OPTIONS? prompt. The last option was B6WU (in any order). Press the ENTER/RETURN key. Strike Esc when the ***NOT FOUND*** prompt is displayed.

13. Return the cursor to the position before the last find command.

14. Enter a place marker at this point. The number of the marker should be 0.

15. Position the cursor at position 16 on the first line of the next screen. Set another place marker here and number it 1.

16. Go to the end of the document.

17. Find the text at the first place marker.

18. Find the text at the second place marker.

19. Return to the beginning of the document.

20. Find "text." Change "text" to "TEXT" in all capital letters at every occurrence. Strike ^*L* until the ***NOT FOUND*** prompt is displayed.

21. Save the file.

22. Print the file named LESSON14.EX.

15. Replacing Text _____

OBJECTIVES:

1. Explain the replace concept.

2. Describe the replace command.

3. Introduce the replace options.

4. Show how to replace text globally and selectively.

5. Describe how to replace text from the cursor position without operator input.

6. Describe how to replace text globally without stopping.

7. Explain how to return the cursor to its original position.

8. Explain how to delete a string.

9. Explain how to insert a string at different places in the text throughout a file.

10. Summarize the replace command.

THE REPLACE CONCEPT

Replacing one string with another string with one command makes WordStar a powerful editing tool. You have already learned how to find a string with the ^QF command and then enter a new string. But the replace command is much more efficient. For example, you may want to replace the string "word" with the string "character." The replace command will find "word" and ask if you want it replaced with "character." With the replace command, you do not have to reenter the replacement each time the string is found.

To find a string and replace it with another string, enter the command ^QA. When ^QA is entered, the screen displays the prompt as illustrated in Figure 15.1.

```
^S=delete character   ^Y=delete entry    ^F=File directory
^D=restore character  ^R=Restore entry   ^U=cancel command

    FIND?
```

Figure 15.1   The Replace Command Prompt

So far, the prompt is exactly the same as the find command prompt. Enter the string you want to find. Using the example given, enter the string "word" and press ENTER/RETURN at the FIND? prompt. Now the screen will display the prompt as illustrated in Figure 15.2.

```
^S=delete character    ^Y=delete entry    ^F=File directory
^D=restore character   ^R=Restore entry   ^U=cancel command

   FIND? word    REPLACE WITH ?
```

**Figure 15.2   The Replace Command Display After Identifying
                  Text to Find**

Continuing with the example, enter the string "character" at the REPLACE WITH? prompt. The screen will now show the display as illustrated in Figure 15.3.

```
^S=delete character    ^Y=delete entry    ^F=File directory
^D=restore character   ^R=Restore entry   ^U=cancel command

   FIND? word    REPLACE WITH? character
```

**Figure 15.3   The Replace Command Display After New String
                  is Identified**

Press the ENTER/RETURN key after identifying a new string. The screen will now display the "OPTIONS? (? FOR INFO)" prompt as illustrated in Figure 15.4.

```
^S=delete character    ^Y=delete entry    ^F=File directory
^D=restore character   ^R=Restore entry   ^U=cancel command

   FIND? word    REPLACE WITH? character
OPTIONS? (? FOR INFO)
```

Figure 15.4   The Replace Command With Option Display

Press the ENTER/RETURN key again. These two things will happen:

1. From the cursor position, the computer will search for "word" to the file's end. When the first occurrence of "word" is found, the cursor will stop.

2. A prompt will appear in the upper right-hand side of the screen as illustrated in Figure 15.5.

REPLACE (Y/N):

Figure 15.5   The Replace Command Display After String is Found

To make the replacement, enter Y (for yes). The string "word" will be replaced with "character." If you do not wish the replacement at this particular occurrence, enter N (for no) and "word" will not be replaced. Unless the replacement has the exact number of characters as the original text, the paragraph must be reformatted. So enter $^\wedge B$ to reformat the paragraph. Now enter $^\wedge L$ to continue the replace command and to find the next occurrence of "word." Enter either a Y or N again, a $^\wedge B$ if you want to reformat the paragraph, and a $^\wedge L$ until the prompt shown in Figure 15.6 is displayed. After the prompt in Figure 15.6 occurs, strike the Esc key.

*** NOT FOUND: "word" *** Press ESCAPE key

Figure 15.6   Prompt When String is not Found

Sometimes the text to be replaced will not be found, and the prompt in Figure 15.6 will appear at the end of the file. If the string cannot be found, it is possible that the string may not have been entered correctly and the computer cannot find a match. Also, remember that if the text is justified, the computer may have added more than one space between words to form wordwrap. If words have two spaces between them and only one space was entered in the FIND? prompt, the string will not be found. If you have a printout of the file, you can check if extra spaces have been added between the words you identified in the FIND? prompt. Again, this strange spacing will only occur if the text is justified.

In addition to the options available in the find command (B, W, U, and number), the replace command has two additional options:

1. The command can replace text globally and selectively, stopping at each occurrence to ask the operator if the replacement should be executed. (*Globally* means that the entire file will be searched from beginning to end.)

2. The command can replace text from the cursor position without stopping to ask the operator if replacement should be executed.

REPLACING TEXT GLOBALLY AND SELECTIVELY

To replace text globally (from a file's beginning to end) and selectively (to be asked if replacement is desired at each string), enter *G* at the OPTIONS? prompt. Figure 15.7 illustrates how the screen will look when the *G* option is entered for the replace command.

```
^S=delete character   ^Y=delete entry    ^F=File directory
^D=restore character   ^R=Restore entry   ^U=cancel command

  FIND? word    REPLACE WITH? character
OPTIONS? (? FOR INFO) G
```

Figure 15.7   Selective Global Replace Option Display

Press the ENTER/RETURN key after answering the prompt. The search will start from the file's beginning and stop at the first occurrence of "word." The screen will display the prompt illustrated in Figure 15.8 in the upper right-hand corner of the screen.

```
                                        REPLACE (Y/N):
```

Figure 15.8   The Replace Prompt

If *Y* (for yes) is entered, the replacement will be made. "Character" will replace "word" and the search will continue until "word" is found again. If *N* (for no) is entered at the prompt, the replacement will not be made. The search will continue for "word" until the cursor comes to the end of the file.

REPLACING TEXT FROM CURSOR WITHOUT BEING ASKED

To execute the replacement from the cursor position without the "REPLACE (Y/N):" prompt, enter N (for no) at the OPTIONS? prompt. The screen will look like the illustration in Figure 15.9.

```
^S=delete character    ^Y=delete entry    ^F=File directory
^D=restore character   ^R=Restore entry   ^U=cancel command

  FIND?  word    REPLACE WITH ?    character
OPTIONS? (? FOR INFO)   N
```

Figure 15.9   Display to Replace Text from Cursor Without Being Asked

Press the ENTER/RETURN key after answering the prompt. When "word" is found, "character" will replace it automatically. You will not be asked if the replacement is desired. Enter $^\wedge L$ to find and replace the next occurrence.

REPLACING TEXT GLOBALLY WITHOUT STOPPING

To replace text throughout an entire file without stopping, enter N and G in any order after the OPTIONS? prompt. The replacement will start at the beginning of the file regardless of where the cursor was when entering the command. The replacement will continue until the end of the file. Figure 15.10 illustrates the screen display when you want to replace one string with another string throughout the entire file without stopping. (After the replace command has been executed, enter $^\wedge QV$ to return the cursor to the position it was before the command was given.)

```
^S=delete character    ^Y=delete entry    ^F=File directory
^D=restore character   ^R=Restore entry   ^U=cancel command

  FIND?  word    REPLACE WITH ?    character
OPTIONS? (? FOR INFO) NG
```

Figure 15.10   Display for Global Replacement Without Stopping

DELETING A STRING

To delete a string, enter the string to be deleted at the FIND? prompt. When the REPLACE? prompt is displayed, press the ENTER/RETURN key. This means that when "word" is found, it will be deleted.

You can choose the N (delete a string from cursor position and delete without operator input), *G* (delete a string from the beginning of the file while stopping for operator input), or *NG* (delete a string globally without stopping) options. Figure 15.11 illustrates how the screen will look when you want to delete a string throughout the entire document without stopping.

```
^S=delete character    ^Y=delete entry    ^F=File directory
^D=restore character   ^R=Restore entry   ^U=cancel command

   FIND?  word   REPLACE WITH ?
   OPTIONS? (? FOR INFO) NG
```

Figure 15.11   Display to Delete a String Globally Without Stopping

INSERTING A STRING AT DIFFERENT TEXT LOCATIONS

Sometimes you will want to insert the same phrase at different spots throughout a document. To do this, strike ENTER/RETURN after the FIND? prompt. Enter the string you want to insert after the REPLACE? prompt. Press the ENTER/RETURN key. Enter *N* at the OPTIONS? prompt. Move the cursor to the spot where you want the string inserted. Enter ^*L* and the string will be inserted. Then move the cursor to the next spot where you want the string inserted. Enter ^*L*, the string will be inserted, and so forth. Figure 15.12 illustrates how the screen will look to command Word-Star to enter a string at various spots throughout a document.

```
^S=delete character    ^Y=delete entry    ^F=File directory
^D=restore character   ^R=Restore entry   ^U=cancel command

   FIND?  REPLACE WITH ?    See Appendix A For Details.
   OPTIONS? (? FOR INFO) N
```

Figure 15.12   Screen Display for Inserting Strings at Different Positions in a Document

Figure 15.13 on pages 135 and 136 is a summary of the replacement commands. (Notice that to repeat the last find, the last replacement, and/or the last option, the ^R command is entered. This works exactly like the ^R command when using the find command.)

Application	Command	Prompt	Command
Replace text from cursor position; stop for a replacement decision.	^QA	FIND? (*enter string*)	ENTER/RETURN
		REPLACE WITH? (*enter string*)	ENTER/RETURN
		OPTIONS? (? FOR INFO)	ENTER/RETURN
		REPLACE (Y/N):	(*Enter Y or N*)
	^L (*to continue search*)		
Replace text globally, stop for a replacement decision, and continue search.	^QA	FIND? (*enter string*)	ENTER/RETURN
		REPLACE WITH? (*enter string*)	ENTER/RETURN
		OPTIONS? (? FOR INFO) *G*	ENTER/RETURN
			(*Enter Y or N. Search will continue.*)
		REPLACE (Y/N):	
Replace text from cursor position without stopping for a replacement decision.	^QA	FIND? (*enter string*)	ENTER/RETURN
		REPLACE WITH? (*enter string*)	ENTER/RETURN
		OPTIONS? (? FOR INFO) *N*	ENTER/RETURN
	^L (*to continue search*)		
Return cursor to original position before replace command.	^QV		

(Fig. 15.13, continued on p. 136)

Delete a string through an entire file.	^QA	FIND? (*enter string*)	ENTER/RETURN
		REPLACE WITH? (*enter string*)	ENTER/RETURN
		OPTIONS? (? FOR IN-FO) *NG*	ENTER/RETURN
Insert a string at different text locations.	^QA	FIND? (*enter string*)	ENTER/RETURN
		REPLACE WITH? (*enter string*)	ENTER/RETURN
		OPTIONS? (? FOR IN-FO) *N*	ENTER/RETURN
	Move cursor to insert position and enter ^L.		
Repeat last find, last replace, and/or last option.	^QA^R		

Figure 15.13   A Summary of the Replace Commands

LESSON 15 EXERCISE   Name _____   Date _____

TRUE/FALSE

Each of the following statements is either true or false. Indicate your choice in the Answers column by circling T for a true statement or F for a false statement.

1. The replacement string does not have to be reentered if you enter a replace command. (Obj. 1) ....   1.   T   F

2. The replace command is ^QA. (Obj. 2) ....   2.   T   F

3. The first prompt after ^QA is entered is exactly like the first prompt after ^QF is entered. (Obj. 2) ....   3.   T   F

4. After identifying the string to be found in the replace command, the screen displays REPLACE WITH? (Obj. 2) ....   4.   T   F

5. After identifying the replacement text, the screen displays OPTIONS? (? FOR INFO). (Obj. 2) ....   5.   T   F

6. Pressing the ENTER/RETURN at the OPTIONS? prompt will instruct the computer to search the entire file. (Obj. 2) ....   6.   T   F

7. The replace command stops to ask for operator input at the first replacement. (Obj. 2) ....   7.   T   F

8. The computer will automatically search for the next replacement after a Y or an N is entered at the REPLACE (Y/N) prompt. (Obj. 2) ....   8.   T   F

9. Enter ^L to continue the replacement search. (Obj. 2) ....   9.   T   F

10. If text is justified, care should be taken about entering the exact number of spaces between words when identifying strings. (Obj. 2) ....   10.   T   F

11. No options are available for the replace command. (Obj. 3) ....   11.   T   F

12. Enter G at the OPTIONS? prompt to replace text globally and stop for a replacement decision. (Obj. 4) ....   12.   T   F

13. With the G option, strike ^L to continue the search. (Obj. 4) ....   13.   T   F

14. If N is entered at the OPTIONS? prompt, text is replaced from the cursor position without stopping for any operator input. (Obj. 5).................   14.   T   F

15. When replacing text globally without stopping, N must be entered before G at the OPTIONS? prompt. (Obj. 6) ....   15.   T   F

16. The command ^QR will return the cursor to its original position before the replace command. (Obj. 7) ....   16.   T   F

17. Press the ENTER/RETURN key after the FIND? prompt only when you want to delete a string. (Obj. 8)...   17.   T   F

18. Enter NG at the OPTIONS? prompt to insert a string at different positions within a document. (Obj. 9) ....   18.   T   F

19. After entering the correct ^QA commands, the same text can be inserted anywhere in a document by striking ^L. (Obj. 9)........................... 19.   **T**   **F**

20. The ^R command entered after the ^QA prompts will repeat the last string entered in a previous replace command. (Obj. 10)........................ 20.   **T**   **F**

COMPLETION

Indicate the correct answer in the space provided.

1. You do not have to reenter the new string if you are using which command? (Obj. 1)......................... 1. _____

2. The replace command is ? (Obj. 2) .... 2. _____

3. The first prompt of the replace command is exactly like ? (Obj. 2) .... 3. _____

4. The second prompt in the replace command is ? (Obj. 2) .... 4. _____

5. The third prompt in the replace command is ? (Obj. 2) . 5. _____

6. When no options are chosen, the search will begin from the ? (Obj. 2) .... 6. _____

7. What is displayed after the computer finds the first occurrence in the find string? (Obj. 2).................... 7. _____

8. If Y is entered at the "REPLACE (Y/N):" prompt, the replacement will or will not be executed? (Obj. 2) ...... 8. _____

9. Sometimes a string will not be found because extra spaces are added between words when the right margin is ? (Obj. 2) .... 9. _____

10. When the computer searches for a string throughout an entire file, it has performed a ? (Obj. 3) .... 10. _____

11. The command entered at the OPTIONS? prompt to replace text globally and ask the operator if the replacement should be executed is ? (Obj. 4) .... 11. _____

12. The command entered at the OPTIONS? prompt to replace text from the cursor position and not ask the operator for a replacement decision is ? (Obj. 5)............ 12. _____

13. The command entered at the OPTIONS? prompt to replace text globally and without stopping is ? (Obj. 6)... 13. _____

14. The command to return the cursor to its original position before the replace command is ? (Obj. 7)............... 14. _____

15. When at the REPLACE? prompt, what must you enter to delete a string? (Obj. 8) .... 15. _____

16. When at the OPTIONS? prompt, what must you enter to delete a string throughout an entire document without stopping? (Obj. 8)..................................... 16. _____

17. When at the FIND? prompt, what must you enter to insert the same string at different text locations within the document? (Obj. 9) ....   17. _____

18. In order to execute the insert, after the cursor is positioned where the insert is wanted, what must you strike? (Obj. 9) ....   18. _____

19. At the OPTIONS? prompt, what must you enter to insert the same string at different text locations within a document? (Obj. 9) ....   19. _____

20. The command to repeat the last replace strings and options is *?* (Obj. 10) ....   20. _____

COMPUTER EXERCISE ONE

Directions: Follow the step-by-step instructions given to complete Computer Exercise One.

1. Create a file named LESSON15.EX1.

2. Change the following defaults:

   a. Turn hyphen help off.
   b. Turn justification off.
   c. Change help level to 2.
   d. Omit page numbers.

3. Enter the memorandum in Figure 15.14 with margin and tab defaults.

4. Print the file named LESSON15.EX1.

```
TO:        Division Dean of Humanities

FROM:      Committee on Transcript Evaluations

SUBJECT:   Report on Guidelines for Transcript Evaluations

DATE:      December 15, 19--


     On November 1 the Committee mailed a questionnaire to all division

deans as part of a preliminary study to update our guidelines for

evaluating transcripts of our transfer students.  To date, 80 percent of

the questionnaires have been returned and are now being tallied.

     Thank you for taking time to complete the questionnaire.
```

(Fig. 15.14, continued on p. 140)

```
     The findings will be analyzed by Professors John Cortez and Jane

Brady.  When the questionnaire has been evaluated, the Committee will issue

recommendations for any changes that should be considered in our transcript

evaluation procedures.

     Please submit the questionnaire to me by Christmas recess.

     Our recommendations will be presented in a written report at the

January 16 meeting.  All division deans are invited to attend this very

important session.
```

Figure 15.14   Text for Computer Exercises

COMPUTER EXERCISE TWO

Directions: Follow the step-by-step instructions given to complete Computer Exercise Two.

1. Make a copy of the file named LESSON15.EX1. Name the new file LESSON15.EX2.

2. You will now edit the file named LESSON15.EX2.

3. Turn off the help commands.

4. Insert the heading COMPUTER EXERCISE TWO at the top of the file and center it.

5. Find every occurrence of *Humanities* and replace it with *Computer Sciences*.

6. Find *Computer Sciences* with a global search and replace it with *Language Arts*.

7. Find each occurrence of *questionnaire* and replace it with *survey*. Search globally, stopping for a replacement decision.

8. Find every occurrence of *survey* and replace it with *report*. Do a global search without stopping for a replacement decision.

9. Repeat the last command at all the prompts.

10. Find every occurrence of *January 16* from the cursor position and replace it with *January 28* without stopping for a replacement decision.

11. Delete all occurrences of *division* (uppercase or lowercase), globally and all at once.

12. Insert *Have you returned the survey?* at the end of every paragraph.

13. Save the file.

14. Print the file named LESSON15.EX2.

16. Identifying and Finding Blocks

OBJECTIVES:

1. Define a block.

2. Explain how to mark a block.

3. Explain how to hide a block display.

4. Describe how to find a block.

5. Describe how to return the cursor to the original block position.

6. Explain how to delete an incorrect block marker.

7. Summarize the commands for identifying and finding blocks.

DEFINITION OF A BLOCK

A **block** is the beginning and end of text that has been marked for further edit. The text is identified with a WordStar command at its beginning and with a WordStar command at its end. This block command causes the text to be highlighted so that the marked block stands out from the rest of the document. (Some computer terminals will not support this highlighting feature.) A block can be a few words, lines, paragraphs, or even whole pages. Once the block has been identified, it can be moved to another area within the file, copied to another area within the file, copied to a new file, or deleted.

MARKING A BLOCK

The block commands are ^KB and ^KK. The beginning of the block is marked by positioning the cursor at the space before the first character in the block, holding down the Ctrl key and the K key at the same time, and striking *B*. The screen will display <B>. Because the <B> appears on the screen, the text moves over and the line appears to need reformatting. Since the <B> will not print, the line will not need to be reformatted. The cursor is then moved to the end of the text you want to identify. At the block's end, hold down the Ctrl key and the K key at the same time, and strike another *K*. The screen will display <K>. To help you remember the block command, think of the word block. The begin-block command includes the first letter of the word block (the letter b); the end-block command includes the last letter of the word block (the letter K).

The ^K menu appears on top of the screen when you enter ^*K*. However, you can enter ^*KB* and ^*KK* very quickly so that the menu will not display. When the block has been marked with ^*KB* and ^*KK*, the block becomes highlighted so that it is distinguished from the rest of the document.

HIDING THE BLOCK DISPLAY

Once the block is marked and highlighted, you can hide block highlighting by the command ^KH. To help you recall this command, think of the word hide. This is a toggle command; when ^*KH* is entered again, the block will be highlighted again.

FINDING A BLOCK

You can return to the beginning of a marked block quickly by entering the command ^QB (think of quick beginning). You can return to the end of a marked block quickly by entering the command ^QK. If the highlighting of the marked block is hidden, it will highlight again with these quick commands.

When a file is saved with the ^*KD* command, blocks are canceled. However, when files are saved with the ^KS command, you are still in the edit mode and any block command in the file will be saved.

RETURNING THE CURSOR TO THE ORIGINAL BLOCK POSITION

If you identify a block and then move the block to another location within the file, the cursor will be at the new location. You may want to return the cursor to its original location before the block was moved. To return the cursor to the original block position, enter ^*QV*. This is the same command used to return the cursor to the original position before a find and replace command. The ^QV command will return the cursor to the original location before a block, a find, or a replace command, whichever was entered last.

DELETE A BLOCK MARKER

Most commands entered incorrectly can be canceled by striking $\wedge U$ and Esc; the block marker will not delete with this command. Instead, enter the block command as a toggle to cancel an incorrect entry. For example, if you enter $\wedge KB$ at the wrong location, enter $\wedge KB$ again to cancel the display. If you enter $\wedge KK$ at the wrong location, enter $\wedge KK$ again to cancel the display. If incorrect text has been highlighted, you can cancel the highlighting with the $\wedge KH$ command.

Figure 16.1 summarizes the commands to identify and find blocks.

Function	Command
Mark beginning of the block.	$\wedge$KB
Mark end of the block.	$\wedge$KK
Hide block highlighting.	$\wedge$KH
Find beginning of the block.	$\wedge$QB
Find end of the block.	$\wedge$QK
Return the cursor to original block position.	$\wedge$QV
Delete beginning marker <B>.	$\wedge$KB
Delete end marker <K>.	$\wedge$KK

Figure 16.1   Command Summary to Identify and Find Blocks

LESSON 16 EXERCISE   Name _____ Date _____

TRUE/FALSE

Each of the following statements is either true or false. Indicate your choice in the Answers column by circling T for a true statement or F for a false statement.

1. A block is the beginning and end of text that has been marked for further edit. (Obj. 1) ....   1.   **T**   **F**

2. A block cannot be less than a paragraph. (Obj. 1) ....   2.   **T**   **F**

3. The block must be marked at its beginning and at its end. (Obj. 1) ....   3.   **T**   **F**

4. Once a block is marked, it can be moved, copied, or deleted. (Obj. 1).......   4.   **T**   **F**

5. All terminals will support highlighting. (Obj. 2) ....   5.   **T**   **F**

6. The block commands are ^QB and ^QK. (Obj. 2) ....   6.   **T**   **F**

7. A paragraph must be reformatted after a block command. (Obj. 2) ....   7.   **T**   **F**

8. The ^K menu will be displayed if ^KD is entered slowly. (Obj. 2) ....   8.   **T**   **F**

9. You must highlight a block after ^KK is entered by striking ^KH. (Obj. 2) ....   9.   **T**   **F**

10. The toggle command to highlight and hide highlighting of a block is ^KH. (Obj. 3) ....   10.   **T**   **F**

11. The command to find the beginning of a marked block is ^QB. (Obj. 4) ...   11.   **T**   **F**

12. The command to find the end of a marked block is ^KK. (Obj. 4) ....   12.   **T**   **F**

13. The commands ^QB and ^QK will highlight a marked block. (Obj. 4) .....   13.   **T**   **F**

14. When a file is saved with ^KS, any marked block in the file will be canceled. (Obj. 4) ....   14.   **T**   **F**

15. When a file is saved with ^KD, any marked block will be saved. (Obj. 4) .   15.   **T**   **F**

16. The command to return the cursor to its original block position is ^QR. (Obj. 5) ....   16.   **T**   **F**

17. If a find and replace command is entered after identifying a block, ^QV will return the cursor to the block position. (Obj. 5)...........................   17.   **T**   **F**

18. To delete a begin block display, enter ^KK. (Obj. 6) ....   18.   **T**   **F**

19. To delete an end block display, enter ^KK. (Obj. 6) ....   19.   **T**   **F**

20. To delete highlighting, enter ^KH. (Obj. 6) ....   20.   **T**   **F**

COMPLETION

Indicate the correct answer in the space provided.

1. What is the beginning and end of text that has been marked for further edit called? (Obj. 1) ....

    1. _____

2. How many WordStar commands are entered to identify a block? (Obj. 1) ....

    2. _____

3. After the block commands are entered, what causes the marked block to stand out from the rest of the document? (Obj. 1) ....

    3. _____

4. A block can be a few words, lines, paragraphs, or *?* (Obj. 1) ....

    4. _____

5. Once blocks are marked, name two things you can do with the block within the file. (Obj. 1) ....

    5. a. _____
       b. _____

6. The begin-block command is *?* (Obj. 2) ....

    6. _____

7. The end-block command is *?* (Obj. 2) ....

    7. _____

8. After the end-block command, the text will be *?* (Obj. 2) ....

    8. _____

9. If the block commands are entered slowly, which menu will be displayed? (Obj. 2) ....

    9. _____

10. Text block highlighting is hidden by the command *?* (Obj. 3) ....

    10. _____

11. Text can be highlighted again after a $\wedge$KH command by entering *?* (Obj. 3) ....

    11. _____

12. The command to find the beginning of a marked block is *?* (Obj. 4) ....

    12. _____

13. The command to find the end of a marked block is *?* (Obj. 4) ....

    13. _____

14. If the highlighting of the marked block is hidden, when you enter $\wedge QB$ and $\wedge QK$ the text will become *?* (Obj. 4) ....

    14. _____

15. A marked block is canceled when a file is saved with *?* (Obj. 4) ....

    15. _____

16. A marked block is not canceled when a file is saved with *?* (Obj. 4) ....

    16. _____

17. The command to return the cursor to its original block position is *?* (Obj. 5) ....

    17. _____

18. The command to return the cursor to its original position before a find and replace command is *?* (Obj. 5) ....

    18. _____

19. To cancel the highlighting of a beginning block marker,
    enter *?* (Obj. 6) ....   19. _____

20. To cancel the highlighting of an end block marker, enter
    ? (Obj. 6)...   20. _____

COMPUTER EXERCISE

Directions:Follow the step-by-step instructions given to complete the computer exercise.

1. Create a file named LESSON16.EX.

2. Change the left margin to 12. Set the spacing to double. Set help level at 2. Turn off justification. Do not print page numbers.

3. Enter the text in Figure 16.2 and center the title. Triple space after the title.

4. You will complete the rest of these step-by-step instructions to mark and find blocks.

THE TYPEWRITER THEN AND NOW

The first practical typewriter was produced in America in 1874. It was called the Remington and was based on an invention by Sholes. The device worked on this principle: When a key was pressed on a keyboard, the corresponding character on a type bar struck the paper through an inked ribbon causing the character to print on the paper.

When the electric typewriter came upon the scene, the typist expended 95 percent less energy typing. In addition to lessening fatigue, the quality of work increased because all keys pressed struck the paper with uniform pressure regardless of the force used by the typist.

Figure 16.2   Text for Computer Exercise

---

5. Mark the first paragraph as a block. Enter $^\wedge KB$ at column 1 to include the tab. Enter $^\wedge KK$ in the blank line following the paragraph so that the hard return is included in the block.

6. Hide the block highlighting.

7. Move the cursor to the end of the file.

8. Find the beginning of the block.

9. Find the end of the block.

10. Hide the block highlighting.

11. Highlight the block again.

12. Enter a begin block command at the second paragraph. Notice that this will hide highlighting of the first paragraph, but the <K> is still displayed.

13. Cancel the <B> display.

14. Cancel the <K> display. Move the cursor just beyond the display.

15. Mark the last sentence in the last paragraph as a block.

16. Move the cursor to the file beginning.

17. Find the end of the last block.

18. Hide block highlighting.

19. Save the file.

20. Print the file.

17. Working with Blocks _____

OBJECTIVES:

1. Describe how to move a block.

2. Describe how to copy a block.

3. Explain how to delete a block.

4. Show how to restore a deleted block.

5. Describe how to write a block into a new file.

6. Explain how to read one file into another.

7. Describe how to get help for block edits.

8. Summarize the block command edit features.

MOVING A BLOCK

A marked block can be moved from one place to another place within the file. To move a marked block, position the cursor where the block is to be moved. Enter $^\wedge KV$. The marked block will be inserted at the cursor position. The block has been deleted at its original position.

If the block highlighting has been hidden and you try to move the block, an error message will appear on the screen as illustrated in Figure 17.1. Enter $^\wedge KH$ to highlight the block, and try the command again. The same error message will appear if you try to move a block and have not marked the block beginning. Reenter the block commands so that the text is highlighted, and then try to move the block again. The cursor will be at the new block location. You can return the cursor to the original location before the block move (or any other block edit command) by entering $^\wedge QV$.

```
*** ERROR E6:   BLOCK BEGINNING NOT MARKED
                (OR MARKER IS UNDISPLAYED) *** Press ESCAPE Key
```

Figure 17.1   Error Prompt When Marker is not Displayed

COPYING A BLOCK

A marked block can be copied to another place within the file. To copy a marked block to another position within a file, place the cursor where you want the block copied. Enter ^KC. The marked block is now in two places—at the original position and at the cursor. If the block is not highlighted or has been marked improperly, the error message appears as illustrated in Figure 17.1.

DELETING A BLOCK

A marked block can be deleted. The cursor may be anywhere within the file. Enter ^KY. The marked block will be deleted. If the block has been marked improperly or is not highlighted, the error message as illustrated in Figure 17.1 will be displayed.

RESTORING A DELETED BLOCK

If a block is deleted by mistake, and the text within that block has been saved before with ^KD (save and return to opening menu), ^KS (save and still in the edit mode), or ^KX (save and return to operating system), the block can be restored. Enter ^KQ for abandon edit. The screen will display the prompt illustrated in Figure 17.2.

```
ABANDON EDITED VERSION OF FILE B:LESSON17.TXT? (Y/N)
```

Figure 17.2   Prompt to Abandon Edit

Enter Y to the prompt. All of the changes made after the last save command will be deleted; however, the original text before the edit will be restored, including the deleted block.

WRITING A BLOCK INTO A NEW FILE

A marked block can become a new file. You can "write" (meaning *copy*) the text in a marked block into a separate file. Enter ^KW. The screen will display the message shown in Figure 17.3.

```
NAME OF FILE TO WRITE MARKED TEXT ON?
```

Figure 17.3　Prompt to Write a Block into a New File

Enter a suitable file name and ENTER/RETURN. The marked block will become the text in the new file you named, and the marked block will still be highlighted in the original file.

To view the file directory to verify that a new file containing the marked text is now listed, enter $\wedge KF$. This command displays part of the file directory on the screen. The directory will not print. To delete the file directory from the screen, enter $\wedge KF$ again.

READING ONE FILE INTO ANOTHER

If you want the text of one file (file A, for example) to become part of another file (file B), position the cursor in file B at the location you want file A to be inserted. Enter $\wedge KR$. Figure 17.4 illustrates the screen display for this process.

```
NAME OF FILE TO READ?
```

Figure 17.4　Prompt to Read One File into Another

At the prompt, enter FILE A and press ENTER/RETURN. The text of file A will be copied at the cursor position in file B. This command does not affect the text in file A.

Use this feature to "read" (meaning *copy*) standard paragraphs that will go into many different documents. These paragraphs used over and over again are called **boilerplate**. The standard paragraph is entered into a separate file. By creating a file containing the boilerplate material, you do not have to key-in the same words over and over again. Simply read the boilerplate file into the other files with the $\wedge$KR command.

GETTING HELP

You can get on-screen help anytime for block edits by viewing the $\wedge$K menu (strike $\wedge K$) or by entering $\wedge JV$. $\wedge JV$ displays a summary of how to use the block commands. (Figure 17.5 on page 152 summarizes all of the block edit commands.)

Function	Command
Move a marked block.	^KV
Copy a marked block.	^KC
Delete a marked block.	^KY
Restore a marked block.	^KQ
Write a marked block into a new file.	^KW
Read one file into another file.	^KR
Get help for block edits.	^JV
Return cursor to original block position.	^QV

Figure 17.5   Block Command Edit Summary

LESSON 17 EXERCISE   Name _____ Date _____

TRUE/FALSE

Each of the following statements is either true or false. Indicate your choice in the Answers column by circling T for a true statement or F for a false statement.

1. The command to move a marked block is ^KV. (Obj. 1)...................   1. T F

2. With the ^KV command, the block that is moved also remains in its original position. (Obj. 1) ....   2. T F

3. The block highlighting may be hidden before the ^KV command. (Obj. 1).   3. T F

4. An error message appears on the screen when the block marker is not displayed with a ^KV command. (Obj. 1) ....   4. T F

5. To correct a block error, enter the missing block markers and highlight the block if necessary. (Obj. 1) ....   5. T F

6. To return the cursor to the original block location after a block edit, enter ^QV. (Obj. 1) ....   6. T F

7. To copy a marked block, enter ^KC. (Obj. 2) ....   7. T F

8. The block that is copied with the ^KC command will be deleted from its original position. (Obj. 2).......................................   8. T F

9. The command to delete a marked block is ^Y. (Obj. 3) ....   9. T F

10. If a block deleted by mistake is restored from a previous save command, all of the edits made after the last save command will be deleted. (Obj. 4) ...   10. T F

11. In order for a deleted block to be restored, the file must have been saved at least once. (Obj. 4)..   11. T F

12. A prompt saying that the file has been abandoned is displayed after the ^KQ command. (Obj. 4) ....   12. T F

13. "Write" may mean "to copy." (Obj. 5) ....   13. T F

14. The command to write a marked block into a new file is ^KR. (Obj. 5) ...   14. T F

15. The prompt NAME OF FILE TO WRITE MARKED TEXT ON? is displayed after the ^KR command. (Obj. 5) ....   15. T F

16. When a marked block is written into a new file, the block will be deleted from the edited file. (Obj. 5) ....   16. T F

17. The command to view the file directory while in the edit is ^KF. (Obj. 5).   17. T F

18. If the file directory is displayed when a file is saved, the directory will print. (Obj. 5) ....   18. T F

19. To delete the file directory display from a file, enter ^KF. (Obj. 5)........   19. T F

20. To read or copy one file into another file, enter ^KR. (Obj. 6) ....   20. T F

21. You must enter the file name of the file being edited at the ^KR prompt. (Obj. 6) ....   21. T F

22. If file A is copied into file B, the text in file A will not be affected. (Obj. 6) ....   22. T F

23. A boilerplate is text that is used over and over in different files. (Obj. 6) .   23.   **T   F**

24. You can get on-screen help for block commands by entering ^K. (Obj. 7) .   24.   **T   F**

25. You can get on-screen help for block commands by entering ^JV. (Obj. 7) ....   25.   **T   F**

COMPLETION

Indicate the correct answer in the space provided.

1. The command to move a block is ? (Obj. 1) ....   1. _____

2. When a block is moved, what happens to the block at its original position? (Obj. 1)..............................   2. _____

3. Before a block is moved, it must first be ? (Obj. 1) .....   3. _____

4. If the block is not marked properly, what will be displayed? (Obj. 1).......................................   4. _____

5. To return the cursor to its original location before a block edit, enter the command ? (Obj. 1)...............   5. _____

6. The command to copy a marked block is ? (Obj. 2) .....   6. _____

7. When a block is copied, the copied block is in how many places? (Obj. 2) ....   7. _____

8. The command to delete a marked block is ? (Obj. 3)....   8. _____

9. If the file has been saved, a deleted block can be ? (Obj. 4) ....   9. _____

10. When ^KQ is executed, all of the current edits will be ? (Obj. 4) ....   10. _____

11. The command to write a marked block into a new file is ? (Obj. 5) ....   11. _____

12. To display the file directory in a file, enter ? (Obj. 5) ..   12. _____

13. To delete the file directory display in a file, enter ? (Obj. 5) ....   13. _____

14. The command to read one file into another is ? (Obj. 6) ....   14. _____

15. A file used over and over again in different documents is called a ? (Obj. 6)....................................   15. _____

16. What must be positioned at the location where the file is to be copied before one file can be read into another? (Obj. 6) ....   16. _____

17. A boilerplate file is copied into another file with the command ? (Obj. 6) ....   17. _____

18. You can get on-screen help with block commands by entering which two commands? (Obj. 7)..................   18. a. _____
    b. _____

COMPUTER EXERCISE

Directions: Follow the step-by-step instructions.

1. This exercise uses the file named LESSON16.EX. If you did not create this file, do so now.

2. Write this entire file called LESSON16.EX into a new file named LESSON17.EX. To do this, follow these steps:
   a. Enter $^\wedge KB$ at the beginning of the file.
   b. Go to the end of the document. Enter $^\wedge KK$ one line after the last line in the file. The file should be completely highlighted.
   c. Enter $^\wedge KW$. The prompt NAME OF FILE TO WRITE MARKED TEXT ON? will appear.
   d. Name the file LESSON17.EX and strike ENTER/ RETURN.
   e. Save LESSON16.EX.

3. You will edit the file named LESSON17.EX.

4. Delete the .OP command at the beginning of the file.

5. The help level should be at 2. Turn off hyphen help.

6. If you get into a wrong command, enter $^\wedge U$ and Esc.

7. Turn insert off. Insert "#1" at column 1 at the beginning of the first paragraph. This is to identify the paragraph by number as you work through these instructions.

8. Insert "#2" at column 1 at the beginning of the second paragraph.

9. Mark and highlight paragraph #1 as a block.
   a. Position the cursor one line above paragraph #1.
   b. Position the cursor one line below paragraph #1.

10. Move paragraph #1 to the end of the document:
    a. Enter $^\wedge QC$ to get to the document's end. The cursor should be on a blank line after paragraph #2.
    b. Enter $^\wedge KV$.

11. *Copy* paragraph #1 to the end of the document:
    a. Enter $^\wedge QC$ to get to the document's end.
    b. Enter $^\wedge KC$. There are now two paragraphs labeled #1 at the end of the file.
    c. Hide highlighting by entering $^\wedge KH$.

12. Save the document with $^\wedge KS$. A prompt is displayed to enter $^\wedge QP$ to return the cursor to its original position before the save command. Enter $^\wedge QP$.

13. Delete the last two occurrences of paragraph #1 at the end of the document by doing the following:
    a. Enter $^\wedge R$ to get to the beginning of the first occurrence of paragraph #1.
    b. Enter $^\wedge KB$.

    c.   Move the cursor to the end of the document and enter $\wedge KK$.

    d.   Delete the last two occurrences of paragraph #1 by entering $\wedge KY$.

14. Restore the paragraphs that were deleted by step 13. To do this, enter $\wedge KQ$ and answer Y to the prompt "ABANDON EDITED VERSION OF FILE B:LESSON17.EX? (Y/N):"

15. Go to the document's end. Edit LESSON17.EX file again. All the paragraphs have been restored.

16. Create a new page (page 2).

17. Read the file named LESSON16.EX into the beginning of the new page. Enter LESSON16.EX and ENTER/ RETURN at the prompt NAME OF FILE TO READ?

18. Copy all of page 2 into a new file named WRITE.17:

    a.   Mark all of page 2 with a block command.

    b.   Enter $\wedge KW$. Prompt displays NAME OF FILE TO WRITE MARKED TEXT ON?

    c.   Enter WRITE.17 and ENTER/RETURN.

    d.   Hide highlighting.

19. Check the file directory ($\wedge KF$) to see that a file named WRITE.17 has indeed been created. You may have to $\wedge Z$ or $\wedge W$ to see the file name.

20. Delete the file directory.

21. Create a new page (page 3).

22. Copy the file named LESSON16.EX onto page 3.

23. Read the help menu for the block command by entering $\wedge JV$. Space to get out of this menu.

24. Return to paragraph #2 at the document's beginning.

25. Copy paragraph #2 to the file's end:

    a.   Mark and highlight paragraph #2. You may have to insert a blank line between the paragraphs by entering $\wedge N$ with the insert on.

    b.   Position the cursor at the file's end.

    c.   Enter $\wedge KC$.

    d.   Hide highlighting.

26. Return the cursor to the position before the block copy.

27. Reformat the entire document to the WordStar defaults. You may have to insert a blank line between some of the paragraphs.

28. Delete the .OP command on pages 2 and 3.

29. Save the document.

30. Print the file named LESSON17.EX.

18. Columns

OBJECTIVES:

1. Define a column.

2. Explain the column mode.

3. Explain how to turn the column mode off.

4. Describe how to move a marked column.

5. Describe how to copy a marked column.

6. Describe how to delete a marked column.

7. Explain how to format a two-column newsletter.

8. Summarize column mode applications.

DEFINITION OF A COLUMN

A **column** is vertical (up and down) text in the form of a rectangle. Figure 18.1 illustrates column text.

```
      111111              222222
      111111              222222
      111111              222222        COLUMN TEXT IN A TABLE
      111111              222222
      111111              222222


XXXXXXXXXXXXXXX      XXXXXXXXXXXXXXX
XXXXXXXXXXXXXXX      XXXXXXXXXXXXXXX    COLUMN TEXT IN A NEWSLETTER
XXXXXXXXXXXXXXX      XXXXXXXXXXXXXXX
XXXXXXXXXXXXXXX      XXXXXXXXXXXXXXX
XXXXXXX.             XXXXXXXXXXX.
```

Figure 18.1   Columns in a Table and a Newsletter

Look closely at the columns labeled "COLUMN TEXT IN A TABLE" in Figure 18.1. To move column 1 in the table to the right of column 2, it is necessary to first highlight column 1 for the move.

But if you enter the begin-block command (^KB) at the beginning of column 1 and the end-block command (^KK) at the end of column 1, column 2 will also be highlighted and included in the block move. This is because WordStar cannot distinguish separate vertical text from the entire document without a special command.

THE COLUMN MODE

The special command to edit columns is not available in WordStar versions before 3.0. If you have an earlier version, skip this lesson and go on to the next lesson.

A column is marked in the same way horizontal (across) text is marked, except that a special command must be entered before WordStar can recognize the column. The command ^KN is for the **column mode**. Entering ^KN will enable you to mark vertical text for edit.

After ^KN is entered, use the same begin (^KB) and end (^KK) mark block commands to highlight the column. After the column is marked, the text can be moved to another location within the document (^KV), copied to another location within the document (^KC), or deleted (^KY).

Marked columns cannot be copied to a new file (^KW) or read into another file (^KR). If you try, the prompt in Figure 18.2 will display.

```
*** ERROR E13 COLUMN READ / WRITE NOT ALLOWED *** Press ESCAPE key
```

Figure 18.2   The Column Error Message With ^KW and ^KR

TURNING OFF THE COLUMN MODE

After the marked column has been moved, copied, or deleted, turn off the column mode by entering ^KN again. If ^KN is on, you can manipulate only column blocks. The status of the column mode is viewed by reading the ^K menu. Enter ^K to read the menu, and strike the space bar to exit from it.

MOVING A MARKED COLUMN

Look at Figure 18.1 again. You may now move column 1 (of the column text in a table) to the right of column 2. With ^KN entered to turn on the column block mode, position the cursor at the beginning of column 1 and enter ^KB. The text will move to the right. Then position the cursor at the end of column 1 and enter $^\wedge KK$. The column is now highlighted. Move the cursor to the right of column 2 at the position you want column 1 moved. Enter $^\wedge KV$. The table will now look like the illustration in Figure 18.3. To turn off the column mode after the move, strike $^\wedge KN$.

```
222222     111111
222222     111111
222222     111111
222222     111111
222222     111111
```

Figure 18.3   Table After Moving a Column

COPYING A MARKED COLUMN

To *copy* column 1 to the right of column 2 (in Figure 18.1), enter $^\wedge KN$ to turn on the column block mode. Mark the beginning and the end of column 1. Move the cursor to the right of column 2 at the position you want column 1 copied and enter $^\wedge KC$. Column 1 is now on both sides of column 2 as illustrated in Figure 18.4. Turn off the column mode by striking $^\wedge KN$.

```
111111     222222     111111
111111     222222     111111
111111     222222     111111
111111     222222     111111
111111     222222     111111
```

Figure 18.4   Table After Copying a Column

DELETING A MARKED COLUMN

To delete column 1 in Figure 18.1, enter $^\wedge KN$ and mark the beginning and the end of the column with $^\wedge KB$ and $^\wedge KK$. Then enter $^\wedge KY$ to delete the column. Turn off the column mode with $^\wedge KN$. The table now appears as illustrated in Figure 18.5.

```
222222
222222
222222
222222
222222
```

Figure 18.5   Table After Deleting Columns

FORMATTING A NEWSLETTER

WordStar version 3.0 will format two-column newsletters using the $^\wedge KN$ column mode. Follow these step-by-step instructions to format a newsletter:

1. Enter all of the text horizontally with margins at the defaults. The right margin should be justified.

2. Correct all the errors before you divide the text into columns. It becomes more difficult to correct errors after the text is moved into two columns. Turn hyphen help off ($^\wedge OH$). Your newsletter will look like the text in Figure 18.6.

```
Text  that  is to be formatted into two  columns  should
first  be  entered  into  the file  using  the  complete
screen.   Be sure to proofread and correct errors  while
the  text is in this format,  because corrections become
much more difficult after the text has been  reformatted
into two columns.
```

**Figure 18.6   Text Entered With Full Margins Before
                Reformatting**

3. Reset the right margin where you want the first column to end. For example, if you decide that the first column width will be 30 characters, set the right margin at 30 ($^\wedge OR$). Remember, there are 10 characters to an inch at the defaults, so the right column will be 3 inches wide (30 characters wide divided by 10 characters to an inch).

4. Turn hyphen help back on ($^\wedge OH$) and reformat each paragraph with $^\wedge B$. Now the text is one long column at the left margin as illustrated in Figure 18.7.

```
Text that is to be formatted
into two columns should first
be entered into the file using
the complete screen.   Be sure
to  proofread  and correct er-
rors while the text is in this
format,   because  corrections
become  much  more  difficult
after the text has been refor-
matted into two columns.
```

Figure 18.7   Text Reformatted to Left Margin for a Newsletter

5. Make a backup copy of this newsletter formatted completely in the left column. This is a precaution against the text getting scrambled during the two-column formatting which you will do. To make a backup copy, the column mode must be off (^*KN*). Highlight the text and enter ^*KW* to write the marked block into a new file. Another way of making a backup copy is to save the document and copy the file from the opening menu.

6. Now you must "harden" any hyphens at the end of the lines, because soft hyphens will not print in the first column. A hard hyphen is a required hyphen and will print. To make all hyphens required, use the following search and replace feature.

   a. Enter the command ^QA.
   b. At the FIND? prompt, enter ^*P*^- and press ENTER/RETURN. (Hold down the Ctrl key and the P key at the same time; then hold down the Ctrl key and the hyphen key at the same time.)
   c. At the REPLACE WITH? prompt, strike the hyphen key and press ENTER/RETURN.
   d. At the OPTIONS? prompt, enter *NG* and press ENTER/RETURN.

7. Enter the column mode (^KN).

8. Highlight the text that will make up the second column. Enter ^*KB* at column 1 of this text so that all vertical text on each line from column 1 will be included in the highlighting. If ^*KB* is entered beyond column 1, the highlighting will not include the beginning of each line. Enter ^*KK* one space after the right margin setting so that all the vertical text on each line at the right margin will be highlighted. If you enter ^*KK* short of the right margin setting, the highlighting will not include the end of each line.

9. Position the cursor at the end of the first line of the first column. Release the margins with ^OX. Enter five spaces (or the number of spaces you want between columns). This is where the second column will begin.

10. Enter ^KV. The highlighted text will move to the cursor position. The document will look like the illustration in Figure 18.8.

```
Text  that is to be  formatted     errors  while the text  is  in
into two columns should  first     this format,  because  correc-
be entered into the file using     tions become  much more  diffi-
the complete screen.   Be sure     cult after  the text  has been
to   proofread   and   correct     reformatted into two columns.
                                                              <
                                                              <
                                                              <
                                                              <
                                                              <
```

Figure 18.8   Newsletter After Column Move With ^KN Mode

Notice the return graphics (<) on the right side of the screen. This is all that is left to indicate where the lines have been. Delete these returns with a line delete (^Y) or a block delete (^KY). ^KN must be off to do the block delete.

11. Turn column mode off with ^KN after each use.

12. Before printing, the following dot commands must be entered for printers with microjustification. (Check the manual that came with your printer or check with your instructor to see if your printer has microjustification.) With the cursor at position 1 at the file's beginning, enter .UJ0 (using zero). Then at the file's end, enter .UJ1 at column 1. If these commands are not entered, the inner margins of the two columns will be ragged instead of justified.

Figure 18.9 summarizes the steps for working with columns in tables.

Tables	Procedures
Move columns	1. ^KN, column mode on. 2. ^KB at full column beginning. 3. ^KK at full column end. 4. ^KV at new column position. 5. ^KN, column mode off.
Copy columns	1. ^KN, column mode on. 2. ^KB at full column beginning. 3. ^KK at full column end. 4. ^KC at new column position. 5. ^KN, column mode off.
Delete columns	1. ^KN, column mode on. 2. ^KB at full column beginning. 3. ^KK at full column end. 4. ^KY for block delete. 5. ^KN, column mode off.

Figure 18.9   Column Edit Summary For Tables

Figure 18.10 summarizes the steps in preparing two-column newsletters. The summary commands in Figure 18.10 are not applicable for versions of WordStar before 3.0.

PROCEDURES FOR NEWSLETTERS

1. Enter text horizontally at defaults.

2. Turn hyphen help off with ^OH.

3. Correct errors.

4. Reset first column right margin with ^OR.

5. Turn hyphen help on with ^OH.

6. Reformat each paragraph with ^B.

7. Make a backup copy.
   a. Highlight the text with the commands ^KB and ^KK.
   b. Strike ^KW.

(Fig. 18.10, continued on p. 164)

8. Harden the hyphens.
   a. Strike $^\wedge QA$.
   b. At the prompt FIND, enter $^\wedge P^\wedge$- and press ENTER/RE-TURN.
   c. At the prompt REPLACE WITH?, strike the hyphen key and press ENTER/RETURN.
   d. At the prompt OPTIONS?, enter *NG* and press ENTER/RETURN.

9. Turn the column mode on with $^\wedge KN$.

10. Strike $^\wedge KB$ at full left column of the beginning text that will make up the right-hand column.

11. Strike $^\wedge KK$ at full right column of text that will end the right-hand column.

12. Move the cursor to the end of the first line in column 1.

13. Strike the margin release with $^\wedge OX$.

14. Space to where you want the second column to begin.

15. Strike $^\wedge KV$.

16. Delete the hard return graphics with $^\wedge Y$.

17. Enter the dot command .UJ0 at the beginning of the file.

18. Enter the dot command .UJ1 at the end of the file.

Figure 18.10   Summary For Creating Two-Column Newsletters

LESSON 18 EXERCISE   Name _____ Date _____

TRUE/FALSE

Each of the following statements is either true or false. Indicate your choice in the Answers column by circling T for a true statement or F for a false statement.

1. A column is vertical text in the form of a rectangle. (Obj. 1) ....   1. T

2. WordStar versions before 3.0 cannot distinguish between horizontal and vertical text. (Obj. 2) ....   2. T   F

3. The command for the column mode is ^KN. (Obj. 2) ....   3.   F

4. Marked columns can be copied to another file. (Obj. 2) ....   4.   F

5. Marked columns can be read into another file. (Obj. 2) ....   5. T   F

6. The column mode is turned off by entering ^KN. (Obj. 3) ....   T   F

7. The column mode status is given in the ^K menu. (Obj. 3)................   T   F

8. To move a marked block after it is highlighted, enter ^KC. (Obj. 4).......   8. T   F

9. To copy a marked block after it is highlighted, enter ^KV. (Obj. 5)........   9. T   F

10. To delete a marked block after it is highlighted, enter ^KY. (Obj. 6)......   10. T   F

11. Newsletters can be formatted with the column mode featur (Obj. 7) ....   11. T   F

12. The first step in creating a newsletter is to enter the two columns. (Ob)   12. T   F

13. It is not necessary to hyphenate when correcting errors in the first ne etter draft before reformatting into columns. (Obj. 7)................. ...   13. T   F

14. If the left column in a newsletter is to be two inches wide, set the ri margin at 30. (Obj. 7).. ......   14. T   F

15. When finished with corrections in the first newsletter draft, turr yphenation help on before reformatting the text into a column. (Obj. 7 ....   15. T   F

16. A backup copy of the newsletter should be made before attemp   g to divide it into two columns. (Obj. 7)...   16. T   F

17. If a backup copy is made with the ^KW command, the column mode can be on. (Obj. 7)...   17. T   F

18. A backup copy can be made from the opening menu. (Obj. 7) ....   18. T   F

19. Soft hyphens can be "hardened" by using the search and replace command. (Obj. 7) ....   19. T   F

20. Enter ^P^- after the FIND? prompt to harden all hyphens. (Obj. 7).......   20. T   F

21. After a part of a column of text has been highlighted to be made into a second column, you should move the cursor directly to where you want the second column to be. (Obj. 7)..   21. T   F

22. With the cursor at the beginning of the second column, enter $\wedge KV$ to move the highlighted text. (Obj. 7) .... 22. **T**   **F**

23. The column mode should be turned off after each use. (Obj. 7) .... 23. **T**   **F**

24. Dot commands must be entered in the newsletter file so that the inner margins will be justified. (Obj. 7) .... 24. **T**   **F**

25. Enter *.UJ0* at the end of the newsletter file. (Obj. 7) .... 25. **T**   **F**

COMPLETION

Indicate the correct answer in the space provided.

1. Vertical text in the form of a rectangle is called a *?* (Obj. 1) .... 1. _____

2. WordStar cannot distinguish separate vertical text from the entire document without a special *?* (Obj. 1) .... 2. _____

3. The special command to edit columns is not available before WordStar version *?* (Obj. 2) .... 3. _____

4. The column mode command is *?* (Obj. 2) .... 4. _____

5. Before columns can be moved, they must be *?* (Obj. 2) . 5. _____

6. After the column mode is on, the begin block is entered with the command *?* (Obj. 2) .... 6. _____

7. After the column mode is on, the end block is entered with the command *?* (Obj. 2) .... 7. _____

8. Marked columns cannot be copied to a new file with which command? (Obj. 2) .... 8. _____

9. Marked columns cannot be read into another file with which command? (Obj. 2) .... 9. _____

10. If an error message appears on the screen, which key must be struck? (Obj. 2) .... 10. _____

11. The column mode is turned off by entering *?* (Obj. 3) .. 11. _____

12. The command to move a marked column is *?* (Obj. 4) .. 12. _____

13. The command to copy a marked column is *?* (Obj. 5) ... 13. _____

14. The command to delete a marked column is *?* (Obj. 6).. 14. _____

15. The first step in formatting a newsletter is to enter text with the margins at *?* (Obj. 7) .... 15. _____

16. The hyphen help should be turned on or off when correcting and editing the first input of a newsletter? (Obj. 7) .... 16. _____

17. If the first column of a newsletter is to be three inches wide, set the right margin at *?* (Obj. 7) .... 17. _____

18. After the right margin for the first column has been set, reformat the text with hyphen help on or off? (Obj. 7) . 18. _____

19. To make a backup copy of the newsletter with the ^KW command before the two columns are formatted, the column mode should be on or off? (Obj. 7) ....

19. _____

20. What is entered for the FIND? prompt to search and replace soft hyphens with hard hyphens? (Obj. 7) ....

20. _____

21. What is entered at the REPLACE WITH? prompt to search and replace soft hyphens with hard hyphens? (Obj. 7) ....

21. _____

22. What is entered at the OPTIONS? prompt to search and replace soft hyphens with hard hyphens? (Obj. 7) ....

22. _____

23. After positioning the cursor at the end of the first line in the first column, what must be entered to permit you to space over to set the left margin of the second column when creating newsletters? (Obj. 7) ....

23. _____

24. With the text for the second column highlighted and the column mode on, what must be entered to move the marked block? (Obj. 7)..................................

24. _____

25. The return graphics left after the column block move should or should not be deleted? (Obj. 7) ....

25. _____

COMPUTER EXERCISE ONE

Directions: Follow the step-by-step instructions given to complete Computer Exercise One.

1. Create a file named LESSON18.EX1.

2. Turn off page numbering.

3. Clear all tabs.

4. Set tabs at columns 10, 20, and 30.

5. Enter the following table. The first column should start at the first tab.

COLUMN BLOCK EXERCISE

Team	Won	Lost
1	1	9
2	5	5
3	7	3
4	4	6
5	8	2
6	0	10
7	4	6
9	2	8

Figure 18.11   Computer Exercise One

6. You will move the "Team" column ten spaces to the right of the "Lost" column. To do this, follow these steps:

   a. Turn column mode on.
   b. Enter ^KB before "Team."
   c. Enter ^KK four spaces after the last score in the "Team" column.
   d. Position the cursor at column 40 on the same line as the column headings.
   e. Enter ^KV. The "Won" column and the "Lost" column will move to the left four spaces, because the "Team" column is four spaces wide. The move command will cause the preceding text to move to the left the number of spaces in the moved column.

7. Hide the text highlighting.

8. Copy the "Won" column ten spaces to the right of the "Team" column by following these steps:

   a. Highlight the entire "Won" column. Enter ^KB before "Won." Enter ^KK three spaces after the last score in the column. (Use ^X and ^D to move the cursor.)
   b. Position the cursor at position 50 on the same line as the column headings.
   c. Enter ^KC. Because this is a copy command, the previous text does not move over as it did in the move command.
   d. Hide the text highlighting.

9. Delete the "Won" column on the left. To do this, follow these steps:

   a. Highlight the entire column.
   b. Enter ^KY.
   c. Hide the text highlighting.
   d. Hide the markers.

10. Copy the entire text ten lines below the original text at position 1. To do this, follow these steps:

    a. Turn the column block off.
    b. Enter ^KB at column 1 on the column heading line.
    c. Enter ^KK at end of the entire file.
    d. Press ENTER/RETURN ten times.
    e. Enter ^KC at column 1.

11. Hide the text highlighting.

12. Print the file named LESSON18.EX1.

COMPUTER EXERCISE TWO

Directions: Follow the step-by-step instructions given to complete Computer Exercise Two.

1. Create a file named LESSON18.EX2.

2. Turn off page numbering. Margins should be at the defaults and justified.

3. If you get into a wrong command, enter $\wedge U$ and Esc.

4. You will key-in and format the newsletter in Figure 18.12 by following the step-by-step instructions.

HIDDEN COSTS OF PERSONAL COMPUTERS

There is no doubt that owning a personal computer for word processing and data management is a very good investment. However, the costs of fully equipping your computer with features and materials that make it truly efficient can run five to eight times as much as the original computer cost.

For example, a personal computer may cost anywhere from $2,000 to $5,000. This cost is for the computer and the very minimum amount of equipment to make the computer work; in other words, for the basic equipment.

Most users will begin to buy additional software and hardware within the first year of purchase.

Additional disk storage is needed to handle large quantities of data: A floppy disk drive costing from $500 to a faster, larger capacity "hard disk" drive costing up to $6,000 can be purchased for this purpose.

A good letter-quality printer is often required for business correspondence. This can add another $1,000 to $5,000 to your personal computer cost.

A connection to telephone lines gives access to data banks. These modems cost anywhere from $500 to $1,500. In addition to the modem itself, telephone bills will be higher, not to mention the connection charges to on-line data bases.

Local networks connect one computer with other computers so that information can be shared. Add another $500 to $700 for each computer in the network.

Graphic capability is often desired, so a graphics plotter can be purchased. Add another $2,000 for this piece of hardware.

Software, of course, makes the computer valuable. Programs can run from $150 to $500 each.

Supplies such as paper, disks, ribbons, and print wheels, must be purchased at regular intervals.

Maintenance contracts and service calls will add another five to ten percent to the system's purchase price. The cost of "down time" while the computer is being repaired must also be considered when computing costs.

Figure 18.12   Computer Exercise Two

5. Enter the newsletter first in the default line length with the margins at 1 and 65. Center the title. Indent each paragraph five spaces. Double space between paragraphs.

6. Correct all errors. Reformat with the hyphen help off.

7. Each column of the newsletter will be three inches wide. Reset the right margin at 30.

8. Reformat each paragraph with the hyphen help turned on.

9. Make a backup copy of this file for safety reasons. Name the backup file BACKUP.18. To do this, follow these instructions:

   a. Column mode should be off. View the ^K menu to see if it is off. If it is not, enter N. If it is off, strike the space bar to exit from the menu.
   b. Highlight the entire text.
   c. Enter ^KW. When the prompt NAME OF FILE TO WRITE MARKED TEXT ON? appears, enter BACKUP.18.

10. Hide the text highlighting.

11. View the file directory to see that the file named BACKUP.18 is now listed. Enter ^KF.

12. Clear the file directory from the screen.

13. Harden all the hyphens so that even the soft hyphens at the end of column one will print. To do this:

   a. Enter ^QA. When the prompt FIND? appears, enter ^P^-.
   b. When the prompt REPLACE WITH? appears, strike the hyphen key; when the OPTIONS? prompt appears, enter NG.

14. Mark the block you will move to make the newsletter appear as shown in Figure 18.12.

15. Move the marked text by following these instructions:

   a. With the cursor at the end of the first line of column one, enter ^OX to release the margin.
   b. Space over five times.
   c. Turn on the column mode with ^KN. Enter ^KV.

16. Delete the return graphics left over from the moved text.

17. Turn off the column mode.

18. Enter .UJ0 at the beginning of the file.

19. Enter .UJ1 at the end of the file.

20. Save the document.

21. Print the file named LESSON18.EX2.

19. Disk and File Operations and ^K Menu Review _____

OBJECTIVES:

1. Describe how to copy a file from the ^K menu.

2. Explain how to delete a file from the ^K menu.

3. Describe how to print a file from the ^K menu.

4. Explain how to rename a file from the ^K menu.

5. Describe how to change logged disk drives from the ^K menu.

6. Summarize the ^K menu commands.

THE ^K MENU FUNCTIONS

All of the ^K menu commands, except the file and disk operation features, have been introduced in previous lessons. File and disk operations can be executed from the ^K menu while you are still editing a file, making the ^K menu very powerful.

Files can be copied, deleted, printed, and renamed from the ^K menu, and the logged disk drive can be changed from the ^K menu. The commands for these features can also be made from the opening menu and from the operating system. The WordStar functions are easy and more flexible because of the many prompts and messages that are displayed for the user.

COPYING A FILE FROM THE ^K MENU

You have had some experience in copying a file from the opening menu. It is also possible to copy a file, while editing a document, from the ^K menu. Files may be copied

1. onto the same disk, using a different file name.

2. from one disk drive to another disk drive.

The command to copy a file from the ^K menu is ^KO. When *^KO* is entered, a prompt is displayed to name the file that is to be copied. After the file name is entered, another prompt is displayed asking for the name of the file to copy to. The prompts are illustrated in Figure 19.1.

```
NAME OF FILE TO COPY FROM?    LESSON19.TXT

NAME OF FILE TO COPY TO?    LSN19TXT
```

Figure 19.1   Copying a File onto the Same Disk from the ^K Menu

---

The file named LESSON19.TXT will be copied to another file named LSN19TXT on the same disk drive. There will now be two copies of the same material under two different names on the same disk.

Files may be copied to and from different disk drives by entering the drive letter and a colon before the file name. To copy a file named TEST from Disk Drive A to Disk Drive B, enter ^KO. To the prompt NAME OF FILE TO COPY FROM?, enter *A:TEST*, and to the prompt NAME OF FILE TO COPY TO?, enter *B:TEST*. There will now be a copy of the same file on two different disks.

If you try to use the source file name in the destination file name, or if you enter a file name that already appears in the file directory, the prompt displayed in Figure 19.2 will appear.

```
B:LSN19TXT EXISTS -- OVERWRITE (Y?N)
```

Figure 19.2   Prompt When File Name Already Exists

If you strike *N* in answer to the prompt, you will be asked again to name the file to copy to. If you strike *Y* in answer to the prompt, text in the file with the same name will be replaced by text in the source file. If you try to copy a file that is in edit, the prompt in Figure 19.3 will be displayed.

```
FILE B:LESSON19.TXT IN USE BY WordStar
```

Figure 19.3   Prompt When File to be Copied is in Edit

The copy file command from the ^K menu is helpful when you need to make room on a full disk so that the file in edit can be saved.

A file can be copied to another disk and then deleted, leaving room to save the current file.

DELETING A FILE FROM THE ^K MENU

A file can be deleted from the opening menu or it can be deleted from the ^K menu. The command to delete a file from the ^K menu is ^KJ. Files from the current logged disk drive or from another disk drive may be deleted. If the file is on another disk drive, enter the drive letter and a colon before the file name. If the file name is incorrect, a prompt illustrated in Figure 19.4 will appear on the screen.

```
FILE B:LESSON19.TXT NOT FOUND
```

Figure 19.4   Prompt When File is not Found

You can enter the correct file name, or you can enter ^U and Esc to delete the command. The delete command from the ^K menu is helpful in order to make room on a disk so that the file in edit can be saved.

PRINTING A FILE FROM THE ^K MENU

You can print one file while editing another with the ^KP command. When ^KP is entered, a prompt is displayed asking for NAME OF FILE TO PRINT? When the name of the file has been entered, press Esc and the file will begin to print. If you strike ENTER/RETURN after the prompt NAME OF FILE TO PRINT?, the print questions will appear on the screen. Strike ENTER/ RETURN after each question.

To stop the print, enter ^KP again. The prompt illustrated in Figure 19.5 will then be displayed. Strike Y to abandon the printing. A file from another disk drive can be printed by entering the drive number and a colon before the file name.

```
NOW PRINTING FILE B:LESSON6.TXT
"Y" TO ABANDON PRINT, "N" TO RESUME, ^U TO HOLD
```

Figure 19.5   Prompt to Stop Print with ^KP

RENAMING A FILE FROM THE ^K MENU

A file can be renamed from the ^K menu by entering ^*KE*. A prompt appears asking the NAME OF FILE TO RENAME? To rename a file on another disk drive, enter the drive letter and a colon before the file name. A prompt is displayed asking for the NEW NAME?

CHANGING LOGGED DISK DRIVES FROM THE ^K MENU

To change logged disk drives from the ^K menu, enter ^*KL*. The prompt illustrated in Figure 19.6 is displayed.

```
The LOGGED (or Current Disk or Default Disk) is the
disk drive used for files except those files for which
you enter a disk drive name as part of the file name.
WordStar displays the File Directory of the Logged Disk.

THE LOGGED DISK DRIVE IS NOW B:
NEW LOGGED DISK DRIVE (letter, colon, RETURN)?
```

Figure 19.6　Prompt to Change Logged Disk Drives

Enter the new drive letter, a colon, and press ENTER/RETURN. After the file you are editing is saved, the new logged disk file directory is displayed.

^K MENU SUMMARY

The ^K menu is viewed by holding down the Ctrl key and the K key at the same time when editing a file. The menu is exited by striking the space bar. Commands from the ^K menu save time because you do not have to leave the edit mode to execute disk and file commands such as copying and deleting disk files, viewing the file directory, or changing disk drives. Figure 19.7 illustrates the ^K block menu displayed on the screen when ^K is entered.

```
^K        B:LESSON19.TXT  PAGE 1 LINE 1 COL 01          INSERT ON
                    < < <   B L O C K   M E N U   > > >
 -Saving Files- ! -Block Operations- ! -File Operations- !   -Other Menus-
 S Save & resume ! B  Begin  K  End   ! R  Read  P  Print  ! (from Main only)
 D Save--done    ! H  Hide / Display  ! O  Copy  E  Rename  ! ^J Help  ^K Block
 X Save & exit   ! C  Copy   Y  Delete! J  Delete           ! ^Q Quick ^P Print
 Q Abandon file  ! V  Move   W  Write ! -Disk  Operations-  ! ^O Onscreen
 -Place Markers- ! N  Column  now OFF !L Change logged disk! Space Bar returns
 0-9 set/hide 0-9!                    !F Directory now OFF ! you to Main Menu.
 L----!----!----!----!----!----!----!----!----!----!--------R
```

Figure 19.7　The ^K Menu

All of the ^K menu commands have been presented. The following tables in Figure 19.8 summarize each command and its feature.

TABLE ONE: SAVING FILES

Command	Feature
^KS	Save the file currently in edit and stay in the file to resume the edit. Cursor returns to the file beginning after save. Enter ^QP to return the cursor to the location before the save.
^KD	Save the file and return to the opening menu.
^KX	Save the file and return to the operating system.
^KQ	Will not save the current edit. Return to the opening menu.

TABLE TWO: PLACE MARKERS

Command	Feature
^K0-9	Enter ^K and any number between 0 and 9 to mark text for a quick find. To find the place marker, enter ^Q and the number. Ten markers are possible. Enter ^K and the number again to delete the display. Markers are not saved except with the ^KS command.

TABLE THREE: BLOCK OPERATIONS

Command	Feature
^KB	Mark block beginning display <B>. If the begin-block marker is already displayed, entering ^KB will delete it.
^KK	Mark block end and display <K>. If the end block is already marked, entering ^KK will delete it.
^KH	Hide the block highlighting. Entering ^KH again will highlight the block.

(Fig. 19.8, continued on p. 176)

^KC	Copy or duplicate a marked block from one location to another location within a file.
^KV	Move a marked block from one location to another location within a file.
^KN	Turn on column mode to permit high-lighting of vertical columns for block operations. Enter ^KN again to turn off column mode.
^KY	Delete a highlighted block.
^KW	Write or copy a highlighted block into a new file.

TABLE FOUR: FILE OPERATIONS

Command	Feature
^KR	Read or copy one file into another file.
^KO	Copy a file from one disk onto another disk or copy a file onto the same disk using a different file name.
^KJ	Delete a file from current disk or from another disk.
^KP	Print a file while still in the edit mode. Enter ^KP again to abandon print.
^KE	Rename a file while still in the edit mode.

TABLE FIVE: DISK OPERATIONS

Command	Feature
^KL	Change the logged disk drive. After the document in edit is saved, the file directory of the new disk drive will be displayed.
^KF	Display the file directory into the edited file. The file directory will not print. Enter ^KF again to delete the display.

Figure 19.8   Summary of ^K Block Menu Commands

LESSON 19 EXERCISE

Name _____ Date _____

COMPLETION

Indicate the correct ^K command for each of the functions stated below. (Obj. 6)

1. Save the file currently in edit and stay in the file to resume the edit. Cursor returns to the file beginning after the save. Enter $\wedge QP$ to return the cursor to the location before the save. ....

2. Save the file and return to the opening menu. ....

3. Save the file and return to the operating system. ......

4. Will not save the current edit. Return to the opening menu. ....

5. Mark text for a quick find. To find the place marker, enter $\wedge Q$ and the number. Ten markers are possible. Enter $\wedge K$ and the number again to delete the display. Markers are not saved except with the $\wedge KS$ command. .

6. Mark block beginning display <B>. If the begin-block marker is already displayed, entering $\wedge KB$ will delete it.

7. Mark block end and display <K>. If the end block is already marked, entering $\wedge KK$ will delete it. ....

8. Hide the block highlighting. Entering $\wedge KH$ will highlight the block again. ....

9. Copy or duplicate a marked block from one location to another location within a file. ....

10. Move a marked block from one location to another location within a file. ....

11. Turn on column mode to permit highlighting of vertical columns for block operations. Enter $\wedge KN$ to turn off column mode. ....

12. Delete a highlighted block. ....

13. Write or copy a highlighted block into a new file. ......

14. Read or copy one file into another file. ....

15. Copy a file from one disk onto another disk or copy a file onto the same disk using a different file name. ....

16. Delete a file from current disk or from another disk. ..

17. Print a file while still in the edit mode. Enter $\wedge KP$ to abandon print. ....

18. Rename a file while still in the edit mode. ....

1. _____

2. _____

3. _____

4. _____

5. _____

6. _____

7. _____

8. _____

9. _____

10. _____

11. _____

12. _____

13. _____

14. _____

15. _____

16. _____

17. _____

18. _____

19. Change the logged disk drive. After the document in edit is saved, the file directory of the new disk drive will be displayed. .... 19. _____

20. Display the file directory into the edited file. The file directory will not print. Enter ^KF to delete the display.   20. _____

COMPUTER EXERCISE ONE

Directions: Follow the step-by-step instructions given to complete Computer Exercise One.

1. You will create several files and then do some block and file operations with the files. Create a file for the document shown in Figure 19.9 and name it INDEPEND.19. Enter the document. Turn off page numbering and use all the defaults. Proofread your entry and make the necessary corrections.

```
                  IN CONGRESS, JULY 4, 1776
                  THE UNANIMOUS DECLARATION OF
                  THE THIRTEEN UNITED STATES OF
                             AMERICA


        When  in the Course of human events it becomes necessary for one  people
   to  dissolve the political bands which have connected them with another,  and
   to  assume among the powers of the earth,  the separate and equal station  to
   which the Laws of Nature and of Nature's God entitle them,  a decent  respect
   to the opinions of mankind requires that they should declare the causes which
   impel them to the separation.

        We hold these truths to be self-evident,  that all men are created equal,
   that they are endowed by their Creator with certain unalienable Rights,  that
   among these are Life,  Liberty,  and the pursuit of Happiness.  That to secure
   these  rights,  Governments  are instituted among Men,  deriving  their  just
   powers  from  the  consent  of  the  governed.   That  whenever  any Form  of
   Government becomes destructive of these ends,  it is the Right of the  People
   to  alter  or  to abolish it,  and to institute new Government,  laying  its
   foundation on such principles and organizing its powers in such form,  as  to
   them shall seem most likely to effect their Safety and Happiness.
```

Figure 19.9   Computer Exercise One, Step One

---

2. Create a file for the document shown in Figure 19.10 and name it RIGHTS.19. Enter paragraph tabs (^OG) three times to indent the main text.Proofread the file and make any necessary corrections.

BILL OF RIGHTS

Amendment
One
Congress shall make no law respecting an establishment of religion, or prohibiting the free exercise thereof; or abridging the freedom of speech, or of the press; or the right of the people peaceably to assemble, and to petition the Government for a redress of grievances.

Amendment
Two
A well regulated Militia being necessary to the security of a free State, the right of the people to keep and bear Arms, shall not be infringed.

Amendment
Three
No Soldier shall, in time of peace be quartered in any house, without the consent of the Owner.

Amendment
Four
The right of the people to be secure in their persons, houses, papers, and effects, against unreasonable searches and seizures, shall not be violated, and no Warrants shall issue, but upon probable cause, supported by Oath or affirmation, and particularly describing the place to be searched, and the persons or things to be seized.

Amendment
Five
No person shall be held to answer for a capital, or otherwise infamous crime, unless on a presentment or indictment of a Grand Jury, except in cases arising in the land or naval forces, or in the Militia.

Amendment
Six
In all criminal prosecutions, the accused shall enjoy the right to a speedy and public trial, by an impartial jury of the State and district wherein the crime shall have been committed, which district shall have been previously ascertained by law, and to be informed of the nature and cause of the accusation; to be confronted with the witnesses against him; to have compulsory process for obtaining Witnesses in his favor, and to have the assistance of counsel for his defence.

Amendment
Seven
In Suits at common law, where the value in controversy shall exceed twenty dollars, the right of trial by jury shall be preserved.

Amendment
Eight
Excessive bail shall not be required, nor excessive fines imposed, nor cruel and unusual punishments inflicted.

Amendment
Nine
The enumeration in the Constitution, of certain rights, shall not be construed to deny or disparage others retained by the people.

Amendment
Ten
The powers not delegated to the United States by the Constitution, nor prohibited by it to the States, are reserved to the States respectively, or to the people.

Figure 19.10   Computer Exercise One, Step Two

3. Create a third file and name it COPY.19. Read the file named INDEPEND.19 into this file. Read the file named RIGHTS.19 into this file.

4. Turn off page numbering. Save and print the file named COPY.19.

COMPUTER EXERCISE TWO

Directions: Follow the step-by-step instructions given to complete Computer Exercise Two.

1. You will edit the file named COPY.19 that you made in Computer Exercise One.

2. Make the corrections which are handwritten in the file COPY.19 shown in Figure 19.11. Continue to follow these step-by-step instructions for Figure 19.11.

```
                    IN CONGRESS, JULY 4, 1776
                   THE UNANIMOUS DECLARATION OF         move to the
                   THE THIRTEEN UNITED STATES OF       end of the file
                             AMERICA


        When  in the Course of human events it becomes necessary for one  people
   to  dissolve the political bands which have connected them with another,  and
   to  assume among the powers of the earth,  the separate and equal station  to
   which the Laws of Nature and of Nature's God entitle them,  a decent  respect
   to the opinions of mankind requires that they should declare the causes which
   impel them to the separation.

        We hold these truths to be self-evident, that all men are created equal,
   that they are endowed by their Creator with certain unalienable Rights,  that
   among these are Life,  Liberty, and the pursuit of Happiness.  That to secure
   these  rights,  Governments  are instituted among Men,  deriving  their  just
   powers  from  the  consent  of  the governed.   That  whenever  any  Form  of
   Government becomes destructive of these ends,  it is the Right of the  People
   to  alter  or  to abolish it,  and to institute new  Government,  laying  its
   foundation on such principles and organizing its powers in such form,  as  to
   them shall seem most likely to effect their Safety and Happiness.
```

←——————————————————————— BILL OF RIGHTS

```
   Amendment
   One
                   Congress  shall  make  no law respecting  an  establishment  of
                   religion,  or  prohibiting  the  free  exercise  thereof;   or
                   abridging the freedom of speech,  or of the press; or the right
                   of  the  people  peaceably to assemble,  and  to  petition  the
                   Government for a redress of grievances.

   Amendment
   Two
                   A  well regulated Militia being necessary to the security of  a
                   free  State,  the  right  of the people to keep and  bear Arms,
                   shall not be infringed.
```

(Fig. 19.11, continued on p. 181)

Amendment
~~Three~~ *l*

No Soldier shall, ~~in time of peace be~~ quartered in any house, *delete*
~~without the consent~~ of the Owner.

Amendment
~~Four~~ *l*

~~The right~~ of the people to be secure in their persons, ~~houses,~~
papers, and ~~effects,~~ against unreasonable ~~searches~~ and *delete*
seizures, shall not be ~~violated, and no~~ Warrants shall issue,
but upon probable cause, ~~supported by Oath or~~ affirmation, and
particularly ~~describing~~ the place to be ~~searched, and~~ the
~~persons~~ or things to be seized.

Amendment
~~Five~~ *l*

~~No person shall~~ be held to answer for a capital, or ~~otherwise~~ *delete*
infamous crime, ~~unless on a presentment or indictment~~ of a
Grand Jury, ~~except in cases~~ arising in the ~~land or naval~~
~~forces, or~~ in the Militia.

Amendment
Six

*copy after
Amendment
Ten*

In all criminal prosecutions, the accused shall enjoy the right
to a speedy and public trial, by an impartial jury of the State
and district wherein the crime shall have been committed, which
district shall have been previously ascertained by law, and to
be informed of the nature and cause of the accusation; to be
confronted with the witnesses against him; to have compulsory
process for obtaining Witnesses in his favor, and to have the
assistance of counsel for his defence.

Amendment
~~Seven~~ *l*

~~In Suits at common law,~~ where the value in ~~controversy shall~~ *delete*
exceed twenty dollars, ~~the right of trial by jury shall be~~
~~preserved.~~

Amendment
Eight

Excessive bail shall not be required, nor excessive fines
imposed, nor cruel and unusual punishments inflicted.

Amendment
Nine

The enumeration in the Constitution, of certain rights, shall
not be construed to deny or disparage others retained by the
people.

Amendment
Ten

*copy column
to the end of
the file*

The powers not delegated to the United   States   by the
Constitution, nor prohibited by it to the States, are reserved
to the States respectively, or to the people.

Figure 19.11   Computer Exercise Two

3. Move the title and the first two paragraphs to the end of
the file. To do this, highlight all of the text in the move
with ^KB and ^KK. Then move the cursor to the end of
the file. Strike ^KV. Insert two blank lines between the
last line of the amendments and the moved text if
necessary.

4. Move the title BILL OF RIGHTS to the left margin.

5. To delete the text where indicated in the file, highlight it and then enter ∧*KY*.

6. To copy Amendment Six after Amendment Ten, highlight the text. Move the cursor two lines after Amendment Ten. Insert some blank lines if necessary with ∧*N*. Enter ∧*KC*.

7. To copy the circled column to the end of the file, follow these steps:

   a. Turn the column mode on with ∧*KN*.
   b. Highlight the complete column with ∧*KB* and ∧*KK*.
   c. Move the cursor to the end of the file with ∧*QC*.
   d. Insert some blank lines between the text to be moved and the previous text if necessary.
   e. Enter ∧*KC*.

8. Save the document.

9. Print the document named COPY.19.

COMPUTER EXERCISE THREE

Directions: Follow the step-by-step instructions given to complete Computer Exercise Three.

1. Edit the file named COPY.19. You will practice using the file and disk features in the ∧K menu while editing the

2. You should be in the file named COPY.19. Copy the file named INDEPEND.19 created in Computer Exercise One and call the copied file INDEPEND.COP.

3. Delete the file named INDEPEND.19.

4. Print the file named INDEPEND.COP.

5. Rename the INDEPEND.COP file INDEPEND.19.

6. View the file directory by entering ∧*KF*.

7. Save the file.

20. Quick Cursor Moves and the ^Q Menu Review _____

OBJECTIVES:

1. Describe how to move the cursor quickly to the top of the screen.

2. Describe how to move the cursor quickly to the bottom of the screen.

3. Present the quick cursor diamond.

4. Summarize the ^Q menu.

All of the ^Q (quick menu) commands have been introduced except for the commands that move the cursor quickly to the top and the bottom of the screen. These two commands will be introduced in this lesson followed by a summary of all of the ^Q menu commands.

THE ^QE AND ^QX COMMANDS

The cursor is moved quickly to the text at the top of the screen by striking the Ctrl key and the Q key at the same time and then striking the letter E. Of course, the status line and the ruler line are at the very top of the screen. The ^QE command will move the cursor to the top of the text, not to the status line display.

To move the cursor quickly to text at the bottom of the screen, hold down the Ctrl key and the Q key at the same time and strike the letter X.

THE QUICK CURSOR DIAMOND

You will recall that the command to move the cursor up one line is $\wedge E$; to move the cursor down one line is $\wedge X$; to move the cursor to the left one character is $\wedge S$; and to move the cursor to the right one character is $\wedge D$. The cursor diamond (shown in Figure 20.1) should help you to remember the cursor movement keys.

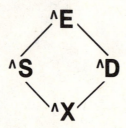

Figure 20.1   The Cursor Diamond

Think of the cursor diamond again to help you remember the quick cursor movement keys. You have already been introduced to the $\wedge QS$ command that moves the cursor directly to the beginning of a line and the $\wedge QD$ command that moves the cursor directly to the end of a line. Figure 20.2 illustrates the quick cursor diamond.

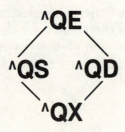

Figure 20.2   The Quick Cursor Diamond

$\wedge$Q MENU SUMMARY

The $\wedge Q$ menu is displayed by striking $\wedge Q$ while editing a document. The $\wedge Q$ menu is exited by striking the space bar. Figure 20.3 illustrates the $\wedge Q$ menu.

```
^Q       B:LESSON20.TXT     PAGE 2    LINE 53    COL   47       INSERT ON
                 < < <    Q U I C K    M E N U    > > >
---Cursor Movement---       ¦ -Delete- ¦ --Miscellaneous-- ¦--Other   Menus--
S left side D right side    ¦Y line   rt¦F Find text in file¦ (from Main only)
E top scrn  X bottom scrn   ¦DEL lin lf ¦A Find & Replace    ¦^J Help ^K Block
R top file  C end file      ¦           ¦L Find Misspelling  ¦^Q Quick ^P Print
B top block K end block     ¦           ¦Q Repeat command or ¦^O Onscreen
0-9 marker  W up  Z down    ¦           ¦ key until space    ¦Space bar returns
P previous  V last Find or Block        ¦ bar or other key   ¦you to Main Menu.
L----!----!----!----!----!----!----!----!----!----!----!--------R
```

Figure 20.3   The ^Q Menu

The ^Q menu commands execute quick cursor and scroll movements. They also delete parts of a line and find and replace text. Figure 20.4 summarizes all of the ^Q (quick menu) commands.

Command	Feature
^QS	Move the cursor quickly to the beginning of a line.
^QD	Move the cursor quickly to the end of a line.
^QE	Move the cursor quickly to the text at the top of the screen.
^QX	Move the cusor quickly to the text at the bottom of the screen.
^QC	Move the cursor quickly to the end of the file.
^QR	Move the cursor quickly to the beginning of the file.
^QB	Move the cursor to begin-block marker.
^QK	Move the cursor to end-block marker.
^Q0-9	Move the cursor to the corresponding place marker. For example, to find the place marker ^K2 (<2>), enter ^Q2.
^QP	Move the cursor to where it was before the previous command; use this command to return the cursor to its position before a save (^KS) or a paragraph reformat (^B).

(Fig. 20.4, continued on p. 186)

^QV	Move the cursor to its location before the last block copy, block move, block delete, or find and replace command, whichever was entered last.
^QW	Scroll to the beginning of a document. Enter any number between 1 and 9 to vary the speed. The lower the number, the faster the speed. Space to stop the scroll.
^QZ	Scroll to the end of a document. Enter any number between 1 and 9 to vary the speed. The lower the number, the faster the speed. Space to stop the scroll.
^QY	Delete a line to the right of the cursor.
^QDel	Delete a line to the left of the cursor.
^QF	Find text in a document.
^QA	Find text and replace it with other text.
^QL	This is a SpellStar command. (To learn about SpellStar, another disk and another book are necessary.)
^QQ	Repeat the next command or key entered. The repeat rate can be varied by entering a number from 1 to 9. The lower the number, the faster the speed. Use to reformat an entire document at once.

Figure 20.4   The ^Q Menu Command Summary

LESSON 20 EXERCISE   Name _____ Date _____

COMPLETION

Indicate the correct command for each feature in the space provided. (Obj. 4)

1. Move the cursor quickly to the beginning of a line......   1. _____

2. Move the cursor quickly to the end of a line. ....   2. _____

3. Move the cursor quickly to the text at the top of the screen. ....   3. _____

4. Move the cursor quickly to the text at the bottom of the screen. ....   4. _____

5. Move the cursor quickly to the end of the file. ....   5. _____

6. Move the cursor quickly to the beginning of the file....   6. _____

7. Move the cursor to begin-block marker.................   7. _____

8. Move the cursor to end-block marker...................   8. _____

9. Move the cursor to the corresponding place marker.....   9. _____

10. Move the cursor to where it was before the previous command; use this command to return the cursor to its position before a save (^KS) or a paragraph reformat (^B). ....   10. _____

11. Move the cursor to its location before the last block copy, block move, block delete, or find and replace command, whichever was entered last. ....   11. _____

12. Scroll to the beginning of a document. Enter any number between 1 and 9 to vary the speed. The lower the number, the faster the speed. Space to stop the scroll. .   12. _____

13. Scroll to the end of a document. Enter any number between 1 and 9 to vary the speed. The lower the number, the faster the speed. Space to stop the scroll............   13. _____

14. Delete a line to the right of the cursor.................   14. _____

15. Delete a line to the left of the cursor. ....   15. _____

16. Find text in a document. ....   16. _____

17. Find text and replace it with other text. ....   17. _____

18. This is a SpellStar command...........................   18. _____

19. Repeat the next command or key entered. The repeat rate can be varied by entering a number from 1 to 9. The lower the number, the faster the speed. Use to reformat an entire document at once. ....   19. _____

COMPUTER EXERCISE

Directions: Follow the step-by-step instructions to complete the computer exercise.

1. Create a file named LESSON20.EX and enter the directors' report shown in Figure 20.5. You will practice the quick cursor movements and other ^Q menu commands in this file. Follow the step-by-step instructions to gain practice using the ^Q menu commands.

```
                         DIRECTORS' REPORT


To the Shareholders,
Urban Toronto Mines Limited:

     Presented herewith are the financial statements of your Company
for the year ended December 31, 19-- with Auditors' Report thereon
dated March 1, 19--.

     During the past year, and as previously reported, two diamond
drill holes were completed on your Company's 15 claim groups in the
Cold Branch Brook area of New Brunswick, adjacent to the east of the
property of Key Anacon, Incorporated, which returned important
geological information.  It is not proposed to undertake further
exploration work on these claims until information might be available
from the neighboring property.

     Surface examination was made of the Company's group of 15
patented claims in Cardiff Township, Eastern Toronto Mining Division,
and further work is planned to explore these claims for their uranium
potential.  Also, an exploration program is planned on the Company's
group of 14 claims in San Clemente Township, Ontario, to test these
claims for their nickel-copper potential.

     In addition to the aforementioned claim groups, your Company holds
a good standing in 57 claims in the Red River area, County of
Gloucester, New Brunswick.

     Arrangements have been made which, when completed, will provide
your Company with further finances to carry on its exploration
activities.  It is expected that an announcement in this regard will
be made in the near future.

                         On behalf of the Board,



                         Alan Boyton, President
```

Figure 20.5   Text for Computer Exercise

2. Omit page numbers. Insert should be on. Set help level at 2. Turn hyphen help off.

3. Practice the following quick cursor movements several times:

   a. Move the cursor to the beginning and the end of the document with ^QR and ^QC.

   b. Move the cursor to the first line in the first paragraph. Move the cursor to the end of the line and the beginning of the line with ^QD and ^QS.

   c. Move the cursor directly to the top of the screen and the bottom of the screen with ^QE and ^QX.

4. Enter a place marker at the beginning of the second paragraph. Call this place marker number 1. Enter ^K1 at the beginning of the paragraph.

5. Mark the third paragraph for a block move with ^KB and ^KK. The block will be moved later. Hide the block highlighting.

6. Scroll at the fastest speed to the beginning of the document.

7. Find place marker number 1.

8. Find the begin-block marker.

9. Find the end-block marker.

10. Move the block to the end of the report just before the complimentary close.

11. Hide the block highlighting. Enter a blank line between the paragraphs if necessary.

12. Move the cursor to its location before the block was moved. Delete any extra blank lines between the paragraphs that may have been left after the block move.

13. Scroll to the end of the document and vary the speed by entering numbers between 1 and 9.

14. Find "Red River." Use the search backwards option because you are now at the end of the document.

15. Save the document with ^KS. Return the cursor to its location before the save.

16. Find and replace every occurrence of "Company" with "Corporation."

17. Move the cursor to the middle of the first line in the first paragraph. Delete the line to the right of the cursor. Delete the line to the left of the cursor.

18. Delete the rest of the paragraph.

19. Change the margins to 5 and 60. Turn justification off.

20. Reformat the entire document without stopping.

21. Save the document with $^\wedge KD$.

22. Print the file named LESSON20.EX.

21. Headers _____

OBJECTIVES:

1. Define a header.

2. Describe the header command.

3. Print headers starting from page one.

4. Print headers after page one.

5. Explain canceling headers.

6. Explain page numbers in headers.

7. Alternating page number position in headers.

8. Page numbers and titles in headers.

9. Describe how to change spacing from top of page to header.

10. Describe how to change spacing between header and text.

11. Summarize the header features.

HEADERS

A **header** is one line of text at the top of a page that is repeated on subsequent pages. Examples of headers include the following:

1. Page number at the top of every page.

2. Chapter title at the top of every page.

3. Page number and chapter title at the top of every page.

THE HEADER COMMAND

The header command is .HE (uppercase or lowercase) and a space. Think of the first two letters of the word *header* to remember this command. It is a dot command because it begins with a dot (.). This command takes up four character spaces (*.HE* and a space) on the screen, but the *.HE* will, of course, not print. So the header text on the screen will always appear four spaces to the right of where it will actually print.

Several points should be made about the header command:

1. The dot (.) must be entered at column 1 or the dot command will print.

2. There must be at least one space after .*HE* or the header will not print.

3. The command can be entered anywhere in the document, but it must begin at column 1.

4. The header line does not conform to the set right margin. Text can be entered up to column 250.

5. The header default is a blank line. In other words, no header will print unless the dot command is entered.

When the dot is entered at column 1, a question mark appears on the right side of the screen signaling that WordStar is waiting for a dot command to be executed.

HEADERS STARTING FROM PAGE ONE

If you want a heading to print on every page beginning with the first page of the document, enter .*HE* (and a space) at the very beginning of the document before any text has been entered. Figure 21.1 illustrates a heading that will print from page one.

```
B:BOOK.TEXT        PAGE 1  LINE 1  COL 12      INSERT ON
L----!----!----!----!----!----!----!----!--------------------R

.HE CHAPTER ONE

This  chapter will instruct you about headers.   When the chapter

is printed, "CHAPTER ONE" will appear at the top of each page in

the document.
```

Figure 21.1   Header Command to Print Header From Page One

Notice that the title "Chapter One" begins at column 5 because the first four columns are taken up by the header command. The title will print out at column 1.

HEADERS STARTING AFTER PAGE ONE

The command to print headers after page one can be entered anywhere in the document except at the very beginning. The header will print on the pages following the command. Figure 21.2 illustrates a header command that will cause the title to print on the pages following the command.

```
This WordStar command saves lots of time; you no longer have to

retype the same title on every page of the document.

.HE CHAPTER ONE
```

Figure 21.2   Header Command to Print on the Pages Following the Command

---

CANCELING HEADERS

To cancel the printing of a header, enter the header command again but this time do not enter a title. No titles will print on subsequent pages until another header dot command and a title are entered.

PAGE NUMBERS IN HEADERS

Page numbers will print by default at the bottom of every page. Suppose you want the page numbers to print at the top of the page. The header command will print page numbers as well as titles.

If page numbering is in the header, you must omit the page numbering that prints by default at the end of the page. To omit page numbers at the bottom of the page, enter *.OP* at column 1 at the beginning of the file.

The symbol # stands for *number*. Where this symbol appears in the header, WordStar substitutes a number which increases by one as each page prints. For example, to print page numbers in the upper right corner of each page, the header line will look like the illustration in Figure 21.3.

```
.HE                                                              #
```

Figure 21.3   Header Command to Print Page Numbers at Right

If the document has a right margin set at 65, the # symbol should appear at column 69 because the command itself takes up four spaces on the line (65 spaces to the right margin plus 4 header command characters).

Numbers can print at any column position on the header line. If you want the numbers to print at the center of the line, enter # and center it with ^OC. Then move the cursor to the beginning of the line with ^QS and enter .HE and a space. Figure 21.4 shows the header line for numbers to print at the center.

. HE   #

**Figure 21.4   Header Command to Print Page Numbers at
Center**

If you want numbers to print at the upper left corner of each page, enter the number symbol # immediately after .HE at column 1. Do not space before the #. Figure 21.5 illustrates the header command to print numbers at left.

. HE#

Figure 21.5   Header Command to Print Page Numbers at Left

ALTERNATING PAGE NUMBER POSITION

Sometimes you may want to alternate or vary the page number position between the upper right side and upper left side of the page, as in a book. Think of the page numbering in a book. The right-hand pages have odd numbers that occur on the right side of the page; the left-hand pages have even numbers that occur on the left side of the page. In other words, the page numbers are always on the outside of the page (on the side away from the book's binding).

WordStar will alternate the position of page numbers by a special command .HE^P^K. Nothing appears on the screen when ^P is entered. When ^K is entered, the screen will display ^K. Figure 21.6 illustrates the header line command to alternate the printing of page numbers between the right and left side of the page.

. HE^K   #

**Figure 21.6   Header Command to Alternate Page Numbers to
the Right and Left (.HE^P^K)**

Notice that there is no space between *.HE* and ^*K* and that the ^*K* takes up two more spaces on the header line. So now there are actually five characters that appear on the screen but will not print (.HE^K).

PAGE NUMBERS AND TITLES

Headers can display page numbers and titles. Simply enter the text as well as the # symbol at the positions you want the text and numbers printed. Figure 21.7 illustrates different configurations of a header with a title and page numbering.

```
.HE                        CHAPTER ONE                              #

(Centered Title with page numbers at right.)


.HE# CHAPTER ONE

(Page numbers and title at left.)


.HE^K                                            CHAPTER ONE #

(Page numbers and title alternating right and left.)
```

Figure 21.7   Header Commands With Title and Page Numbers

Suppose you want each page to print as "Page #1," "Page #2," "Page #3," and so on, using the # symbol as part of the printed header. WordStar will mistake this symbol (#) for a command to print page numbers. To print the # symbol, strike the backslash key (\) before the # symbol. WordStar interprets the backslash symbol to mean "print the next character." Figure 21.8 illustrates the header line command to print the number symbol. (If you want to print the backslash symbol (\) in the header, enter two backslashes. The first backslash would indicate that the second backslash is to print.)

```
.HE                        Page \##
```

Figure 21.8   Header Command to Print # Symbol in Header

CHANGING THE SPACING BETWEEN
TOP OF PAGE AND HEADER

When a header is entered in a document, it is considered to be part of the margin top and will print by default on the first line of the page. The text will print by default two lines after the header. Figure 21.9 illustrates the vertical line spacing on a page with and without a header.

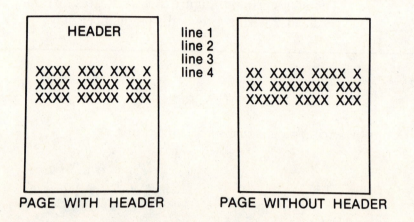

Figure 21.9   Vertical Page Layout With and Without a Header

The default for the margin top is three lines and can be expressed by the dot command .MT 3 (MT means *margin top*). But when a header is entered, the header will print on line one, and the other two lines of the top margin default are dropped.

The default for the vertical spacing between the header and the text is two blank lines and can be expressed by the dot command .HM 2 (HM means *header margin*). To increase the spacing between the top of the page and the header, add the number of blank lines wanted between the top of the page and the header and the number of blank lines wanted between the header and the text. For example, if you want six lines from the top of the page to the header and two lines between the header and the text, add six and two. The margin top will be entered as the dot command .MT 8 at column 1 at the file's beginning. Since the header margin is at the default (two lines), no dot command is needed to change the header margin.

CHANGING THE SPACING BETWEEN
HEADER AND TEXT

Text prints by default on the third line after the header, leaving two blank lines. This can be expressed by the dot command .HM 2. To change the default spacing, enter the dot command .HM and the number of blank lines wanted between the header and the text. For example, if you want four blank lines between the header and the text, enter *.HM 4* at column one at the beginning of the document.

Figure 21.10 defines the header command and its variations.

Feature	Command or Default
Print from page 1	Enter *.HE* and a space at column 1 at the very beginning of the document.
Print from page 2	Enter *.HE* and a space at column 1 anywhere before page 2 except at the very beginning of the file.
Cancel a heading	Enter *.HE* and a space at column 1 or delete the header line.
Page numbers at left	Enter *.HE #* at column 1.
Page numbers at center	Enter # and center it. Enter *.HE* and a space at column 1.
Alternate position	Enter *.HE^P^K* at column 1.
Header print line	Default: Header prints on line 1.
Change spacing from top of page to header	Enter *.MT* and the number of lines wanted from top of page to header plus number of lines between header and text.
Spacing from header to text	Default: two blank lines (*.HM 2*).
Change spacing from header to text	Enter *.HM* and a space at column 1 and number of blank lines wanted between header and text.

Figure 21.10   Summary of Header Command Features

TRUE/FALSE

Each of the following statements is either true or false. Indicate your choice in the Answers column by circling T for a true statement or F for a false statement.

Answers

1. A header is more than one line of text at the top of a page that is repeated on subsequent pages. (Obj. 1) ....

   1.   **T**   **F**

2. Page numbers can only be printed at the bottom of each page. (Obj. 1) ....

   2.   **T**   **F**

3. The header command is .HE and a space. (Obj. 2) ....

   3.   **T**   **F**

4. The dot in the header command must be entered at column 1. (Obj. 2) .....

   4.   **T**   **F**

5. The header line does not conform to the right margin setting. (Obj. 2).....

   5.   **T**   **F**

6. A question mark appears on the right side of the screen when a dot is entered at column 1. (Obj. 2) ....

   6.   **T**   **F**

7. Headers will always start from page one. (Obj. 3).........................

   7.   **T**   **F**

8. The header command takes up four columns of space on the screen. (Obj. 3) ....

   8.   **T**   **F**

9. To print a header beginning on page two, enter the .HE command at the very beginning of the document. (Obj. 4) ....

   9.   **T**   **F**

10. Enter the header command again to cancel a header. (Obj. 5) ....

   10.   **T**   **F**

11. Page numbers will print by default at the bottom of every page. (Obj. 6)..

   11.   **T**   **F**

12. To print a page number at the top of every page, enter # anywhere on the header line. (Obj. 6) ....

   12.   **T**   **F**

13. To print page numbers in the upper left corner of every page, enter *.HE*, a space, and # (.HE #). (Obj. 6) ....

   13.   **T**   **F**

14. A book usually has an odd page number printed at the outside of a right-hand page. (Obj. 7)...

   14.   **T**   **F**

15. The entire command for alternating page numbers is displayed on the screen as ^P^K. (Obj. 7)...

   15.   **T**   **F**

16. The entire ^P^K command takes up eight spaces in the header line. (Obj. 7) ....

   16.   **T**   **F**

17. If page numbers are in the header, chapter titles cannot be in the header. (Obj. 8) ....

   17.   **T**   **F**

18. The page number symbol will print in a header if it is preceded by a backslash in the header line. (Obj. 8) ....

   18.   **T**   **F**

19. The header will print on the first line from the top of the page by default. (Obj. 9) ....

   19.   **T**   **F**

20. The dot command to change a margin top with headers is *.MT* and the sum of the margin top lines and the header margin lines. (Obj. 9) ....   20. **T**   **F**

21. To print a margin top of six lines with a header, enter the dot command .MT 8. (Obj. 9)...   21. **T**   **F**

22. The dot command that expresses the default margin between the header and text is .MT 3. (Obj. 10) ....   22. **T**   **F**

23. To print four blank lines between the header and the text, enter the dot command .HM 4. (Obj. 10)...   23. **T**   **F**

24. To print text on the fifth line after a header, enter the dot command .HM 4. (Obj. 10) ....   24. **T**   **F**

COMPLETION

Indicate the correct answer in the space provided.

1. A header is one line of text at the top of a page that is repeated or not repeated on subsequent pages? (Obj. 1)...   1. _____

2. The header command is a space following what three characters? (Obj. 2) ....   2. _____

3. The header command takes up how many character spaces on the line? (Obj. 2) ....   3. _____

4. The header command must always be entered at column *?* (Obj. 2) ....   4. _____

5. What is the maximum number of characters that can be entered on the header line? (Obj. 2) ....   5. _____

6. What appears on the screen when the dot (.) is entered at column 1? (Obj. 2)...   6. _____

7. To print a header starting on page one, enter the header command before the document *?* (Obj. 3)...............   7. _____

8. To print headers starting on page two, on what page should you enter the header command? (Obj. 4)........   8. _____

9. To cancel a header, you can delete the header line or enter *?* (Obj. 5)...   9. _____

10. If page numbers are to print in the header, you should cancel the page numbering default by what command? (Obj. 6)...   10. _____

11. What symbol stands for page numbers in the header? (Obj. 6)...   11. _____

12. To print page numbers at the top left corner of each page, enter *?* (Obj. 6) ....   12. _____

13. In a book, the odd page numbers are usually printed on what pages? (Obj. 7) ....   13. _____

14. To alternate page number positions, enter *?* (Obj. 7)....   14. _____

15. The command to alternate page numbers in the header uses how many character spaces in the line? (Obj. 7) ...

16. The ^P character will or will not display on the screen when entered as part of the command .HE^P^K? (Obj. 7) ....

17. What symbol does WordStar interpret to mean "print the next character"? (Obj. 8) ....

18. What is the header line command to print "Page #1," "Page #2," "Page #3," and so on? (Obj. 8)............

19. The header will print by default on which line? (Obj. 9) ....

20. What is the header margin dot command if the margin top is to be six lines and the header margin is to be three lines? (Obj. 10) ....

15. _____

16. _____

17. _____

18. _____

19. _____

20. _____

COMPUTER EXERCISE ONE

Directions: Follow the step-by-step instructions to complete Computer Exercise One.

1. Create a file and name it LESSON21.EX1.

2. Enter the text in Figure 21.11. Turn justification off and double-space the document. Turn hyphen help off.

EVALUATION

The Board shall complete an official evaluation of each contract certificated employee at least once every academic year and of each regular certificated employee at least once every two academic years. Each temporary certificated employee, if employed by the District for three quarters, whether or not successive, shall be evaluated at least once during that period and, if employed thereafter, at least once every six quarters of employment. The Board may utilize either an appropriate management employee or a regular certificated employee designated by management to conduct such an evaluation. The use of nonmanagement personnel for conducting official evaluations shall be pursuant to the stipulations outlined in this Agreement.

The official evaluation of a certificated employee shall be recorded on an appropriate evaluation form and promptly placed in the certificated employee's on-campus personnel file. The evaluation form shall be signed by an appropriate management employee and the certificated employee, unless, after reviewing the evaluation, the certificated employee elects to sign a separate form stating his or her reasons for refusing to sign the official evaluation form. This form shall be attached to the official evaluation form promptly placed in the employee's on-campus personnel file.

(Fig. 21.11, continued on p. 202)

If, after 25 working days, the certificated employee fails or refuses
to sign either the official evaluation form or the separate form specified
by this Agreement, the official evaluation form shall be placed in the
employee's personnel file and a copy shall be sent to the employee by
certified mail. The certified mail receipt shall be attached to the
official evaluation in the employee's personnel file.

PERSONNEL FILES

Every certificated employee shall have the right, at reasonable times,
to inspect any employment record retained in the personnel files of the
school that may serve as a basis for affecting the status of the employee's
certificated employment.

Information from the employment records of a certificated employee
shall not be released without the consent of the certificated employee
unless the release is compelled by law or by a judicial order or lawfully
issued subpoena. All written material that may serve as a basis for a
certificated employee's suspension, dismissal, or reprimand shall be kept
in the employee's personnel file.

If a certificated employee believes that any portion of his or her
personnel file is not accurate, relevant, timely, or complete, the
certificated employee may request correction of the record or deletion of
the offending portion. Such a request should be in writing and should
include a statement of the corrections and deletions that the certificated
employee believes are necessary and the reasons. The request will become
part of the certificated employee's employment record unless the request is
granted.

In addition to the right to request correction or deletion in the
personnel file, each certificated employee shall have the right to include
a relevant response to any negative material in his or her personnel file.

WORKING HOURS

The normal academic workday means the period of time between 7:30 a.m.
and 5:30 p.m.

The normal academic workweek begins at 7:30 a.m. on Monday and ends at
5:30 p.m. on Friday of any week of instruction in the regular academic
year.

The regular academic year begins the first week in September and ends
the second week in June.

Figure 21.11   Text for Computer Exercises

---

3. Proofread and correct any errors. Reformat the document
if necessary. You will now create different headings for
this document and print the document with the various
heading formats.

4. The first printing for this file will have the header "CON-
TRACT PROPOSAL" centered on every page. To do this
follow these steps:

a. Enter a blank line with ^N. Enter "CONTRACT PRO-
POSAL" and center it with ^OC at the beginning of
the file.

   b. Position the cursor at column 1 with $\wedge QS$.

   c. Enter *.HE* and a space.

5. Save and print the file named LESSON21.EX1.

COMPUTER EXERCISE TWO

Directions: Follow the step-by-step instructions to complete Computer Exercise Two.

1. Make a copy from the opening menu of the file named LESSON21.EX1 created in Computer Exercise One and name the new file LESSON21.EX2.

2. Create a new header for page numbering in this file (LESSON21.EX2) so that the number prints in the upper right corner beginning on the second page of the document. Precede the page number with the word "Page" (as in Page 1, Page 2, Page 3, and so on). To do this, follow these steps:

   a. Delete the header line from the previous exercise.

   b. On the first page, enter *.HE* at column 1 on any line except the first line.

   c. Enter the word *Page*, a space, and the symbol # at column 63 of the header line. (The 65-space line, plus 4 spaces in the header command, minus 6 spaces in the title gives you column 63 to begin this entry.)

   d. Insert a blank line ($\wedge N$) to replace the line used for the header command.

   e. Omit the page numbering default with the dot command *.OP* at the file's beginning. Add a blank line with $\wedge N$ to insert this command.

3. Save and print the file named LESSON21.EX2.

COMPUTER EXERCISE THREE

Directions: Follow the step-by-step instructions to complete Computer Exercise Three.

1. Make a copy of the file named LESSON21.EX2 from the opening menu and name the new file LESSON21.EX3.

2. Create a new header in the file named LESSON21.EX3 with the following format. Follow the instructions in step 3 to complete the header format.

   a. Alternate page number positions. The first page number is to print in the upper right corner of the page; the second page number is to print in the upper left corner of the page.

   b. Print the # symbol before the page number (#1, #2, #3, and so on).

   c.   The header should start one inch (6 lines) from the top of the page.

   d.   The text should start five blank lines after the header.

3. Follow these steps to complete the header format:

   a.   At the very beginning of the file, insert a blank line with ^N. To alternate page number position, enter *.HE^P^K* at column 1.

   b.   Enter \ # # at column 67 on the header line (the 65-space line, plus 5 spaces in the header command, minus 3 spaces in \ # # gives you column 67 to begin this entry).

   c.   Change the margin top default. At the very beginning of the file enter a blank line with ^N and insert at column 1 *.MT*, a space, and *11* (6 lines at the top of the page for the one-inch margin top plus 5 blank lines for the header margin). The margin top command must be on the very first line of the file.

   d.   Add a blank line after the .MT 11 command. At column 1, enter *.HM*, a space, and *5* to change the header margin default.

   e.   Delete the previous header line on page 1.

4. Save and print the file named LESSON21.EX3.

22. Footers

OBJECTIVES:

1. Define a footer.

2. Describe the footer default.

3. Explain the footer command.

4. Explain canceling the footer command.

5. Print a footer from page one.

6. Print a footer after page one.

7. Describe page numbers in footers.

8. Explain how to alternate footer position.

9. Show how to change spacing between text and footer line.

10. Describe how to change spacing between footer line and page end.

11. Summarize the footer command features.

FOOTERS

A **footer** is one line of text at the bottom of the page that is repeated on subsequent pages. Footers consist of any text such as titles, page numbers, or messages.

THE FOOTER DEFAULT

The centered page number printed at the bottom of each page is the footer default. The numbering begins at column 33, which is at the center of the 65-space line. When the margins are changed, the page numbers will still print at column 33 causing the page numbers to be off center.

You can control the column where the page number prints with the dot command .PC. Suppose the right margin is changed to 50. The center of that margin setting is 25. Enter *.PC 25* so that the page number prints at center. When the footer command is entered, the footer default for page numbers is canceled. The footer default is also canceled by the dot command .OP (OP means *omit page*).

THE FOOTER COMMAND

The command to enter a line of text at the bottom of every page is the dot command .FO and a space. (You should think of the first two letters of the word *footer* to remember this command.) The rules for headers outlined in the previous lesson also apply to footers. The rules include the following:

1. The dot (.) must be entered at column 1 or the dot command will print.

2. There must be at least one space after the .FO or the footer will not print.

3. The command can be entered anywhere in the document, but it must begin at column 1.

4. The footer line does not conform to the set right margin. Text can be entered up to column 250.

5. The footer command uses four character spaces on the screen; therefore, the footer message will appear four spaces to the right of where it actually will print.

CANCELING AND PRINTING FOOTERS

To cancel the printing of a footer, enter *.FO* and a space with nothing on the rest of the line. The command is keyed-in on the page you want the footer to be canceled. The page numbering default will be turned on with the canceling of the footer command unless the page numbering is suppressed by *.OP*.

To print a footer beginning at page one, enter the footer line anywhere on page one. To print a footer after page one, enter the footer line on the page the footer is to be printed. The command must be entered at column 1.

PAGE NUMBERS IN FOOTERS

The # symbol in the footer line tells WordStar to print page numbers. The number will increase by one on each subsequent page. If the number is to print at the bottom left corner of the page, the # symbol is entered on the footer line immediately after the .FO command (.FO#).

If the number symbol (#) is to print out in the footer line as in "Chapter #1," "Chapter #2," "Chapter #3," and so on, a backslash (\) must be entered immediately before the number symbol (#). Remember, the backslash symbol entered immediately before a character tells WordStar to print the character exactly as entered and not to interpret it as a special command.

ALTERNATING FOOTER POSITION

To alternate the printing of text between the lower right and lower left corner of the page, enter *.FO^P^K*. Use this command to print footer text at the outside of the page, as if to allow for binding. Odd page numbers are printed at the lower right and even page numbers are printed at the lower left side of the page. The footer line for alternate page number positions is illustrated in Figure 22.1.

```
.FO^K                                                              #
```

Figure 22.1   Footer Line for Alternate Page Number Positions

The ^P does not display when you enter the command .FO^P^K. The alternate position footer command uses up five character spaces on the screen; therefore, the footer text should appear five spaces beyond where you want the text printed. In Figure 22.1, the # symbol is entered at column 70 (the 65-space line plus the 5 spaces in .FO^K indicate column 70 for the # symbol).

CHANGING SPACING BETWEEN TEXT AND FOOTER

The default for vertical line spacing between the document text and the footer message is two blank lines. This footer margin default can be expressed in the dot command .FM 2. (Think *footer margin* to help remember the command.) To change the default spacing between the text and the footer message, enter *.FM*, a space, and the number of blank lines required. For example, to print four blank lines between the text and the footer, enter the dot command .FM 4 at column 1.

CHANGING SPACING BETWEEN FOOTER AND END OF PAGE

The footer message prints within the margin bottom. The margin bottom default is eight blank lines and can be expressed by the dot command .MB 8. (Think *margin bottom* to help remember the command.) So when a footer prints at the footer margin default, there are five lines left over for the margin bottom. (Subtract the footer line and the two blank lines for the footer margin default from the eight lines in the margin bottom default: 8 − 3 = 5 lines for the margin bottom.)

To change the margin bottom of five blank lines from the

footer to the bottom of the page, add the blank lines in the footer margin and the number of blank lines wanted for the margin bottom. Enter the sum of these lines in the dot command .MB. For example, to leave a margin bottom of eight lines, enter the dot command .MB 10 (2 blank lines between text and footer plus 8 blank lines between footer and end of the page). The margin bottom command must be entered at the beginning of the file at column 1.

Figure 22.2 is a summary of the footer command and its features.

Feature	Command or Default
Footer default	Default: page numbers at column 33 (half of the 65-space line).
Change print column in footer default	Enter *.PC*, a space, and column required.
Footer command	Enter *.FO* and a space at column 1.
Cancel footer command	Enter *.FO* and a space or delete footer line.
Begin footer from page one	Enter footer command anywhere on page one.
Begin footer after page one	Enter footer command on page footer is printed.
Page numbers in footer	Enter # symbol in footer line.
Page numbers at left	Enter *.FO#* (with no spaces) at column 1.
Alternate footer position	Enter *.FO^P^K* at column 1.
Footer margin default	Default: *.FM 2* (two blank lines).
Change footer margin	Enter *.FM*, a space, and number of blank lines required.
Margin bottom default	Default: *.MB 8* (eight blank lines).
Change margin bottom with footer	Add number of lines between text and footer plus margin bottom required. Enter sum of the lines in .MB command.

Figure 22.2   Footer Command Summary

TRUE/FALSE

Each of the following statements is either true or false. Indicate your choice in the Answers column by circling T for a true statement or F for a false statement.

Answers

1. Footers are only page numbers. (Obj. 1) ....   1. **T**   **F**

2. The page numbers begin by default at column 33. (Obj. 2) ....   2. **T**   **F**

3. The command .PC will change the column number of the page default. (Obj. 2) ....   3. **T**   **F**

4. If the margin line has 75 spaces in it, change the number column default with the command .PC 25. (Obj. 2) ....   4. **T**   **F**

5. The dot command to print a footer line is .FO and a space. (Obj. 3) ....   5. **T**   **F**

6. The footer line conforms to the right margin setting. (Obj. 3) ....   6. **T**   **F**

7. The footer command uses three character spaces on the screen. (Obj. 3)....   7. **T**   **F**

8. To cancel the footer, enter *.FO* and a space with no text after it on the page before the canceled footer. (Obj. 4) ....   8. **T**   **F**

9. The page numbering default will be turned on when the footer is canceled, unless the dot command .OP is entered at the beginning of the file. (Obj. 4) ....   9. **T**   **F**

10. To print the footer from page one, enter the command anywhere on page one. (Obj. 5) ....   10. **T**   **F**

11. To print the footer after page one, enter the footer line on the page the footer is to be printed. (Obj. 6) ....   11. **T**   **F**

12. To print a number in the lower left corner of the page, enter *.FO*, a space, and # at column 1. (Obj. 7) ....   12. **T**   **F**

13. To print "Chapter #4" in a footer line, enter *Chapter \ # 4*. (Obj. 7) ....   13. **T**   **F**

14. The command .FO^P^K will alternate page number positions in the footer line. (Obj. 8) ....   14. **T**   **F**

15. The alternate page number command takes up seven character spaces in the display. (Obj. 8)...   15. **T**   **F**

16. The command to change the footer margin is .FM and a space. (Obj. 9)....   16. **T**   **F**

17. The footer margin default is three blank lines. (Obj. 9) ....   17. **T**   **F**

18. To print five blank lines between the text and the footer, enter *.FM 5*. (Obj. 9) ....   18. **T**   **F**

19. The margin bottom default without footers is six lines. (Obj. 10) ....   19. **T**   **F**

20. To print a margin bottom of six blank lines with a footer margin of four blank lines, enter the dot commands .MB 10 and .FM 4. (Obj. 10)..........   20. **T**   **F**

COMPLETION

Indicate the answer for each of the following statements in the space provided.

1. A line of text repeated at the bottom of consecutive pages is called a *?* (Obj. 1) ....   1. _____

2. What does the footer default print at the bottom of each page? (Obj. 2) ....   2. _____

3. The page number default prints at which column? (Obj. 2) ....   3. _____

4. To change the page number default column, you should enter which command? (Obj. 2) ....   4. _____

5. If the right margin is changed to 70, what must be entered to change the page number default column? (Obj. 2) ....   5. _____

6. When the footer command is entered, the footer default is *?* (Obj. 2) ....   6. _____

7. The dot command to cancel the page number default is *?* (Obj. 2) ....   7. _____

8. The footer command is *?* (Obj. 3) ....   8. _____

9. The dot command must be entered at which column? (Obj. 3) ....   9. _____

10. Text can be entered up to which column in the footer line? (Obj. 3) ....   10. _____

11. The footer command uses how many character spaces on the screen? (Obj. 3) ....   11. _____

12. To cancel a footer, what must be entered? (Obj. 4) .....   12. _____

13. The page number default will be turned on or off when the footer is canceled? (Obj. 4)...........................   13. _____

14. The command to omit page numbers is *?* (Obj. 4) ....   14. _____

15. To print a footer on the first page of a document, enter the footer line anywhere on *?* (Obj. 5) ....   15. _____

16. To print a footer beginning on page three, enter the footer line on page *?* (Obj. 6) ....   16. _____

17. The symbol to print a page number in the footer is *?* (Obj. 7) ....   17. _____

18. To print the page number in the bottom left corner of the page, enter *?* (Obj. 7) ....   18. _____

19. If the # symbol is to print in a footer, what must be entered before the #? (Obj. 7) ....   19. _____

20. To print "Chapter #1" at the lower left corner of the page, enter *?* (Obj. 7) .... 20. _____

21. The command to alternate footer positions is *?* (Obj. 8)... 21. _____

22. What does the screen display for the command to alternate footer positions? (Obj. 8) .... 22. _____

23. Odd numbers usually print on which side of a page in a book? (Obj. 8) .... 23. _____

24. The dot command for the footer margin default is *?* (Obj. 9)... 24. _____

25. The margin bottom default can be expressed by which dot command? (Obj. 10).................................. 25. _____

COMPUTER EXERCISE

Directions: Follow the step-by-step instructions given to complete the computer exercise.

1. For this exercise, use the file named LESSON21.EX1 created in Lesson 21, Computer Exercise One. If you have not created this file, do so now.

2. Copy the file named LESSON21.EX1 from the opening menu. Name the copied file LESSON22.EX.

3. Create a footer line that reads "First Draft of Contract Proposal." Center this footer title. Start the footer from page one. To do this:

   a. Position the cursor at the beginning of the file.
   b. Insert a blank line for the footer message. Enter *First Draft of Contract Proposal.*
   c. Center the line with ^*OC.*
   d. Position the cursor at the beginning of the line with ^*QS.* Enter *.FO* and a space with insert on.

4. The page number should print in the lower right corner of the page. Precede the page number with the number symbol (#) in the footer line (as in #1, #2, #3, and so on). To do this:

   a. Position the cursor at column 62 of the footer line. Enter \##.

5. Set four blank lines between the text and the footer. To do this:

   a. Position the cursor at the beginning of the file. Insert a blank line for the dot command.

b. Enter *.FM 4.*

6. Set a margin bottom of 10 lines. To do this:

a. Position the cursor on line 1 àt column 1. Insert a blank line for the dot command.

b. Enter *.MB 10.*

7. Cancel the footer on the last page.

8. Save the file.

9. Print the file named LESSON22.EX.

23. Special Print Features _____

OBJECTIVES:

1. Describe the printer and WordStar print features.

2. Explain how to underscore words.

3. Explain continuous underscoring.

4. Describe superscripts.

5. Describe subscripts.

6. Explain how to change superscript and subscript roll.

7. Explain bold print effect.

8. Explain double strike.

9. Summarize special print features.

THE PRINTER AND WORDSTAR

WordStar has a variety of print features to enhance document appearance. Underscoring text, raising numbers for footnote notations, lowering numbers for equations, and bold text are the most common print enhancements. Other print enhancements such as overstriking lines, changing ribbon color, changing horizontal print size, printing special characters or symbols, changing the daisy wheel, and special user-defined print features are explained in a later lesson.

Your printer must be able to support WordStar's special print features; otherwise, the commands will not work. Daisy-wheel printers and some dot-matrix printers with microjustification will be able to execute these special print enchancements. **Microjustifying printers** make fine space adjustments between characters in the text, permitting proper placement in formulas and justified margins. Printers not capable of microjustification will print in a fixed position.

UNDERSCORING WORDS

The underscore key is not used to underline text as it is on a typewriter. If you try to use this key, the underscore will appear as a separate character (with insert on) or will replace the character you try to underscore (with insert off). Enter ∧*PS* before and after the word or words you want underscored. (Think of *print underscore* when entering this command.) Several things should be pointed out about the ∧PS underscore command:

1. The ∧P will not display on the screen.

2. The ∧S will display on the screen.

3. The ∧PS command must be entered before the word or words you want underscored and again after the underscored text.

4. Four character spaces are used up in the display with the underscore command. The ∧S is displayed before the underscored text, and ∧S is displayed after the underscored text. The on-screen layout, therefore, will not be the same as the printout.

5. To view the text in the format in which it will print out, enter ∧*OD*. You will recall that this command turns off print displays such as the ∧S and displays text as it will appear in print. Turn the print display back on with ∧*OD* after checking the print layout.

6. Spaces between words will not underscore.

7. The ∧S can be deleted from the screen with ∧*G* or ∧*T*.

8. If ∧*P* is entered by mistake, strike the space bar to cancel.

Figure 23.1 shows how underscored words look on the screen when the underscore command is entered and how the command prints out.

```
SCREEN DISPLAY                          PRINTOUT

^SWordStar^S                            WordStar

^SWordStar Word Processing^S            WordStar Word Processing
```

Figure 23.1   Screen Display and Printout of Underscored Words

---

CONTINUOUS UNDERSCORING

Look at Figure 23.1. The space between the words did not underscore. If you want to print a solid line under both words and spaces, enter ∧*PS* and strike the underscore key instead of the space bar between words. Enter ^PS again to cancel the underscore. Figure 23.2 illustrates how the screen should look in order to print a continuous line under a sentence and how the sentence will print out.

SCREEN DISPLAY

^SStrike_the_underscore_key_between_words_instead_of_the_space_bar.^S

PRINTOUT

Strike_the_underscore_key_between_words_instead_of_the_space_bar.

Figure 23.2   Screen Display and Printout of Continuous Underscoring

SUPERSCRIPTS

A **superscript** is a character printed slightly above the line as in a footnote (footnote[1]) or an equation ($X^2 = Y^2$). The command to print a character slightly above or on top of the line is ^PT, entered before and after the raised text. (Think of *print top* when entering this command.) As in the underscore command, the ^P does not display; however, the ^T will show on the screen. Four character spaces are used up on the screen with ^T entered before and after the raised text. Enter the ^OD command to view the text as it actually will print out. Figure 23.3 illustrates how text with superscripts displays on the screen and how it prints out.

SCREEN DISPLAY

See notation below.^T1^T

X^T3^T-Y^T3^T

PRINTOUT

See notation below.[1]

$X^3 - Y^3$

Figure 23.3   Screen Display and Printout of Superscripts

SUBSCRIPTS

A **subscript** prints slightly below the line of text as in a formula (H_2O). The command to print a subscript is $\wedge$PV. It is entered before and after the character or characters you want to make into subscripts. The $\wedge$P will not display, but $\wedge$V will show on the screen. Enter $\wedge OD$ to delete the print character display and to view the text as it actually will print. Figure 23.4 illustrates how the screen will look when a subscript is entered and how the text will print out.

```
        SCREEN DISPLAY                          PRINTOUT

LOG^Vb^V XY = LOG^Vb^V X+LOG^Vb^V Y     LOG  XY = LOG  X+LOG  Y
                                            b          b        b
```

Figure 23.4   Screen Display and Printout of Subscripts

CHANGING THE SUPERSCRIPT AND SUBSCRIPT ROLL

The superscript and the subscript are printed 3/8 of a line above or below the text by default. This default can be expressed by the dot command *.SR 3*. (Think of *script roll* when entering this command.) If you want to change the roll to half an inch above or below the line (4/8 of a line), enter *.SR 4*. To decrease the roll by 1/8 of a line, enter *.SR 2*.

BOLD PRINT

Bold print is darkened text used to emphasize portions of a document. The command to instruct the printer to use boldface is $\wedge$PB (think of *print bold*), entered before and after the text to be darkened. The $\wedge$P will not appear on the screen, but the $\wedge$B will be displayed. The command, like the previous print commands, will cause the on-screen text display to appear further to the right than it will print. To see how the text will actually print, turn the print display off with $\wedge OD$. It is a good idea to turn the print display on again (^OD) after checking the print layout. Figure 23.5 illustrates how the screen looks when ^PB is entered and how the text will look when it is printed.

SCREEN DISPLAY

This sentence demonstrates the ^Boutstanding^B effect of ^Bbold type^B.

PRINTOUT

This sentence demonstrates the **outstanding** effect of **bold type**.

Figure 23.5   Screen Display and Printout of Bold Type

DOUBLE STRIKE

All printers can produce double strike. When double strike is started, the text is darker because the printer strikes the same letter twice. Double strike is similar to bold type in that they both darken text.

Printers that do not microjustify will not differ between double strike and boldface print. Microjustifying printers will show a difference between the two commands: Boldface will be even darker than double strike.

The command to produce double strike is ^PD (think of *print dark*), entered before and after the text to be darkened. The ^P will not display on the screen. Figure 23.6 illustrates the keyed-in double strike command, the screen display, and the printout. Boldface is also displayed to illustrate the difference between the bold and the double strike commands.

Enter	Screen Display	Printout
^PDdouble strike^PD	^Ddouble strike^D	**double strike**
^PBbold type^PB	^Bbold type^B	**bold type**

Figure 23.6   Double Strike and Bold Type Commands, Screen Display, and Printout

Figure 23.7 summarizes the commands for the most frequently used print features.

Command	Screen Display	Printout
^PS	^Sunderscore^S	underscore
^PS_	^Scontinuous_line^S	continuous line
^PT	footnote^T3^T	footnote[3]
^PV	H^V2^V0	H_2O
.SR (and number)		Will change by eighths of a line. Default: *.SR 3*
^PB	^Bbold type^B	**bold type**
^PD	^Ddouble strike^D	**double strike**

Figure 23.7   Summary of the Special Print Controls

LESSON 23 EXERCISE   Name _____ Date _____

TRUE/FALSE

Each of the following statements is either true or false. Indicate the correct answer by circling T for a true statement or F for a false statement.

1. Printers with microjustification will support WordStar's special print features. (Obj. 1) .... 1. **T**   **F**

2. Microjustifying printers make fine space adjustments between characters. (Obj. 1) .... 2. **T**   **F**

3. To underscore text, strike the underscore key. (Obj. 2)..................... 3. **T**   **F**

4. To underscore text, enter $\wedge PS$ once. (Obj. 2) .... 4. **T**   **F**

5. The print commands will not affect on-screen layout. (Obj. 2) .... 5. **T**   **F**

6. To check how a document will look in the printout, enter $\wedge OD$. (Obj. 2).... 6. **T**   **F**

7. Spaces between words will not underscore with just the $\wedge PS$ command. (Obj. 2) .... 7. **T**   **F**

8. The $\wedge S$ characters can be deleted with $\wedge G$ or $\wedge T$. (Obj. 2) .... 8. **T**   **F**

9. If $\wedge P$ is entered by mistake, strike the space bar. (Obj. 2) .... 9. **T**   **F**

10. WordStar will not underscore spaces between words. (Obj. 3).............. 10. **T**   **F**

11. A superscript is a character printed slightly below the line. (Obj. 4)........ 11. **T**   **F**

12. To print a superscript, enter $\wedge PT$ before and after the text to be raised. (Obj. 4) .... 12. **T**   **F**

13. Subscripts print slightly below the line of text. (Obj. 5).................... 13. **T**   **F**

14. The command to print a subscript is $\wedge V$. (Obj. 5) .... 14. **T**   **F**

15. The subscript command must be entered before and after the text to be lowered. (Obj. 5) .... 15. **T**   **F**

16. The superscript and subscript position can be changed. (Obj. 6)............. 16. **T**   **F**

17. The default for the superscript and subscript position is .SR 3. (Obj. 6)..... 17. **T**   **F**

18. To print in bold type, enter $\wedge PB$ before and after the text to be darkened. (Obj. 7) .... 18. **T**   **F**

19. It is good practice to always reset the print display control to the on mode after checking the print layout. (Obj. 7) .... 19. **T**   **F**

20. The command to double strike is $\wedge PD$. (Obj. 8)............................. 20. **T**   **F**

COMPLETION

Indicate the correct answer in the space provided.

1. Daisy-wheel printers and some dot-matrix printers need what to be able to execute the WordStar special print enhancements? (Obj. 1) ....

1. _____

2. The underscore command is *?* (Obj. 2) ....

2. _____

3. Name the two places $^\wedge PS$ must be entered to have the word or words underscored. (Obj. 2) ....

3. a. _____

    b. _____

4. To display the text as it will print out, enter *?* (Obj. 2) ....

4. _____

5. Spaces between words will or will not underscore with just the $^\wedge PS$ command? (Obj. 2) ....

5. _____

6. If $^\wedge P$ is entered by mistake, what must you strike to cancel the command? (Obj. 2) ....

6. _____

7. To have continuous underscoring, what must you strike between words? (Obj. 3) ....

7. _____

8. The command to print a superscript is *?* (Obj. 4) ....

8. _____

9. Indicate what is displayed on the screen when $^\wedge PT$ is entered? (Obj. 4) ....

9. _____

10. The command to print a subscript is *?* (Obj. 5) ....

10. _____

11. Where is the command to lower text entered in relation to the character or characters to be lowered? (Obj. 5) ..

11. a. _____

     b. _____

12. Indicate what is displayed on the screen when $^\wedge PV$ is entered. (Obj. 5) ....

12. _____

13. The default dot command for the superscript and subscript roll is *?* (Obj. 6) ....

13. _____

14. The command to print in boldface is *?* (Obj. 7) ....

14. _____

15. Indicate what the screen displays when $^\wedge PB$ is entered. (Obj. 7) ....

15. _____

16. It is a good idea to turn the print control display on or off after checking how the text will print out? (Obj. 7) ....

16. _____

17. Indicate what is displayed on the screen to print H_2O. (Obj. 5) ....

17. _____

18. Indicate what is displayed on the screen to print <u>WordStar</u>. (Obj. 2) ....

18. _____

19. To print <u>continuous underscore</u>, what should be displayed on the screen? (Obj. 3) ....

19. _____

20. The dot command to change the superscript roll to 4/8 of a line is *?* (Obj. 8) ....

20. _____

COMPUTER EXERCISE

Follow the step-by-step instructions to complete the computer exercise.

1. Create a file and name it LESSON23.EX.

2. Enter the text titled "CARBONATES, NITRATES, AND BORATES" in Figure 23.8. Enter the text as shown with boldface, superscripts, subscripts, and underscoring. If your printer will not print boldface, enter the double strike command instead.

3. Use double spacing. Omit the page numbers.

CARBONATES, NITRATES, AND BORATES

CARBONATES[1]

Calcite	$CaCO_3$
Dolomite	$CaMg(CO_3)_2$
Magnesite	$MgCO_3$
Siderite	$FeCO_3$

NITRATES[2]

| Sodium nitrate | $NaNO_3$ |
| Potassium nitrate | KNO_3 |

BORATES[3]

| Boracite | $Mg_7Cl_2B_{16}O_{30}$ |
| Borax | $Na_2B_4O_7$ |

- -

[1] Hurlbut, Cornelius, Dana's Manual Of Mineralogy, (New York, John Wiley & Sons, Inc., 1949), p. 47.

[2] See Chapter 5.

[3] See Figure 2.

Figure 23.8   Text for Computer Exercise

---

4. Enter the footnotes at the end of the page using the commands for superscripts and continuous underscoring when necessary.

5. Turn the print display off to see how the display will print out, then turn the print display back on again.

6. Save the file.

7. Print the file named LESSON23.EX.

24. Printing and the Print Questions

OBJECTIVES:

1. Show how to print from the opening menu.
2. Introduce the print options.
3. Explain the disk file output.
4. Explain the "start at page number" option.
5. Explain the "stop after page number" option.
6. Describe the form feeds option.
7. Describe how to suppress page formatting.
8. Explain pause for paper change between pages.
9. Decribe how to ready the printer.
10. Explain how to cancel the print request.
11. Explain how to cancel the print options.
12. Explain how to stop the printing.
13. Describe how to print the file directory.

PRINTING FROM THE OPENING MENU

Printing can be initiated in three different ways. You can print from

1. the opening menu.
2. a document in edit.
3. MailMerge.

Printing from a document in edit has been introduced in a previous lesson. You will recall that striking $\wedge KP$ while editing a file will permit you to print another file. MailMerge is a separate word processing program designed to merge data for form-letter production.

You have been printing documents from the opening menu by striking *P*, entering the name of the file to print, and striking the Esc key. The printing starts immediately. If you press ENTER/RETURN instead of the Esc key after the NAME OF FILE TO PRINT?, a number of print options are displayed. The print option questions are as follows:

1. DISK FILE OUTPUT (Y/N):

2. START AT PAGE NUMBER (RETURN for beginning)?

3. STOP AFTER PAGE NUMBER (RETURN for end)?

4. USE FORM FEEDS (Y/N):

5. SUPPRESS PAGE FORMATTING (Y/N):

6. PAUSE FOR PAPER CHANGE BETWEEN PAGES (Y/N):

7. READY PRINTER, press RETURN

Pressing ENTER/RETURN after these options is the same as striking the Esc key immediately after naming the file to print; the file will print from page one to the end, implementing all of the WordStar instructions in the file.

DISK FILE OUTPUT

"DISK FILE OUTPUT (Y/N):" is the first print option. Pressing ENTER/RETURN, *N*, or any key except *Y* will send the file immediately to the printer as desired and display the next print option. If *Y* is entered, the prompt OUTPUT FILE NAME? will display.

Enter an appropriate file name to the OUTPUT FILE NAME? prompt. The printout of the file will go directly to the newly named file on the disk instead of to the printer. That is to say, instead of printing out the file on paper, the printed version goes directly into a disk file. You can then call up the output file and see the version that will print displayed on the screen. Commands for headers and footers will not display, but they will execute.

PRINTING FROM SELECTED PAGES

"START AT PAGE NUMBER (RETURN for beginning)?" is the second print option. Enter the page number you want the print to start from and then press ENTER/RETURN to continue the print option questions. If you want the printing to start from page one, press ENTER/RETURN or *1*.

"STOP AFTER PAGE NUMBER (RETURN for end)?" is the

third print option. To print the document to the end, press ENTER/RETURN. To stop the print at a specific page, enter the page number and press ENTER/RETURN. You may want to print out only one page. For example, to print out only the third page of a document, enter *3* and press ENTER/RETURN after the START AT PAGE NUMBER? option. After the STOP AFTER PAGE NUMBER? option, enter *3* and ENTER/RETURN.

THE FORM FEEDS OPTION

"USE FORM FEEDS (Y/N):" is the fourth print option. This option is used for paper that is not the standard 8 1/2 by 11 inch size. Answer *Y* and press ENTER/RETURN to advance the paper to the top line desired on the next page. The printer must be set for the paper size in use, and the paper should be loaded into the printer with the top of the form in the desired position.

SUPPRESS PAGE FORMATTING

"SUPPRESS PAGE FORMATTING (Y/N):" is the fifth print option. Answer *N* or press ENTER/RETURN to cause the file to print with all of the formatting instructions executed. Enter *Y* to print out the file with the dot commands printed but not executed. This allows you to proofread the dot commands. Enter *Y* to this option to print out a file generated by the DISK FILE OUTPUT option.

PAUSE PRINT FOR PAPER CHANGE

"PAUSE FOR PAPER CHANGE BETWEEN PAGES (Y/N):" is the sixth print option. If you strike *N*, ENTER/RETURN, or any character except *Y*, WordStar will assume you are printing on continuous form paper. The printer will advance the paper to the next page and continue printing without stopping.

A *Y* response will stop the printer after a page is printed. The prompt PRINT PAUSED appears on the screen. This option permits you to feed single sheets of paper such as letterheads manually into the printer. To resume printing, enter *P* and press ENTER/RETURN.

THE READY PRINTER OPTION

"READY PRINTER, press RETURN:" is the final print option. This is a reminder to check that the printer is switched on and that the paper is properly inserted. Press ENTER/RETURN to initiate printing.

CANCEL THE PRINT COMMAND AND OPTIONS

The print command can be canceled after any of the print option questions by striking $\wedge U$ and the Esc key. Strike the Esc key after any of the options to bypass the remaining options and start the printing. (Early versions of WordStar will not permit this short-cut.) Of course, you can strike the Esc key after naming the file to print, and all of the print option questions will be canceled. Printing will start immediately.

STOPPING THE PRINTING

Printing can be stopped by striking P. Figure 24.1 illustrates the message displayed when printing is stopped.

```
TYPE "Y" to ABANDON PRINT, "N" TO RESUME, ^U TO HOLD:
```

Figure 24.1   The Stop Print Display

Enter Y to cancel the printing. Enter N to continue the printing from the place where it stopped. Enter $\wedge U$ to interrupt the printing so you can return to the opening menu to edit another file or check the file directory. Enter P again when you want to return to the printing. (The printing will start at the place where it stopped.)

PRINTING THE FILE DIRECTORY

It is a good idea to keep a printout of the file directory of a disk. This printout—a record of all the files that a disk contains—can be stored in the jacket with the disk. The file directory is printed from the operating system. Exit WordStar to get back into the operating system by striking X from the opening menu. If your operating system is CP/M, at the **B**>, enter $\wedge PDIR$ and press ENTER/ RETURN. The printer will start to print the file names, and the screen will display the files as they are printed. Enter $\wedge P$ again to stop the printer. Consult your operating system manual on printing the file directory if you do not have the CP/M operating system.

LESSON 24 EXERCISE

Name _____ Date _____

TRUE/FALSE

Each of the following statements is either true or false. Indicate your choice in the Answers column by circling T for a true statement or F for a false statement.

1. Printing can only be initiated from the opening menu. (Obj. 1) ....   1. **T**   **F**

2. Enter ^*KP* to print while in a document file. (Obj. 1) ....   2. **T**   **F**

3. The opening menu is sometimes called the no-file menu. (Obj. 1) ....   3. **T**   **F**

4. MailMerge is a word processing program that will merge data for form-letter production. (Obj. 1) ....   4. **T**   **F**

5. Strike Esc after naming the file to print from the opening menu to display print options. (Obj. 1) ....   5. **T**   **F**

6. Pressing the ENTER/RETURN after the print options is the same as striking the Esc key after naming the file to print. (Obj. 2) ....   6. **T**   **F**

7. Pressing the ENTER/RETURN or *N* after the DISK FILE OUTPUT option will send the file to the printer. (Obj. 3) ....   7. **T**   **F**

8. Striking *Y* after the DISK FILE OUTPUT option will send the file to the printer. (Obj. 3) ....   8. **T**   **F**

9. To display the version of a file that will print, call up the output file. (Obj. 3) ....   9. **T**   **F**

10. Printing must always start from page one. (Obj. 4) ....   10. **T**   **F**

11. You cannot print out just one page. (Obj. 5) ....   11. **T**   **F**

12. The printer must be set properly for the FORM FEEDS option to work correctly. (Obj. 6) ....   12. **T**   **F**

13. To print out the dot commands, enter *Y* to the SUPPRESS PAGE FORMATTING option. (Obj. 7) ....   13. **T**   **F**

14. To print a file generated by the DISK FILE OUTPUT option, enter *Y* to SUPPRESS PAGE FORMATTING. (Obj. 7) ....   14. **T**   **F**

15. To insert paper after each printed page, press ENTER/RETURN after the PAUSE FOR PAPER CHANGE option. (Obj. 8) ....   15. **T**   **F**

16. Press ENTER/RETURN after the READY PRINTER option to initiate printing. (Obj. 9) ....   16. **T**   **F**

17. To cancel the print command after any of the print options, enter ^*U* and Esc. (Obj. 10) ....   17. **T**   **F**

18. To cancel the remaining print option displays, strike the Esc key. (Obj. 11) ....   18. **T**   **F**

19. Printing can be stopped by striking the Esc key. (Obj. 12) ....   19. **T**   **F**

20. To print the file directory, enter PDIR and press ENTER/RETURN at the **>**. (Obj. 13) ....   20. **T**   **F**

COMPLETION

Indicate the correct answer in the space provided.

1. Name the three places where printing can be initiated. (Obj. 1) ....

    1. a. _____
       b. _____
       c. _____

2. What must be entered to print while editing a document? (Obj. 1) ....

    2. _____

3. MailMerge is a program designed to merge data for ? (Obj. 1) ....

    3. _____

4. What must be entered to print from the opening menu? (Obj. 1) ....

    4. _____

5. The opening menu is sometimes called the ? (Obj. 1)....

    5. _____

6. To display the print options, what must you press after the letter P? (Obj. 1) ....

    6. _____

7. Pressing ENTER/RETURN after all of the print options is the same as striking which key after the letter P? (Obj. 2) ....

    7. _____

8. Pressing ENTER/RETURN or *N* after the DISK FILE OUTPUT option will send the file to the ? (Obj. 3) .....

    8. _____

9. Striking *Y* after the DISK FILE OUTPUT option will send the printed version of the document to what type of file? (Obj. 3)...

    9. _____

10. To start printing from page ten, what must be entered after the START AT PAGE NUMBER? option before you press ENTER/RETURN? (Obj. 4) ....

    10. _____

11. To stop the printing after page ten, what must you enter after the STOP AFTER PAGE NUMBER? option before you press the ENTER/RETURN? (Obj. 5) ....

    11. _____

12. The printer should be set for the proper paper size, and the paper must be loaded into the printer at the desired position when what is entered after the FORM FEEDS option? (Obj. 6)...

    12. _____

13. To print out a file with the dot commands printed but not executed, what must be entered in response to the SUPPRESS PAGE FORMATTING option? (Obj. 7).....

    13. _____

14. To print a file generated by the DISK FILE OUTPUT option, you should enter *Y* to what other option? (Obj. 7) ....

    14. _____

15. To feed letterheads into the printer manually, you should enter *Y* to what option? (Obj. 8).......................

    15. _____

16. What must be entered to resume printing after the printing has paused for a paper change? (Obj. 8) ....

    16. _____

17. What must you strike to start printing after the READY PRINTER option? (Obj. 9) ....   17. _____

18. To cancel the print command, what must be entered? (Obj. 10) ....   18. _____

19. To stop the printing, what must be entered? (Obj. 12) ..   19. _____

20. To print the file directory from the operating system, what must be entered before pressing ENTER/RETURN? (Obj. 13) ....   20. _____

COMPUTER EXERCISE

Directions: Follow the step-by-step instructions to complete the computer exercise.

1. Create a file named LETTER.24.

2. Enter the letter illustrated in Figure 24.2. This is a basic form letter to be sent to various people.

3. Single space the letter. Turn off the justification. Format the letter in full block-letter style. Do not indent paragraphs or the complimentary close. Use the underscore and bold print where indicated. The numbered text should be indented five spaces from the left margin.

```
Recently I arranged a plan for several residents in your area that had a
favorable response.  I was, therefore, prompted to mail it to the entire
community.

The plan I refer to is the "Mortgage Cancelation Plan."  It accomplishes
the following:

     1.    If the homeowner dies, the mortgage is canceled, and the home is
           left free and clear to the spouse and children.

     2.    If the homeowner lives to the end of the mortgage, every dollar
           of the deposit is returned plus a profit.

                         -OR-

     3.    The ever-increasing cash fund of this plan enables you to
           liquidate the mortgage years before it is due, saving you
           thousands of dollars in interest.

Please complete the form below and return it to Mike Olmsted in the
enclosed envelope.

Sincerely,



Carol McWilliams

sg

Enclosure
```

Figure 24.2   Letter for Computer Exercise

4. Create a separate file for each of the addresses shown in Figure 24.3. Name each file with the last name of the addressee followed by a period (.) and *24*. The first file will be named *Castle.24*.

```
Mr. Richard Castle
1390 Fell Street
San Francisco, CA 94302-1232

Ms. Carla Blake
560 Golden Gate Avenue, 2nd Floor
San Francisco, CA 94102-2166

Mrs. Diane Klages
2530 Sutton Place
Stanford, CA 95014-3125
```

Figure 24.3   Names and Addresses for Computer Exercise

---

5. Create another file named LESSON24.EX. The files created in steps 1 and 4 will be read into this file and then this file will be printed.

6. Omit the page numbers.

7. Read the first address file (Castle.24) into LESSON24.EX. Key-in *Dear Mr. Castle:* on the second line after the inside address. Leave one blank line.

8. Read the file named LETTER.24 into LESSON24.EX.

9. Create a new page at the end of the letter.

10. Read the next address file (Blake.24) into this file. Key-in *Dear Ms. Blake:* on the second line after the inside address. Leave one blank line.

11. Read the file named LETTER.24 into this file.

12. Create a new page at the end of the second letter.

13. Read the last address file and the form letter once again into LESSON24.EX, using the format in steps 7 and 8.

14. Save the file named LESSON24.EX.

15. Print out page 2 of the file named LESSON24.EX with the following print options:

    a. Press the ENTER/RETURN after the first print option.
    b. Enter *2* and press the ENTER/RETURN after the START AT PAGE NUMBER? option.

c. Enter *2* and press the ENTER/RETURN after the STOP AFTER PAGE NUMBER? option.

d. Press the ENTER/RETURN after the FORM FEEDS option.

e. Press the ENTER/RETURN at the SUPPRESS PAGE FORMATTING option.

f. Press the ENTER/RETURN at the PAUSE PRINT option.

g. Check the printer; the power should be on, and the paper should be positioned properly. Press the ENTER/RETURN.

16. Print out the file directory and circle the three address files created above. To do this, follow these steps:

a. Strike *X* from the opening menu to get into the operating system.

b. At **B**> key-in ^PDIR and press the ENTER/RETURN.

25. More Print Features ⎯⎯⎯⎯⎯⎯

OBJECTIVES:

1. Explain nonbreak or required space.
2. Describe the strikeout print.
3. Describe how to overprint a character.
4. Describe how to overprint a line.
5. Explain how to underscore continuously with overprint line command.
6. Describe how to double underscore.
7. Explain how to enter equations.
8. Explain how to pause print for a daisy-wheel change.
9. Explain how to alternate pitch.
10. Explain how to change ribbon color.
11. Describe special characters and user-defined features.
12. Summarize the special print features introduced in this lesson.

THE SPECIAL PRINT FEATURES

Many of the special print features have been introduced in a previous lesson. This lesson will complete the discussion on special print effects available through WordStar. Your printer must be able to support these special features and must be properly installed; otherwise, some of these print features will not work.

You will recall the following:

1. The print command starts with ^P, but ^P does not display on the screen.
2. The ^ symbol and the second letter of the command are displayed.
3. The ^ print character distorts the on-screen text layout. To see how the text will actually print out, enter ^*OD*. The print control characters will be deleted. Enter ^*OD* again to turn the print display back on.
4. The print commands are entered once to activate the command and entered again to cancel the command.

NONBREAK OR REQUIRED SPACE

Some words such as certain names, titles, and dates should not be separated. Enter required spaces between these words so that they will not split between lines when you reformat a paragraph. Names such as "Henry VIII" and dates such as "May 19" should be printed on the same line. WordStar calls required spaces **nonbreak spaces**. Nonbreak spaces are entered by using the command ^PO when you would normally strike the space bar. The computer will read the words with *^PO* between them as one word. Figure 25.1 illustrates the command entry, screen display, and printout.

Enter	Screen Display	Printout
Henry^POVIII	Henry^OVIII	Henry VIII
May^PO19	May^O19	May 19

Figure 25.1   **Nonbreak or Required Space Command, Screen Display, and Printout**

THE STRIKEOUT

Legislative drafts and legal documents will sometimes require that text be crossed out. This strikeout format is accomplished through the strikeout command. When the strikeout command is executed, a line of hyphens is printed through the middle of the text. The command to strike out words is ^PX keyed-in before and after the text. Figure 25.2 illustrates the command entry, screen display, and printout.

Enter	Screen Display	Printout
^PXstrikeout^PX	^Xstrikeout^X	~~strikeout~~

Figure 25.2   **Strikeout Command, Screen Display, and Printout**

OVERPRINTING A CHARACTER

Overprint means to print one character over another. The overprint command is entered only once, because it affects only one character. Enter the command ^PH and then key-in the character that is to overprint. For example, to enter the ˜ symbol over "n" in the word "señor," key-in sen^PH˜or. Figure 25.3 illustrates the command entry, screen display, and printout when *^PH* is entered.

Enter	Screen Display	Printout
re^PH´pondre	re^H´pondre	répondre
voila^PH`	voila^H`	voilà
O^PH/	O^H/	Ø

Figure 25.3   Character Overprint Command, Screen Display, and Printout

OVERPRINTING A LINE

One line will print over another line by entering ^*P* and pressing ENTER/RETURN at the end of the line to be overprinted. For example, to cross out an entire line, strike ^*P* and press ENTER/RETURN at the end of the line. A flag (-) will display on the far right of the screen to indicate that the next line is to print on top of the previous line. Enter a complete line of a character such as *X* (or another character such as a /). When the document prints, XXX will print over the line. Figure 25.4 illustrates the overprint line command entry, screen display, and printout.

ENTER

```
This line will be overprinted with the next line.^P ENTER/RETURN
XXXXXXXXXXXXXXXXXXXXXXXXXXXXXXXXXXXXXXXXXXXXXXXXXXX ENTER/RETURN
```

SCREEN DISPLAY

```
This line will be overprinted with the next line.       -
XXXXXXXXXXXXXXXXXXXXXXXXXXXXXXXXXXXXXXXXXXXXXXXXXXX      <
```

PRINTOUT

```
XXXXXXXXXXXXXXXXXXXXXXXXXXXXXXXXXXXXXXXXXXXXXXXXXXX
```

Figure 25.4   Overprint Line Command, Screen Display, and Printout

CONTINUOUS UNDERSCORING

By entering ^*P* and pressing ENTER/RETURN at the end of a line, you can do continuous underscoring. In a previous lesson you learned how to do continuous underscoring with the ^PS command by striking the underscore key instead of the space bar between words (^PScontinuous_underscore^PS). Another way to underscore continuously is to enter text, strike ^P and press ENTER/RETURN at the end of the line, and enter the next line with underscores. Figure 25.5 illustrates how to underscore continuously with the overprint line command.

ENTER

```
It was the best of times, it was the worst of times.^P ENTER/RETURN
------------------------------------------------------ ENTER/RETURN
```

SCREEN DISPLAY

```
It was the best of times, it was the worst of times.        -
----------------------------------------------------        <
```

PRINTOUT

```
It was the best of times, it was the worst of times.
```

Figure 25.5   Continuous Underscore with Overprint Line Command, Screen Display, and Printout

---

Notice the hyphen on the right side of the screen display in Figure 25.5. This flag symbol is displayed to indicate that the next line will overprint the previous line. In the illustration, for example, the next line is a line of underscores; these underscores will print over the previous line causing a continuous underscore to print over the text.

DOUBLE UNDERSCORING

It is possible to double underscore using the overprint line command together with the subscript command. To double underscore, strike the underscore key several times for a solid line. Strike ^P and press ENTER/RETURN. A hyphen appears on the right side of the screen. Enter the ^PV subscript command and strike the underscore key again to match the previous underscore. Enter ^PV again to cancel the subscript. Figure 25.6 illustrates the double underscore command entry, screen display, and printout.

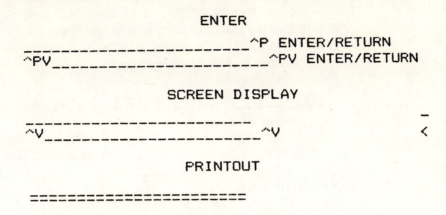

```
                            ENTER

_____^P ENTER/RETURN
^PV_____^PV ENTER/RETURN


                        SCREEN DISPLAY

_____                      _
^V_____^V                    <


                          PRINTOUT

=======================
```

Figure 25.6   Double Underscore with Overprint Line Command, Screen Display, and Printout

EQUATIONS

Mathematical equations can be entered by using the overprint line command (enter $^\wedge$P and press ENTER/RETURN), the superscript command ($^\wedge PT$), and the subscript command ($^\wedge PV$). Figure 25.7 illustrates an equation entry, screen display, and printout with these commands.

```
                          ENTER
.SR 2
          y =      1  ^P    ENTER/RETURN
                              ENTER/RETURN
                _____
                x^PT2^PT - 1 ENTER/RETURN


                      SCREEN DISPLAY

          y =      1                     -
                                         <
                _____                   <
                x^T2^T - 1


                        PRINTOUT

          y =     ___1__
                  x  - 1
                   2
.SR 3
```

Figure 25.7   Equation Entry, Screen Display, and Printout

Notice in Figure 25.7 that the superscript roll has been decreased by the dot command .SR 2 at the beginning of the illustration. If the superscript prints out at the .SR 3 default, the superscript will overlap the solid line because the default sets the printout too high for equations. Notice also that the default superscript roll was reset to .SR 3 after the equation was keyed-in.

PAUSE PRINT TO CHANGE DAISY WHEEL

Some documents will require that a different daisy wheel be installed in the printer in order to achieve a special typeface. Daisy wheels come in 10 pitch (10 characters to an inch) and 12 pitch (12 characters to an inch), italic type, mathematical symbols, Greek symbols, and so on. To stop the printer to change a daisy wheel, enter $^\wedge PC$ in the document where the print is to stop. The prompt PRINT PAUSED is displayed on the screen. After changing the wheel, enter P to continue the print. Enter $^\wedge PC$ again in the document where you want the print to pause so that the original daisy wheel can be installed.

ALTERNATING PITCH

The default character pitch is 10 characters per inch. To change from 10 characters per inch to 12 characters per inch, enter $^\wedge PA$ (think *pitch alternate*) before the text to be changed. To cancel the 12 characters per inch printout and return to the default, enter $^\wedge PN$. If the daisy wheel is to be changed, enter $^\wedge PC$ in the document so that the print will pause for the wheel change. Figure 25.8 illustrates the command entry, screen display, and printout when the alternate pitch command ($^\wedge PA$) and return to original pitch command ($^\wedge PN$) is entered.

```
              ENTER

This line is 10 pitch.^PA
This line is 12 pitch.^PN


        SCREEN DISPLAY

This line is 10 pitch.^A
This line is 12 pitch.^N


           PRINTOUT

This line is 10 pitch.
This line is 12 pitch.
```

Figure 25.8   Alternate Pitch Commands, Screen Display, and Printout

CHANGING RIBBON COLOR

Some ribbons are both red (on the top half) and black (on the bottom half). To change the print from black to red, enter $^\wedge PY$ at the text to be printed red. Enter $^\wedge PY$ again to return to black print. (This command is also used to print on the upper and lower half of other types of ribbons.)

SPECIAL PRINT CHARACTERS AND FEATURES

WordStar has a number of special commands to print special symbols and custom, user-defined features. Two of the special print characters executed by the commands $^\wedge PG$ and $^\wedge PF$ are determined by the daisy wheel or print element installed on your printer. The command $^\wedge PF$ may print the British pound symbol or the American cent symbol. The command $^\wedge PG$ may print a double underscore.

The custom, user-defined features are printed by the commands $^\wedge PQ$, $^\wedge PW$, $^\wedge PE$, and $^\wedge PR$. These features allow you to switch from one printer to another, change type fonts, and start special form feeders. In any case, they are user-defined and are programmed into WordStar with the WordStar INSTALL program. Figure 25.9 summarizes the special print enhancements introduced in this lesson.

FEATURE	ENTER	DISPLAY	PRINTOUT
Required Space	required^POspace	required^Ospace	required space
Strikeout	^PXstrikeout^PX	^Xstrikeout^X	strikeout
Overprint Character	O^PH/	O^H/	Ø
Overprint Line	overprint^P RETURN XXXXXXXX RETURN	overprint — XXXXXXXX <	☒☒☒☒☒☒☒☒
Continuous Underscore	solid line^P RETURN _____ RETURN	solid line — _____ <	solid line
Double Underscore	_____^P RETURN ^PV_____^PV RETURN	_____ — ^V_____^V <	==========
Equations	X = Y^PT2^PT^P RETURN _____ RETURN X + Y	X = Y^T2^T — _____ < X + Y	$X = \dfrac{Y^2}{X + Y}$

(Fig. 25.9, continued on p. 240)

Pause Print	^PC	^C	
Alternate Pitch	10 characters ^PA	^A	10 characters
	12 characters ^PN	^N	12 characters
Change Ribbon Color	^PY	^Y	
Special Characters	^PF ^PG	^F ^G	Depends on daisy wheel
User Defined	^PQ, ^PW, ^PE, ^PR	^Q, ^W, ^E, ^R	Install with printer

Figure 25.9   Special Print Enhancement Summary

LESSON 25 EXERCISE   Name _____ Date _____

TRUE/FALSE

Each of the following statements is either true or false. Indicate
your answer in the Answers column by circling T for a true statement or F
for a false statement.

Answers

1. WordStar refers to required spaces as nonbreak spaces. (Obj. 1) ....   1. T   F

2. To execute a required space, enter ^PO and a space between words.
   (Obj. 1) ....   2. T   F

3. The required space command will display ^PO. (Obj. 1) ....   3. T   F

4. When the strikeout command is executed, a line of XXX is printed over a
   previous line. (Obj. 2) ....   4. T   F

5. Overprint means to print one character over another. (Obj. 3) ....   5. T   F

6. To overprint a character, enter ^PH twice. (Obj. 3) ....   6. T   F

7. To print out señor, the screen displays sen^H˜or. (Obj. 3) ....   7. T   F

8. You can overprint a line with any character. (Obj. 4) ....   8. T   F

9. There are at least two different commands to execute the continuous underscore. (Obj. 5) ....   9. T   F

10. A flag is displayed on the screen after entering the command ^P and press-
    ing ENTER/RETURN. (Obj. 5) ....   10. T   F

11. The double underscore is executed with the overprint line command and the
    subscript command. (Obj. 6) ....   11. T   F

12. Equations are executed with the overprint line command. (Obj. 7) ....   12. T   F

13. The superscript roll cannot be changed. (Obj. 7) ....   13. T   F

14. The printer will pause during printing if you enter the command ^PC while
    the document is being printed. (Obj. 8) ....   14. T   F

15. Alternate pitch is initiated with the command ^PA. (Obj. 9) ....   15. T   F

16. To return to the original pitch, enter ^PN. (Obj. 9) ....   16. T   F

17. The command to change ribbon color is ^PC. (Obj. 10) ....   17. T   F

18. The print features are limited to WordStar's definitions. (Obj. 11) ....   18. T   F

19. The special print characters are determined by the particular printing ele-
    ment. (Obj. 11) ....   19. T   F

20. The user-defined features are programmed with the WordStar INSTALL
    program. (Obj. 11) ....   20. T   F

COMPLETION

Indicate the correct answer in the space provided.

1. What does WordStar call required spaces? (Obj. 1)......

2. To enter a required space, you should enter what command instead of striking the space bar? (Obj. 1) ....

3. If May^PO19 is entered, indicate what the screen will display. (Obj. 1) ....

4. The strikeout command is *?* (Obj. 2) ....

5. When the strikeout command is printed out, what is printed through the middle of the line of text? (Obj. 2).

6. Name the two places where you enter the strikeout command in relation to the text to be crossed out. (Obj. 2) .

7. The command to overprint a character is *?* (Obj. 3) .....

8. When ∅ is printed, the screen displays *?* (Obj. 3) ....

9. What will display on the far right side of the screen when ^P and ENTER/RETURN is keyed-in? (Obj. 4) ..

10. To overprint a line of text with a line of XXX, what do you enter after the line of text to be overprinted? (Obj. 4) ....

11. Continuous underscoring is achieved by the ^PS_ command and what other command? (Obj. 5)...............

12. To double underscore, what must be entered before and after the second solid line? (Obj. 6) ....

13. A double underscore is achieved through which command? (Obj. 6) ....

14. When entering some equations, the superscript or subscript roll may have to be decreased from .SR 3 to *?* (Obj. 7) ....

15. What must be entered to resume printing after a print pause? (Obj. 8) ....

16. How many characters are there to an inch in the default character pitch? (Obj. 9) ....

17. The command to begin the alternate pitch print is *?* (Obj. 9) ....

18. The command to return to original pitch is *?* (Obj. 9) ...

19. The command to change ribbon color is *?* (Obj. 10)......

20. The special print characters and features are determined by the print wheel and which of WordStar's programs? (Obj. 11)...

1. _____

2. _____

3. _____

4. _____

5. _____

6. a. _____
   b. _____

7. _____

8. _____

9. _____

10. _____

11. _____

12. _____

13. _____

14. _____

15. _____

16. _____

17. _____

18. _____

19. _____

20. _____

COMPUTER EXERCISE

Directions: Follow the step-by-step instructions to complete the computer exercise.

1. Create a file named LESSON25.EX. Enter the following text with the appropriate special print features. Do not key-in the directions which are in parentheses.

(Enter the following two lines. Enter items at columns 5, 21, 36, and 51. Enter a required space between each # symbol and each group of digits by using the ^PO command.)

Required Spaces ^PO

    Part# 12345   Part# 767676   Part# 2456   Part# 34378

(Block copy the line above. Change the right margin to 55 spaces and reformat the copied line. Your copy will look like the text below.)

    Part# 12345   Part# 767676   Part# 2456
Part# 34378

(Enter the following line.)

Strikeout ^PX

(Return the right margin to 65. Enter the following sentence.)

Now is the time for all good men to come to the aid of the party.

(Enter it again, but this time strikeout the line with ^PX.)

~~Now is the time for all good men to come to the aid of the party.~~

(Enter the following text.)

Overprint A Character ^PH

¢ Ø Señorita Piñata 75¢ ⌀

Overprint A Line ^P ENTER/RETURN

I pledge allegiance to the flag of the United States of America.

(Now enter the line above and overprint it with a line of /.)

I̸/p̸l̸e̸d̸g̸e̸/a̸l̸l̸e̸g̸i̸a̸n̸c̸e̸/t̸o̸/t̸h̸e̸/f̸l̸a̸g̸/o̸f̸/t̸h̸e̸/U̸n̸i̸t̸e̸d̸/S̸t̸a̸t̸e̸s̸/o̸f̸/A̸m̸e̸r̸i̸c̸a̸.

(Enter the following line. Do continuous underscoring with the ^PS and _.)

Continuous_Underscore

(Enter the following line with continuous underscoring, using ^P ENTER/RETURN at the end of the line.)

These_are_the_times_that_try_men's_souls.

(Fig. 25.10, continued on p. 244)

(Enter the following lines. Set a decimal tab at column 46 to align
decimal points. To double underscore, enter ^P ENTER/RETURN at the end of
the line, then enter ^PV, solid line, ^PV.)

<u>double underscore</u>

<u>ASSETS</u>

    <u>Current Assets</u>   1,961.99

        Bank Balance   1.00

        Organization Expense   3,388.47

        Deficit   <u>4,452,859.92</u>
                        <u>$4,458,211.38</u>

<u>Equations</u>

(Use the superscript command (^PT) and ^P ENTER/RETURN at end of the line
when entering the equation below. Change the superscript roll to .SR 2.
Return the .SR 3 default after entering the equation.)

$$X = \frac{Y^2 - X^2}{X^3 + Y^3}$$

<u>Alternate Pitch</u> ^PA, ^PN

  This is a 12-pitch line.

  This is a 10-pitch line.

<u>Pause Print</u>

(Enter a pause print command at this point with ^PC. The prompt PRINT
PAUSED will display on the screen when the document prints. The printer
will stop. Strike P to resume the print. If you have a printer available
to experiment with the ribbon color change and the user-defined features,
try them out now).

Figure 25.10   Text for Computer Exercise

2. Save the file.

3. Print the file named LESSON25.EX.

26. The Print Menu Review _____

OBJECTIVES:

1. Define the print menu.

2. Explain how to display the print menu.

3. Explain how to exit the print menu.

4. Summarize the print menu.

THE PRINT MENU DEFINED

The print menu (^P) is a listing of print features and print enhancements available to WordStar users. Your printer must be able to support the enhancements. Microjustifying printers, when properly installed, will execute these commands.

THE PRINT MENU DISPLAY

The print menu is displayed by striking *^P* while editing a document. Figure 26.1 illustrates the print menu that displays when *^P* is entered. All of the print features listed in this menu have been explained in previous lessons.

```
^P          B:LESSON26.TXT    PAGE 1  LINE 1   COL 01        INSERT ON
                      < < <     P R I N T    M E N U    > > >
    ------ Special  Effects -------  ! -Printing  Changes- ! -Other  Menus-
  (begin and end) !  (one time each) ! A Alternate pitch   ! (from Main only)
  B Bold D Double ! H Overprint char ! N Standard pitch    !^J Help   ^K Block
    S Underscore  ! O Non-break space ! C Printing pause   !^Q Quick ^P Print
    X Strikeout   ! F Phantom space  ! Y Other ribbon color!^O Onscreen
    V Subscript   ! G Phantom rubout !   --User  Patches-- !Space Bar returns
    T Superscript ! RET Overprint line ! Q(1) W(2) E(3) R(4) !you to Main Menu.
  L----!----!----!----!----!----!----!----!----!----!--------R
```

Figure 26.1   The Print Menu

EXITING THE PRINT MENU

The print menu can be canceled by either one of the following steps:

1. Strike one of the command letters.

2. Strike the space bar.

Figure 26.2 on page 246 summarizes all of the print menu commands and their features.

Command	Feature
^PB	Bold type. Will darken text.
^PD	Double strike. Will darken text, but will not be as black as bold type.
^PS	Underscore text. Will not underscore spaces between words.
^PX	Strikeout. Text is crossed out with hyphens.
^PV	Subscript. Text is printed slightly below the line.
^PT	Superscript. Text is printed slightly above the line.
^PH	Overprint a character (as in Ø).
^PO	Nonbreak or required space. Used to keep words on one line during reformatting.
^PF	Special character, usually the British pound symbol or the American cent symbol, depending on the print element.
^PG	May be a double underscore, depending on the print element.
^P and ENTER/RETURN	Overprint a line. The character(s) entered on the next line will overprint the previous line.
^PA	Alternate character pitch. The 10-space character pitch default will change to 12-space.
^PN	Will return character pitch to the 10-space-per-inch default.
^PC	Print pause. Command is entered in the document. Print will pause for you to change a daisy wheel. Enter P to resume printing.
^PY	Change ribbon color. Some ribbons are half red and half black. The command will start the printing on the top or red half of the ribbon.
^PQ,^PW,^PE,^PR	User-defined features programmed with the WordStar INSTALL program. Consult WordStar installation manual for custom features.

Figure 26.2   Print Menu Summary

COMPLETION

Indicate the print command to accomplish the task described in the space provided. (Obj. 4)

1. Bold type. Will darken text for emphasis..............   1. _____

2. Double strike. Will darken text, but will not be as black as bold type. ....   2. _____

3. Underscore text. Will not underscore spaces between words. ....   3. _____

4. Strikeout. Text is crossed out with hyphens. ....   4. _____

5. Subscript. Text is printed slightly below the line. ....   5. _____

6. Superscript. Text is printed slightly above the line......   6. _____

7. Overprint a character (as in Ø). ....   7. _____

8. Nonbreak or required space. Used to keep words on one line during reformatting. ....   8. _____

9. Special character, usually the British pound symbol or the American cent symbol, depending on the print element. ....   9. _____

10. May be a double underscore, depending on the print element. ....   10. _____

11. Overprint a line. The character(s) entered on the next line will overprint the previous line. ....   11. _____

12. Alternate character pitch. The 10-space character pitch default will change to 12-space character pitch.........   12. _____

13. Will return character pitch to the 10-space-per-inch default. ....   13. _____

14. Print pause. Command is entered in the document. Print will pause for you to change a daisy wheel. Enter *P* to resume printing. ....   14. _____

15. Change ribbon color. Some ribbons are half red and half black. The command will start the printing on the top or red half of the ribbon. ....   15. _____

16. User-defined features programmed with the WordStar INSTALL program. Consult WordStar installation manual for custom features. ....   16. _____

COMPUTER EXERCISE

Directions: Follow the step-by-step instructions to complete the computer exercise.

1. Create a file named LESSON26.EX.

2. Enter the report in Figure 26.3 using the print features indicated. Do not enter the instructions in parentheses.

3. Use all the defaults. Double space between paragraphs. Enter the footnote at the bottom of the second page on line 54.

4. Save the file.

5. Print the file named LESSON26.EX.

1

GUIDELINES TO GRAPHICS

They say that one picture is worth a thousand words. Charts and graphs help to get the words across. A number of formats are available to draw a picture of your message. The following information is a guideline on using business graphics that work best to convey different types of information.

(Change to 12 pitch with ^PA. Use ^PS and the underscore key for continuous underscoring. Put the text with continuous underscores into bold type with ^PB.)

1.   For_time_series_analysis: These graphics are used to show how a value or values changed over time such as in sales per month, profits per quarter, and units produced per week.

(Use ^PD to double strike the next two paragraphs. Indent the first line of each paragraph 5 spaces from the temporary left margin set at 11.)

        Use a bar_graph when there are few time periods to report and where values vary greatly from one period to another.

        Use a line_graph to connect the points and show a smooth pattern over many time periods. You may want to use color to emphasize differences between time periods.

(Cancel double strike with ^PD. Put the text with continuous underscores into bold type with ^PB.)

2.   For_proportional_analysis: Use these graphics to show one number as a portion of a total amount.

(Fig. 26.3, continued on p. 249)

(Double strike the next two paragraphs with ^PD. Indent the first line of
each paragraph 5 spaces from the temporary left margin set at 11.)

Use a pie_chart when there are more than four ways to

slice the total amount. Use one pie chart for each time

period.

Use a 100_percent_column_chart to facilitate visual analysis

of changes over time. Draw a column the full height of the

chart, representing 100 percent. Divide this column into

proportions representing shares or parts of the whole.

(Cancel double strike with ^PD. Put the text with continuous underscores
into bold type with ^PB.)

3.   For_item_comparisons: Use these graphics to compare

specific item comparisons with actual numbers, not just shares or

percentages.

(Double strike the next paragraph with ^PD.   Indent the first line 5 spaces
from the temporary left margin set at 11.)

Use a sorted_bar_chart to show the most, the least, and

the amounts in between. Bar sizes represent the number of

items on display. Use color and silhouettes of items

compared to add emphasis and visual appeal.

(Cancel double strike with ^PD. Put the text with continuous underscores
into bold type with ^PB. Start a new page here with .PA.)

4.   For_relationships_between_variables: Use graphics to show,

for example, the different tax rate for different income levels.

(Double strike the next paragraph with ^PD. Indent the first line 5 spaces
from the temporary left margin set at 11.)

Use a line_graph to show smooth relationships. As the

X value increases, the Y value changes consistently.

(Cancel double strike with ^PD. Return to 10-space character pitch with ^PN.)

Graphic communications is another language that requires

specialized training. With a computer you can use simple graphics to

communicate information.

1
   "Graphic Guidelines," Office Automation Update (June, 1983), p. 4.

Figure 26.3   Text for Computer Exercise

27. More Page Formatting With Dot Commands _____

OBJECTIVES:

1. Define a dot command.

2. Explain the comment line.

3. Describe conditional page command.

4. Explain microjustification default.

5. Explain how to adjust line height.

6. Describe character width command.

7. Explain how to delete a dot command.

8. Summarize the dot commands.

DOT COMMAND DEFINED

A dot command is an optional feature that enables you to have complete control over the page format. The previous lessons have introduced most of these commands; only a few have not been discussed.

You will recall that a dot command

1. begins with a dot (.) at column 1 followed by two letters.

2. is usually followed by a space.

3. can be embedded anywhere in the document, with a few exceptions.

4. takes up one line.

5. will cause a question mark to appear at the far right of the screen when the dot is entered. After the two-letter code is entered, the question mark will disappear.

6. can be entered in uppercase or lowercase.

THE COMMENT DOT COMMAND

Comments can be entered in a document that will display on the screen but will not print out. These comments or remarks may be embedded to remind you to place an illustration at a particular point or to note when the document was entered and who entered it.

Two dot commands will allow you to enter a comment line. Either one of these commands will permit you to enter remarks that will not print. They are as follows:

1. Two dots (..).

2. *.IG* (think of the first two letters in the word *ignore*). (An example of a nonprinting comment line is illustrated in Figure 27.1.)

```
.IG  First draft entered on 9/5 by SG.

..  Insert Table 8 here.
```

Figure 27.1   Dot Commands for the Nonprinting Comment Line

THE CONDITIONAL PAGE COMMAND

WordStar will automatically set a new page after 55 lines. WordStar will also start a new page if you enter the dot command .PA, which you learned about in a previous lesson.

The conditional page dot command is yet another way to control page breaks. Certain types of text should not split between two pages. For example, a table or illustration should appear on one page if possible. To assure that text will not be divided by a page break, enter the dot command .CP, a space, and the number of lines that must be printed together. For example, to be sure that a chart containing five lines will be printed on one page, enter *.CP*, a space, and *5* before the chart. Figure 27.2 illustrates a conditional page command that will instruct the printer to print five uninterrupted lines.

```
.CP 5

XXX XXXX   XXX   XXXX XXXXXXXXX
XXX XXXX   XXX   XXXX XXXXXXXXX
XXX XXXX   XXX   XXXX XXXXXXXXX
XXX XXXX   XXX   XXXX XXXXXXXXX
XXX XXXX   XXX   XXXX XXXXXXXXX
```

**Figure 27.2   The Conditional Page Break to Print Uninterrupted
              Lines**

CHANGING THE MICROJUSTIFICATION DEFAULT

Microjustifying printers distribute spaces 1/120 of an inch between words when the right margin is justified, producing an even look to the printed line. You will recall from the discussion on printing two-column newsletters in Lesson 18 that microjustification is turned off with the command .UJ0 in order for the inside margins to be even. If this command is not entered, microjustification will cause the spaces to spread out evenly—thus spoiling the alignment of the inner margins. Turn microjustification back on with the command .UJ1. Turn microjustification off (.UJ0) when printing tables to assure that the printout will look exactly like the screen display.

ADJUSTING LINE HEIGHT

You learned in Lesson 11 that line height, or the vertical space between lines, is adjusted by the command ^OS. (To double space, enter ^OS 2, to triple space, enter ^OS 3, and so on.) Now suppose you want 1 1/2 spaces between lines. Or suppose you don't want to take up so much screen space with a triple-space command. The dot command .LH (think *line height*) can be used to achieve unusual vertical spacing and more efficient use of the screen display.

Microjustifying printers can adjust vertical spacing in increments of 1/48 of an inch. The default line height is set at .LH8 which is equivalent to single spacing. Remember, there are six vertical lines to an inch. The line height default of eight equals 1/6 of an inch (8/48 = 1/6).

Suppose you want to print a document with 1 1/2 spaces between lines. Since the default *.LH 8* equals six lines per inch, *.LH 12* (8 + 4) will equal four lines per inch (12/48 = 1/4) or 1 1/2 spaces between lines. Figure 27.3 illustrates the line height settings for various vertical lines per inch.

Command	Lines Per Inch (adjusted at 1/48th of a vertical inch)
.LH 1	48 (1/48)
.LH 8	6 (single space default, 8/48)
.LH 12	4 (1 1/2 spaces, 12/48)
.LH 16	3 (double space, 16/48)
.LH 24	2 (triple space, 24/48)

Figure 27.3 Line Height Commands for Vertical Line Spacing

The line height dot command should come after the paper length dot command. You will recall that the paper length default is .PL 66. There are 66 possible lines on a standard sheet of paper (11-inch paper length times 6 lines to a vertical inch). If you use paper that is 14 inches long, you will change the paper length to .PL 84 (14-inch paper times 6 lines to an inch). Enter the paper length dot command first, and then enter the line height dot command; otherwise the page breaks will not display correctly.

CHANGING CHARACTER WIDTH

The default character width is ten spaces to a horizontal inch. In Lesson 25 you learned that the alternate pitch command ($^\wedge PA$) will change the character width from 10 to 12 and that $^\wedge PN$ will return the character width to 10 again. A dot command will also change the character width but will allow you greater choices.

The smallest distance microjustifying printers can move horizontally (across) is 1/120 of an inch per character. There are 10 horizontal characters to an inch by default; this distance is equivalent to 12/120 microspaces per character or 1/l0 of an inch. Another way to say this is that the default uses 12/120 of an inch per character and is expressed by the dot command .CW 12. To change the character width to 12 spaces per inch, the microjustifying printer will use up 1/12 of an inch per character which is equivalent to 10/120 microspaces per character. Therefore, the dot command is .CW10 for elite spacing or pitch. Changing the character width to 15 characters per inch or 1/15 of an inch per character is the same as 8/120 microspaces per character expressed in the dot command .CW 8. Figure 27.4 illustrates a printout with 15 characters per inch and a printout with 5 characters per inch.

```
Dot command                .CW 8
Characters per inch        15 (15/120 = 1/8)

WORDSTAR DOT COMMANDS AND THEIR APPLICATIONS

Dot command                .CW 24
Characters per inch        5 (5/120 = 1/24

W O R D S T A R   D O T   C O M M A N D S
```

Figure 27.4   Printouts of Various Character Widths

DELETING DOT COMMANDS

Dot commands are deleted in the same way as any other line is deleted. Enter $\wedge Y$ to delete the dot command line. (Figure 27.5 summarizes the dot commands discussed in this lesson.)

Command	Default	Function
Two dots (..) or .IG	_____	Enter comments or remarks in the file display but not in the printout.
.CP and number	_____	Print specified number of lines on one page.
.UJ1	ON	Microjustifying printer will add microspaces to justify the right margin.
.UJ0	OFF	Turns off microjustification
.LH	.LH 8	Change vertical spaces between lines.
.CW	.CW 12	Change horizontal character spacing.
$\wedge Y$	_____	Delete a dot command.

Figure 27.5   Summary of Lesson 27 Dot Commands

LESSON 27 EXERCISE

Name _____ Date _____

TRUE/FALSE

Each of the following statements is either true or false. Indicate the correct answer in the Answers column by circling T for a true statement or F for a false statement.

1. A dot command affects page format. (Obj. 1) ....   1.   **T**   **F**

2. A dot command can be entered at any column. (Obj. 1) ....   2.   **T**   **F**

3. A dot command must be entered in uppercase. (Obj. 1) ....   3.   **T**   **F**

4. A comment line will not print. (Obj. 2) ....   4.   **T**   **F**

5. The comment or remark commands are two dots (..) or *.IG.* (Obj. 2) ....   5.   **T**   **F**

6. WordStar generates a new page after 55 lines of text. (Obj. 3) ....   6.   **T**   **F**

7. To start a required page break, enter *.PA.* (Obj. 3) ....   7.   **T**   **F**

8. A conditional page break will instruct the printer to start a new page if less than a specific number of lines remain on a given page. (Obj. 3) ....   8.   **T**   **F**

9. The command to assure that a chart with 12 lines prints on one page is *.CP 12.* (Obj. 3) ....   9.   **T**   **F**

10. The command to turn off microjustification is .UJ1. (Obj. 4) ....   10.   **T**   **F**

11. Microjustifying printers distribute spaces 1/48 of an inch between words when the right margin is justified. (Obj. 4) ....   11.   **T**   **F**

12. Turn microjustification off when printing a two-column newsletter. (Obj. 4) ....   12.   **T**   **F**

13. Turn microjustification off when printing tables. (Obj. 4) ....   13.   **T**   **F**

14. Turn microjustification on with the command .UJ0. (Obj. 4) ....   14.   **T**   **F**

15. Use the line height command to print 1 1/2 vertical lines between text. (Obj. 5) ....   15.   **T**   **F**

16. The line height command should be entered before the paper length dot command. (Obj. 5) ....   16.   **T**   **F**

17. Microjustifying printers can adjust vertical spacing in increments of 1/48 of an inch. (Obj. 5) ....   17.   **T**   **F**

18. The default line height is *.LH 8.* (Obj. 5) ....   18.   **T**   **F**

19. The default character width dot command is .CW 10. (Obj. 6) ....   19.   **T**   **F**

20. To delete a dot command, enter ^Y. (Obj. 7) ....   20.   **T**   **F**

COMPLETION

Indicate the correct answer in the space provided.

1. What optional feature enables you to have complete control over the page format? (Obj. 1) ....

   1. _____

2. A dot command begins with a dot (.) and is followed by how many letters? (Obj. 1)..............................

   2. _____

3. What will appear on the right side of the screen when a dot is entered at column 1? (Obj. 1) ....

   3. _____

4. A dot command must be entered at which column? (Obj. 1)..

   4. _____

5. What are the two comment dot commands? (Obj. 2) ....

   5. a. _____
      b. _____

6. WordStar begins a new page after how many lines of text? (Obj. 3)..

   6. _____

7. To enter a required page break, use the command *?* (Obj. 3)..

   7. _____

8. To assure that all the lines in a 12-line chart will be printed on the same page, before the chart enter *?* (Obj. 3)..

   8. _____

9. To turn off microjustification, enter *?* (Obj. 4) ....

   9. _____

10. The default for microjustification can be expressed in the dot command *?* (Obj. 4)..............................

    10. _____

11. Name two types of documents which need the microjustification default turned off. (Obj. 4) ....

    11. a. _____
        b. _____

12. To print 1 1/2 lines between text, enter *?* (Obj. 5) ......

    12. _____

13. The line height default can be expressed in the dot command *?* (Obj. 5) ....

    13. _____

14. Microjustifying printers can adjust vertical spacing in increments of what part of an inch? (Obj. 5) ....

    14. _____

15. The line height dot command should come after the *?* (Obj. 5)..

    15. _____

16. The paper length default can be expressed in the dot command *?* (Obj. 5) ....

    16. _____

17. The dot command to change the paper length for paper 14 inches long is *?* (Obj. 5)..............................

    17. _____

18. The smallest distance microjustifying printers can move horizontally is what part of an inch? (Obj. 6) ....

    18. _____

19. The dot command for elite pitch (12 characters per inch) is *?* (Obj. 6)..

    19. _____

20. Dot commands are deleted by the command *?* (Obj. 7) ..

    20. _____

COMPUTER EXERCISE

Directions: Follow the step-by-step instructions to complete the computer exercise.

1. Create a file named LESSON27.EX. Read all the instructions and then enter the document shown in Figure 27.6.

2. Set a line height of 1 1/2 lines between text. If your printer does not microjustify, double space the document.

3. Enter a comment line to read "For Publication in the San Jose News, November 20, 1984."

4. Set a character width of 5 characters per inch for each day's heading with the command .CW 24 (24/120 = 5 characters per inch). If your printer does not microjustify, you cannot change the character width.

5. Set a character width of 13.3 characters per inch for the text following the headings with the command .CW 9 (9/120 = 13.3 characters per inch).

6. Set a conditional page break at 8 lines (.CP 8) before the Thursday agenda to keep all of that day's agenda on one page.

7. When you enter the document, do not key-in the text in parentheses.

8. Print the file named LESSON27.EX.

```
(Enter line height here, .LH 12.)

(Enter the following comment line beginning with .IG.)

For publication in the San Jose News, November 20, 19--.

(Enter character width here of .CW 24.  Headings should be put in bold type
and underscored.  If your printer will not print in bold type, double strike
the headings.)

MONDAY

(Enter character width here of .CW 9.)

Control Systems is offering a series of electronic design seminars,
which will show qualified engineers how a personal computer
workstation can improve design productivity and shorten lead times.
The no-cost half-day sessions include demonstrations of personal
computer use in circuit design.  The seminars will be held at Control
Systems every Monday of this month.  For more information, call 253-
4004.
```

(Fig. 27.6, continued on p. 260)

```
(Enter character width here of .CW 24.)
```

TUESDAY

```
(Enter character width here of .CW 9.)
```

The Electronic Association of California will conduct a workshop
entitled "Stress At Work." The workshop will be held at the training
center from 8:30 a.m. to 12:30 p.m. The cost is $120 for members,
$150 for nonmembers. Contact Roy Whitaker to reserve your place.

Biomedical group of the Professional Consultants Association will meet
at 7:30 p.m. in the Sunnyvale area. Contact Jack Smith at 252-6716.

```
(Enter character width here of .CW 24.)
```

WEDNESDAY

```
(Enter character width here of .CW 9.)
```

"Career Advancement: Trends in the Word Processing Field" will be
presented by Mary Stone, a professional trainer for Systems Analysis
at a meeting of the Valley Word Processing Association. The meeting
will be held at the Black Knight Restaurant at 8:00 p.m.

```
(Enter character width here of .CW 24.)

(Enter conditional page here of .CP 8.)
```

THURSDAY

```
(Enter character width here of .CW 9.)
```

Frank Cross, cohost of the Morning Show on channel 11, will speak to
the South Bay Public Relations Group at the Blue Ox Restaurant and give
a presentation of some TV bloopers from his television show.

The South Bay Chapter Of American Women in Radio will meet at 6:00
p.m. at KLIV 1700 Market Street in San Jose.

```
(Enter character width here of .CW 24.)
```

FRIDAY

```
(Enter character width here of .CW 9.)
```

The Association Of Individual Investors will meet at the Golden
Pheasant in Gilroy. Michael Murphy will be the guest speaker. For
further information contact Linda Gossett.

Figure 27.6   Text for Computer Exercise

28. Dot Command Review _____

OBJECTIVES:

1. Show how to get help with dot commands.
2. Summarize the dot commands.

GETTING HELP FOR DOT COMMANDS

On-screen help for dot commands is obtained by entering $\wedge JD$. The MailMerge dot commands also display. MailMerge is a word processing program that works with WordStar to print and merge files. The MailMerge program is not covered in this book.

Figure 28.1 summarizes the dot commands, their default values, and their functions.

VERTICAL LAYOUT

Command	Default	Function
.LH	.LH 8, 8/48 or 1/6 of an inch, (6 lines per inch)	Line height; adjusts vertical space between lines.
.PL	.PL 66 (6 lines per inch)	Adjusts vertical page length.
.MT	.MT 3, 3 lines, 1/2 inch	Adjusts margin top (space from top of page to text).
.MB	.MB 8, 1 1/3 inches	Adjusts margin bottom (space from text to bottom of page).

HEADERS AND FOOTERS

Command	Default	Function
.HE	No heading	Repeat a heading or message on the top of subsequent pages.
.HM	.HM 2 (2 lines)	Adjusts header margin (space between header and text).

(Fig. 28.1, continued on p. 262)

.FO	No footer	Repeat footer or message at the bottom of subsequent pages.
.FM	.FM 2 (2 lines)	Adjusts footer margin (space between text and footer or page number).

PAGE BREAKS

Command	Default	Function
.PA	New page will begin after 55 lines of text are entered.	Adjusts page advance; starts a new page.
.CP	--	Conditional page break. Makes a certain number of lines print on the same page (as in a table).

PAGE NUMBERS

Command	Default	Function
.PN	Number prints at the bottom and center of each page.	Restores page numbering.
.OP	--	Omit page numbering.
.PC	.PC 33	Print page number at specific column.

OTHER DOT COMMANDS

Command	Default	Function
.CW	.CW 12 (12/120 of an inch per character, 10 characters to an inch)	Adjusts character width.
Two dots (..) or .IG	--	Ignore comment line. Comment will display but will not print.
.SR	.SR 3	Script roll for superscripts and subscripts.
.UJ	.UJ1 *ON*, .UJ0 *OFF*	Microjustification for printers capable of moving in microspaces.
.PO	.PO 8, 8 columns	Adjusts page offset (space from left edge of the paper to column where text begins).

Figure 28.1   Dot Command Summary

COMPLETION

Indicate the correct dot command for the definition given. (Obj. 2)

1. Adjusts page offset (space from left edge of paper to column where text begins). ....   1. _____

2. Line height; adjusts vertical space between lines. ....   2. _____

3. Microjustification for printers capable of moving in microspaces. ....   3. _____

4. Adjusts vertical page length. ....   4. _____

5. Script roll for superscripts and subscripts. ....   5. _____

6. Adjusts margin top (space from top of page to text). ....   6. _____

7. Ignore comment line. Comment will display but will not print. ....   7. _____

8. Adjusts margin bottom (space from text to bottom of page). ....   8. _____

9. Adjusts character width. ....   9. _____

10. Repeat a heading or message on the top of subsequent pages. ....   10. _____

11. Print page number at specific column. ....   11. _____

12. Adjusts header margin (space between header and text).   12. _____

13. Omit page numbering. ....   13. _____

14. Repeat footer or message at the bottom of subsequent pages. ....   14. _____

15. Restores page numbering. ....   15. _____

16. Adjusts footer margin (space between text and footer or page number). ....   16. _____

17. Conditional page break. Makes a certain number of lines print on the same page (as in a table). ....   17. _____

18. Adjusts page advance; starts a new page. ....   18. _____

COMPUTER EXERCISE

Directions: Follow the step-by-step instructions given to complete the computer exercise.

1. Create a file named LESSON28.EX.

2. Enter the text in Figure 28.2 with all the defaults on after reading the instructions. Do not enter the instructions in parentheses.

```
TO:  Office Support Personnel        DATE:  December 19, 19--
(Double space)
FROM:  David Johnson                 SUBJECT:  New Printers
(Triple space)
```

Our department recently received delivery of 150 printers capable of

microjustification. This means that we can now use the WordStar word

processing program with all of its capabilities for changing character

width, line height, and printing features.

The following table will help you to use the proper dot commands for

the line height variables. You are encouraged to use print enhancement

features to add emphasis and eye appeal to your documents.
(Triple space)

LINE HEIGHT
(Triple space)

Command	Lines/Inch
.LH 1	48.0
.LH 4	12.0
.LH 6	8.0
.LH 7	6.8
.LH 8	6.0
.LH 9	5.3
.LH 10	4.8
.LH 12	4.0
.LH 16	3.0
.LH 18	2.6
.LH 20	2.4
.LH 24	2.0

(Fig. 28.2, continued on p. 265)

```
      The character width command will also add to your document's overall

appeal.  The following table gives the dot commands to print characters at

various widths per inch.
(Triple space)

CHARACTER WIDTH
(Triple space)
```

Command	Characters/Inch
.CW 6	20
.CW 7	17.1
.CW 8	15
.CW 9	13.3
.CW 10	12
.CW 11	10.9
.CW 12	10
.CW 13	9.2
.CW 14	8.6
.CW 15	8
.CW 16	7.5
.CW 17	7
.CW 20	6
.CW 24	5

Figure 28.2   Text for Computer Exercise

3. Set a 1 1/2 inch left margin with the page offset command .PO 15 (ten spaces equal one inch). Enter a blank line at the beginning of the document for the dot command.

4. Enter a header for the document that prints "DISTRIBUTE TO ALL PERSONAL COMPUTER USERS" in the upper right corner of the page.

5. Enter a centered footer that reads "SOURCE: WORDSTAR MADE EASY by John D. Lee." Enter and center the text first; then turn insert off and enter .FO. Turn insert on again.

6. Print the document with a line height of four lines per vertical inch with the command .LH 12. This must be the very first dot command.

7. Print the table headings at the left margin in a character width of six characters per inch with the command .CW 20. Remember to return the character width to the default (.CW 12), after each of the two headings. Insert a blank line to replace the line used by the dot command.

8. Enter a conditional page break of 16 lines before each table heading with the command .CP 16. Remember to replace the lines used by the dot commands.

9. Set a margin bottom of ten lines.

10. Set a header margin of two lines.

11. Set a margin top of six lines.

12. Print the file named LESSON28.EX.

29. The Help Menu _____

OBJECTIVES:

1. Define the Help or ^J menu.

2. Explain how to display the ^J menu.

3. Explain how to exit the ^J menu.

4. Describe how to change the help level.

5. Describe how to get help to reformat and hyphenate.

6. Describe how to get help defining flag symbols.

7. Show how to get help for dot commands and print control characters.

8. Show how to get help for the status line.

9. Show how to get help for the ruler line.

10. Describe how to get help for on-screen formatting.

11. Describe how to get help for place markers.

12. Explain how to get help for block commands.

13. Describe how to get help for common editing commands.

14. Summarize the ^J submenus.

THE HELP MENU

One of the strongest features of WordStar, in addition to its sophisticated editing choices, is the on-screen help available to the user. The help menu (^J) is a condensed on-screen reference manual of the WordStar editing commands.

The ^J menu commands display information in submenus. There are ten submenus that review basic editing features.

DISPLAYING THE HELP MENU

The help menu is displayed by entering ^J while editing a document file. Figure 29.1 on page 268 illustrates the help menu. You may exit the menu by striking the space bar.

```
^J      B:LESSON29.TXT    PAGE 1   COL  01              INSERT ON

            < < <  H E L P   M E N U  > > >
                               ¦                      ¦  --Other Menus--
   H  Display & set the help level ¦ S Status line    ¦   (from Main only)
   B  Paragraph reform (CONTROL-B) ¦ R Ruler line      ¦ ^J Help    ^K Block
   F  Flags in right-most column   ¦ M Margins & Tabs  ¦ ^Q Quick   ^P Print
   D  Dot commands, print controls ¦ P Place markers   ¦ ^O Onscreen
   I  Index of commands            ¦ V Moving text     ¦ Space bar returns
                                   ¦                   ¦ you to Main Menu.
   L----!----!----!----!----!----!----!----!----!----!--------R
```

Figure 29.1   The Help Menu (^J)

CHANGING THE HELP LEVEL

There are four help levels (3, 2, 1, 0) programmed to give you maximum help as a beginning WordStar user and then less help as you become more experienced with WordStar.

Help level 3 gives the maximum help, displaying all menus and prompts. Level 3 is the default. The command to set the help level at 3 is ^JH3 while in the edit mode.

Help level 2 does not display the main menu; however, the status line and the ruler line will display. You will want to use help level 2 as soon as possible, because omitting the main menu permits an additional eight lines of text to display on the screen. The command to set the help level at 2 is ^JH2 while in the edit mode.

Help level 1 eliminates access to the ^J, ^K, ^P, ^O, and ^Q menus as well as the main menu. The status line and the ruler line will display. The command to set the help level at 1 is ^JH1 while in the edit mode.

Help level 0 eliminates all messages on the screen. The ^J submenus will display if you can remember the ^J command letter. To set the help level at 0, enter *^JH0* while in the edit mode.

REFORMATTING AND HYPHENATING HELP

Enter *^JB* in the edit mode to get on-screen help for reformatting paragraphs and hyphenating text. This submenu displays three screens of information on the reformat and hyphenation edit features.

Enter *^JF* in the edit mode to get on-screen explanations of the flag symbols that appear on the right side of the screen.

Enter *^JD* in the edit mode to get on-screen help for dot commands and print control characters. Six screens of information will give you a quick review of the most common dot and print commands. (The last screen explains dot commands for the MailMerge program; these commands are not covered in this book.)

Enter ∧JS in the edit mode to get on-screen help to define the status line. Two screens of information are displayed.

Enter ∧JR in the edit mode to get on-screen help for setting margins and tabs. The ruler line symbols are also explained.

Enter ∧JM in the edit mode to get help for margins, tabs, and line spacing. Five screens display information on these on-screen edit features.

Enter ∧JP in the edit mode to get help for place markers. Two screens display place marker information.

Enter ∧JV in the edit mode to get help for block moves, copies, and deletes.

Enter ∧JI to get help for locating information on the basic, most common editing features such as cursor movements, scrolling, or find and replace.

SUMMARY OF ∧J SUBMENUS

Figure 29.2 summarizes the ∧J submenus.

Submenu	Help Display
∧JH	Displays current help level and gives instructions for changing to different help levels.
∧JB	Reformatting paragraphs and hyphenation help.
∧JF	Flag symbols.
∧JD	Dot commands and print control characters.
∧JS	Status line.
∧JR	Ruler line.
∧JM	On-screen formatting: margins, tabs, and line spacing.
∧JP	Place markers.
∧JV	Block commands.
∧JI	Indexes where to find information for the most-used editing commands.

Figure 29.2   Summary of the ∧J Submenus

LESSON 29 EXERCISE   Name _____   Date _____

TRUE/FALSE

Each of the following statements is either true or false. Indicate your choice in the Answers column by circling T for a true statement or F for a false statement.

Answers

1. The help menu (^J) is a condensed on-screen reference manual of the Word-Star editing commands. (Obj. 1)..   1. **T**   **F**

2. The ^J menu has ten submenus. (Obj. 1) ....   2. **T**   **F**

3. To display the help menu, enter ^H. (Obj. 2) ....   3. **T**   **F**

4. To exit the help menu, strike the space bar. (Obj. 3) ....   4. **T**   **F**

5. The default help level is 1. (Obj. 4) ....   5. **T**   **F**

6. The command to change the help levels is ^JH. (Obj. 4) ....   6. **T**   **F**

7. The help level that displays all menus and prompts is 0. (Obj. 4) ....   7. **T**   **F**

8. Help level 2 will display the status line and the ruler line but not the main menu. (Obj. 4) ....   8. **T**   **F**

9. An additional eight lines of text are displayed when the main menu is deleted. (Obj. 4) ....   9. **T**   **F**

10. WordStar users have a choice of three different help levels. (Obj. 4) ....   10. **T**   **F**

COMPLETION

Indicate the correct command in the space provided for the sub-menu definition.

1. Displays help for locating information on the most-used editing commands. (Obj. 13) ....   1. _____

2. Displays help for place markers. (Obj. 11) ....   2. _____

3. Displays current help level and gives instructions for changing to different help levels. (Obj. 4) ....   3. _____

4. Displays help for block commands. (Obj. 12) ....   4. _____

5. Displays help for reformatting paragraphs and hyphenating text. (Obj. 5) ....   5. _____

6. Displays ruler line help. (Obj. 9) ....   6. _____

7. Displays status line help. (Obj. 8)........................   7. _____

8. Displays on-screen formatting commands such as margins, tabs, and line spacing. (Obj. 10)...................   8. _____

9. Displays help for dot commands and print control characters. (Obj. 7) ....   9. _____

10. Displays help for flag symbols. (Obj. 6) ....   10. _____

COMPUTER EXERCISE

Directions: Follow the step-by-step instructions to complete the computer exercise.

1. Create a file named LESSON29.EX.

2. Read the submenu for setting the help level.

    a. Set the help level at 0; then set the help level at 1. Try to bring the ^J menu, the ^K menu, the ^P menu, the ^O menu, and the ^Q menu to the screen. (You will not be able to display these menus with the help level at 1.)

    b. Set the help level at 2. Bring the ^O menu to the screen. Delete the ^O menu from the screen.

    c. Set the help level at 3.

    d. Set the help level at 2.

3. Read the submenu for reformatting and hyphenation.

4. Read the submenu for the flag symbols.

5. Read the submenu for the dot and print control characters.

6. Read the submenu for the status line.

7. Read the submenu for the ruler line.

8. Read the submenu for on-screen formatting—margins, tabs, and line spacing.

9. Read the submenu for place markers.

10. Read the submenu for block commands.

11. Read the submenu for locating information on the most-used editing commands.

12. Abandon the edit with ^KQ.

30. The Opening Menu _____

OBJECTIVES:

1. Define the no-file or opening menu.

2. Describe the file directory.

3. Show how to set the help level from the opening menu.

4. Explain the nondocument file.

5. Describe how to rename a file from the opening menu.

6. Describe how to delete a file from the opening menu.

7. Explain how to run another program.

8. Explain the WordStar, MailMerge, and SpellStar options.

9. Summarize the no-file or opening menu.

THE NO-FILE OR OPENING MENU

The no-file or opening menu is displayed when the WordStar program is entered into the computer with the WS command. The opening menu is also displayed after saving or printing a file. Figure 30.1 illustrates the opening menu when WordStar is entered.

```
              < < <   N O - F I L E   M E N U   > > >
--Preliminary    Commands--  ┆ --File Commands-- ┆ --System Commands--
L  Change logged disk drive  ┆                   ┆   R Run a program
F  File directory   now ON   ┆  P Print a file   ┆   X EXIT to system
H  Set help level            ┆                   ┆
--Commands to open a file--  ┆  E RENAME a file  ┆ -WordStar Options-
  D Open a document file      ┆  O COPY a file    ┆   M Run MailMerge
  N Open a non-document file  ┆  Y DELETE a file  ┆   S Run SpellStar
```

Figure 30.1   The No-File or Opening Menu

Many of the commands from the opening menu such as changing logged disk drives, opening a document file, printing a file, copying a file, and exiting to the operating system have been introduced in previous lessons. This lesson will describe the rest of the opening menu commands.

THE FILE DIRECTORY

The file directory is displayed below the opening menu. If Disk Drive A is activated, the directory for Disk Drive A is displayed; if Disk Drive B is activated, the directory for Disk Drive B is displayed, and so on.

The file directory will display by default. The directory can be deleted by striking F. Strike F again to bring the directory back to the screen.

SETTING THE HELP LEVEL
FROM THE OPENING MENU

In the previous lesson you learned how to set the help level in the edit mode. The help level can also be set from the opening menu by striking *H*. Figure 30.2 illustrates the screen display when *H* is entered from the opening menu. The higher the number of the help level setting, the greater the help. Enter the help level desired or strike the space bar to remain in the current help level.

```
HELP LEVELS
    3 all menus and explanations displayed
    2 main editing menu (1-control-char commands) suppressed
    1 prefix menus (2-character commands) also suppressed
    0 command explanations (including this) also suppressed

CURRENT HELP LEVEL IS 2

ENTER Space OR NEW HELP LEVEL (0, 1, 2, OR 3):_
```

Figure 30.2   Setting the Help Level from the Opening Menu

THE NONDOCUMENT FILE

Strike *N* to produce a nondocument file. The nondocument file command is used to create files for MailMerge and to work with other programs such as BASIC or PASCAL.

RENAMING A FILE

To call an existing file by a new name, enter *E* from the opening menu. A prompt is displayed asking the name of the file to be renamed. After that file name is entered, another prompt is displayed asking for the new name. Figure 30.3 illustrates the screen display to change the name of the file LESSON30.TXT to the new name NO-FILE. (You will remember that a file can also be renamed with the ^KE command while editing a document.)

```
NAME OF FILE TO RENAME?   LESSON30.TXT   (ENTER/RETURN)

NEW NAME?  NO-FILE  (ENTER/RETURN)
```

Figure 30.3   Prompt when Renaming a File from the Opening Menu

---

Files from other disk drives can be renamed by entering the drive letter and a colon before the file name. For example, to rename a file named PRACTICE in Disk Drive C, enter C:PRACTICE.

DELETING A FILE

A file is deleted by entering Y from the opening menu. The prompt NAME OF FILE TO DELETE? appears on the screen display when Y is entered from the opening menu. Enter the name of the file to be deleted and press ENTER/RETURN. The file name will be deleted from the file directory.

WordStar automatically generates a backup file for each file that is edited. Backup files are identified by .BAK after the file name. These files cannot be edited. If you delete a file by mistake, you can retrieve it by copying the backup file to the name of the deleted file. The backup file will not reflect the most current edit; therefore, the copied file will not be an exact duplicate of the deleted file.

Files on drives other than the current logged disk drive can be deleted by entering the drive letter before the file name. For example, to delete a file in Disk Drive A, enter A:FILENAME.

RUNNING A PROGRAM

It is possible to run programs other than WordStar without exiting to the operating system. First, to find out how much space there is left on a disk, enter R. The prompt COMMAND? is displayed. Enter a program command such as STAT (the CP/M program command) to display disk space available.

MAILMERGE AND SPELLSTAR

The M and S commands run the MailMerge and SpellStar programs. These are optional programs that can be purchased to work with WordStar. MailMerge is a program to merge data for large printings. SpellStar is a program designed to check for spelling errors in a document.

Figure 30.4 summarizes all of the opening menu commands.

Command	Function
L	Change the current logged disk drive.
F	File directory display. The default is on. Enter *F* to turn the file directory off; enter *F* to turn the file directory back on.
H	Set help level.
D	Open a document file; the file may be a file already created or a new file.
N	A nondocument file used for MailMerge and other programs.
P	Print a file.
E	Rename a file; the file contents remain the same.
O	Copy a file; file directory displays two different file names containing the same information.
Y	Delete a file.
R	Run another program (such as CP/M's STAT) without exiting WordStar.
X	Exit WordStar and return to the operating system.
M	A MailMerge command. You must have the MailMerge program on disk to use this command.
S	A SpellStar command. You must have the SpellStar program on disk to use this command.

Figure 30.4   No-File or Opening Command Summary

LESSON 30 EXERCISE

Name _____ Date _____

COMPLETION

Indicate the correct answer in the space provided.

1. The opening menu is sometimes called the ? (Obj. 1)....

1. _____

2. Is the file directory on or off by default? (Obj. 2).......

2. _____

3. To turn the file directory off, enter ? (Obj. 2)..........

3. _____

4. The help level can be changed from the opening menu or in which mode? (Obj. 3)...............................

4. _____

5. Which help level gives the most on-screen help? (Obj. 3)...

5. _____

6. To change the help level from the opening menu, enter ? (Obj. 3)...

6. _____

7. To create files for MailMerge and other programs, enter ? (Obj. 4)...

7. _____

8. To change the name of an existing file, what must be entered from the opening menu? (Obj. 5).................

8. _____

9. A file can be renamed from the opening menu with *E* or from a document in edit with what other command? (Obj. 5)...

9. _____

10. To rename a file named TEST in Disk Drive A while you are in Disk Drive B, what must you enter to the NAME OF FILE TO RENAME? prompt? (Obj. 5) ....

10. _____

11. To delete a file from the directory at the opening menu, enter ? (Obj. 6)...

11. _____

12. If a file has been edited once, WordStar will automatically generate a ? (Obj. 6) ....

12. _____

13. Backup files are identified in the directory by ? (Obj. 6)...

13. _____

14. A file deleted by mistake can be retrieved by doing what to the backup file to the name of the deleted file? (Obj. 6)...

14. _____

15. To run another program without exiting WordStar, what must be entered from the opening menu? (Obj. 7)...

15. _____

16. Name two options in the opening menu that are for MailMerge and SpellStar programs. (Obj. 8).............

16. a. _____
    b. _____

17. To change the logged disk drive, what must be entered from the opening menu? (Obj. 9) ....

17. _____

18. To create or edit a file, what must be entered from the opening menu? (Obj. 9) ....   18. _____

19. To copy a file from the opening menu, enter *?* (Obj. 9) .   19. _____

20. To exit WordStar and return to the operating system, what must be entered from the opening menu? (Obj. 9) ....   20. _____

COMPUTER EXERCISE

Directions: Follow the step-by-step instructions given to complete the computer exercise.

1. In this computer exercise you will practice the commands from the opening menu. A master WordStar disk should be in Disk Drive A and a working disk with documents in Disk Drive B. Enter WordStar.

2. Change from Disk Drive A to Disk Drive B.

3. Turn the file directory off.

4. Turn the file directory on.

5. Set the help level at 2.

6. Bring one of your files to the screen.

7. Save that document and return to the opening menu.

8. Create a new file named LESSON30.EX.

9. Save the file.

10. Rename the file called LESSON30.EX to RENAME.30.

11. Copy the file named RENAME.30 to COPY.30.

12. Delete the files named RENAME.30 and COPY.30.

13. Return to the operating system.

14. Print the directory for Disk Drive B.

Appendix A Formatting Diskettes ———

A diskette must be formatted before information can be stored on it. Sometimes the formatting procedure is called initializing. This procedure is necessary to write information on the disk in order to permit the computer to find specific tracks and sectors where information is stored.

The format program allows you to format blank disks or to reformat used disks that contain information no longer needed. When reformatting a used disk, be sure you do not need the information on that disk. Formatting destroys all information on a disk.

Formatting procedures for the MS-DOS Operating System and the CP/M Operating Systems follow. The instructions assume that you have two disk drives and that 5 1/4 inch diskettes are being formatted.

MS-DOS PROCEDURES FOR FORMATTING DISKS

1. Insert a master WordStar disk in Drive A.

2. Insert a blank disk in Drive B.

3. Turn on your computer.

4. At the **A>**, enter FORMAT B: and press the ENTER/ RETURN key. FORMAT may be entered in uppercase or lowercase. A light will appear on Drive B and will stay on until the formatting procedure is completed. When formatting is complete, the screen displays the following question: DO YOU HAVE MORE DISKS FOR FORMAT? (Y/N)? If you do, enter *Y* for yes and the procedure will be repeated. If you answer *N* for no, the screen displays **A>**.

CP/M PROCEDURES FOR FORMATTING DISKS

1. Turn on your computer.

2. Insert a master WordStar disk in Drive A.

3. Insert a blank disk in Drive B.

4. At the **A>**, enter FORMAT and strike the ENTER/ RETURN key.

5. When the prompt IS THAT WHAT YOU WANT? (y/n): is displayed, enter Y.

6. At the prompt WHICH DRIVE DO YOU WISH TO USE FOR THIS OPERATION?, enter *B*.

7. On some computers the question WHICH DENSITY? will display. If your computer shows this question, press *D* for double density or *S* for single density. If your computer does not show this question, go to step 8. On some computers the question NUMBER OF SIDES? is displayed. Enter *1* for one-sided disks and *2* for two-sided disks. If your computer does not display this question, go on to step 8.

8. The prompt DO YOU HAVE MORE DISKS TO FORMAT? (y/n): is displayed. Enter *N* for no.

9. The prompt PLACE A BOOTABLE DISK INTO DRIVE A AND PRESS ANY CHARACTER: will display.

10. Strike ENTER/RETURN.

Appendix B The Keyboard on Selected Computers _____

THE IBM PERSONAL COMPUTER KEYBOARD

The IBM Personal Computer special-function keys (F1-F10) will perform the tasks shown in Figure B.1.

IBM Key	WordStar Function	Equivalent WordStar Command
F1	Set help level.	^JH
F2	Indent paragraph to tab.	^OG
F3	Set left margin at cursor position.	^OL and Esc
F4	Set right margin at cursor position.	^OR and Esc
F5	Underscore text.*	^PS
F6	Put text in boldface.*	^PB
F7	Mark beginning of block.	^KB
F8	Mark end of block.	^KK
F9	Move cursor to end of file.	^QC
F10	Move cursor to beginning of file.	^QR

Put the cursor at the beginning and end of text you want to underscore or put into boldface. Then strike the appropriate special-function key.

Figure B.1   The IBM Special-Function Keys

THE IBM NUMERIC KEYPAD

The operation of the numeric keypad (at the right end of the IBM keyboard) is controlled by the Num Lock toggle switch located at the top of the numeric keypad. To enter numbers, strike the Num Lock key. To use the edit functions, press the Num Lock key again.

Figure B.2 shows the IBM key number, the edit function label, the corresponding WordStar edit function, and the equivalent WordStar command.

IBM Key Number*	Edit Function Label	WordStar Edit Function	Equivalent WordStar Command
4	Left arrow	Move cursor left.	^S
6	Right arrow	Move cursor right.	^D
8	Up arrow	Move cursor up.	^E
2	Down arrow	Move cursor down.	^X
7	Home	Move cursor to top of screen.	^R
9	Pg Up	Display previous screen (scroll down).	^R
3	Pg Dn	Display next screen (scroll up).	^C
1	End	Move cursor to bottom of screen.	^QX
0	Ins	Insert	^V
A decimal point (.)	Del	Delete	Del

*Edit functions on numeric keypad will not operate when pressing Ctrl key.

Figure B.2   The IBM Numeric Keypad

APPLE II KEYBOARD

The Apple II Plus keyboard does not have a shift key. When the directions call for using the shift key, substitute the Esc key while striking the letter you want to capitalize. In other words, if you want to enter a capital letter, you must hold down the Esc key while striking the letter you want to capitalize. To activate a caps lock command, strike the Esc key twice; to exit the caps lock command, again strike the Esc key twice.

The Apple IIe keyboard does have a shift key and works like a typewriter.

TRS-80 MODEL 2000

The backspace key has a dual function: It backspaces and also erases. Strike Ctrl and ENTER/RETURN together to return the cursor to the beginning of the next line. Striking ENTER/RETURN by itself executes a command or program.

Opening_Menu_Commands

Open a document file	D
Rename file	E
File directory on/off	F
Set help level	H
Change logged disk drive	L
Print file	P
Exit to operating system	X
Delete file	Y

Other_Menus

Help Menu	^J
Block Menu	^K
Onscreen formatting	^O
Quick Menu	^Q

Cursor_Movement

Right character	^D
Left character	^S
Up line	^E
Down line	^X
Right word	^F
Left word	^A
Top of screen	^QE
Bottom of screen	^QX
Beginning of file	^QR
End of file	^QC
Right end of line	^QD
Left end of line	^QS

Scrolling

Down by line	^W
Up by line	^Z
Up by screen	^C
Down by screen	^R
Continuous scroll up	^QZ
Continuous scroll down	^QW

Basic Editing Commands

Delete character right	^G
Delete character left	Del
Delete word right	^T
Delete line	^Y
Delete line to right of cursor	^QY
Delete line to left of cursor	^QDel
Insert on/off	^V
Insert blank line	^N
Reformat paragraph	^B

Formatting

Paragraph tab	^OG
Variable tabbing	^OV
Center line	^OC
Set left margin	^OL
Set right margin	^OR
Set margins from file	^OF
Ruler line display	^OT
Tab set	^OI
Tab clear	^ON
Justification on/off	^OJ
Set line spacing	^OS
Page break display	^OP

Search_and_Replace

Find string	^QF
Find and replace	^QA
Find and replace again	^L

Saving_Files

Abandon edit	^KQ
Save-reedit	^KS
Save, return to opening menu	^KD
Save, exit to operating system	^KX

Block_Commands

Mark block beginning	^KB
Mark block end	^KK
Hide marked block	^KH
Copy block	^KC
Delete block	^KY
Move block	^KV
Write block into another file	^KW
Read another file	^KR
Copy file	^KO

Print_Controls

Alternate pitch	^PA
Boldface beg./end	^PB
Double strike beg./end	^PD
Standard pitch	^PN
Strikeout beg./end	^PX
Subscript beg./end	^PV
Superscript beg./end	^PT
Underscore beg./end	^PS

Dot_Commands

Footer	.FO
Header	.HE
New page	.PA
Omit page number	.OP
Page number	.PN
Margin top	.MT
Margin bottom	.MB

INDEX

Advanced Applications _____

PURPOSE

The following exercises provide practical problems to solve with your WordStar knowledge. The applications include:

1. handwritten text to enter into WordStar files.
2. letters and reports that require format changes and text revisions.
3. strings to search and replace.
4. tables using tabulation and column techniques.
5. file manipulations.
6. reports with headers and footers.
7. manuscripts with special print features.

GENERAL DIRECTIONS FOR ALL EXERCISES

1. Two kinds of files will be stored on your Work Disk.
   a. The files you create.
   b. The files that have been created for you on a template disk that accompanies this section. This template disk (stock no. W108-1G) is referred to throughout this section as the Applications Exercise Disk. Copy the files from the Applications Exercise Disk onto your Work Disk. Do not edit from the Applications Exercise Disk.
2. At this time copy all of the files from the Applications Exercise Disk that accompanies this text onto your Work Disk. Follow the steps below. (The instructions are for the DOS Operating System.)
   a. Get into WordStar (WS).
   b. Insert a formatted Work Disk into Drive B and close the door.
   c. Exit WordStar (X). **A**⟩ appears on the screen.
   d. At the **A**⟩ enter in uppercase or lowercase **COPY** (1 space) **A:*.*** (1 space) **B:** Your screen looks like this:

   A⟩COPY A:*.* B:

   e. Remove the WordStar Master Disk from Drive A.
   f. Insert the Applications Exercise Disk into Drive A and close the door.
   g. Strike ENTER/RETURN.

    h. When the red lights stop flashing, insert the WordStar Disk into Drive A and close the door.

    i. Get into WS (WS).

    j. Change to Drive B (L Opening Menu).

3. Use the WordStar defaults unless directed otherwise. Remember, the format of the previous file will be duplicated on the next file's Ruler Line. So reset all the defaults after each file edit by exiting WordStar (X from the Opening Menu) and then re-entering WordStar (WS at the **A**⟩).

4. Do not hyphenate words when reformatting text (^OH).

5. Set the help level at 2 (^JH 2).

6. Print every exercise (P Opening Menu).

7. Allow 30 minutes to complete each exercise. Some problems take less time to finish, but no exercise requires more than 30 minutes of computer time.

EXERCISE 1
(Relating to Lessons 1 through 4)

DIRECTIONS: In this exercise you will enter and print a letter from handwritten text using the WordStar defaults. The letter should be entered in Full Block style (all lines begin at the left margin). Use acceptable business letter format. See the Full Block Style Letter Form example illustrated in Figure A.

1. Create a file named LETTER1.EX1 (D Opening Menu).
2. Enter the letter on page 302.

```
            FULL BLOCK STYLE LETTER FORM
          (Every line begins at the left margin)


(Today's Date) 4 RETURNS



XXXXXXXXXX
XXXXXXXXXX
XXXXXXXXXX   TWO RETURNS

XXXXXXXXXXXXXXXXX   TWO RETURNS

XXXXXXXXXXXXXXXXX   XXX   XXX XXX XXX XXX XXXXX XX X XXXX XX   XXXX
XXX   XX X X XXXX XXXX XXX XXX XX XXX XX X XXXXXXXX XXXXX XXXX   XX
XXXXXXXX XXX XXX XXX XX   XXXXXXX.   2 RETURNS

XXXXXXX   XXX   XXX XX XXXX XXXXXXX XXXXX   XXXXXX   XXXXXXXX   XXXXXX
XXXXXXXXX XXXX XXXX XXX XXX XX XX XXXX XXXX.   2 RETURNS

XXXXXXXXXXXXXXXXX   4 RETURNS



XXXXXXXXXXXXXXX
XXXXXXXXXXXXXXXXXXXX   2 RETURNS

(Typist's Initials)
Enclosure
```

Figure A   Example of Full Block Letter Style Form

(Today's Date)
Mr. Peter Ryan
757 Kennedy Way
Monta Vista, CA 95014

Dear Mr. Ryan

Several weeks ago we sent you a copy of our publication, NEW CAREERS. You no doubt have enjoyed reading about the opportunities available to those who are prepared for the coming demand for qualified workers in every area of advanced technology.

Perhaps you know of someone who would appreciate a copy of this new magazine. Please include on the enclosed form the names of people who may benefit from this informative source of job opportunities.

Sincerely,
Sally Warner
Circulation Manager

(Typist's initials)
Enclosure

Document for LETTER1.EX1

EXERCISE 2
(Relating to Lesson 5)

DIRECTIONS: In this exercise you will insert and delete text from a file copied from the Applications Exercise Disk that accompanies this text.

If you have not copied all of the files from the Applications Exercise Disk onto your Work Disk, do so now. Follow the instructions for copying files from the Applications Exercise Disk to the Work Disk located at the beginning of this section.

Make the additions and deletions indicated below to the file named LETTER1.EX2 (D Opening Menu).

Other Commands to Complete Edit of File LETTER1.EX2:

Reformat Text	^B
Delete Word	^T
Delete Line Right of Cursor	^QY
Delete Line Left of Cursor	^QDEL

(Today's Date)

Mr. Peter Ryan   *(Personnel Manager)*
757 Kennedy Way
Monta Vista, CA 95014

Dear Mr. Ryan
                                    (exciting)
Several weeks ago we sent you a copy of our publication, NEW
CAREERS. You no doubt have enjoyed reading about the
opportunities available to those who are prepared for the coming
demand for qualified workers in every area of advanced
technology.
(Do you)   *(people)*   *(their)*
~~Perhaps you~~ know ~~of someone~~ who would appreciate a copy of this
new magazine~~?~~? Please include the names ~~of people who may benefit~~
~~from this informative source of job opportunities~~ on the enclosed
form.
                                    (subscription)
Sincerely

Sally Warner
Circulation Manager

Enclosure

Document for LETTER1.EX2

EXERCISE 3
(Relating to Lesson 6)

DIRECTIONS: In this exercise you will make some format changes with a dot command and the tab command in a file from the Applications Exercise Disk. If you have not copied all of the files from the Applications Exercise Disk onto your Work Disk, do so now. Follow the instructions for copying files from the Applications Exercise Disk to the Work Disk located at the beginning of this section.

1. Edit the file named EXERCISE.3 (D Opening Menu).

2. Make the following format changes:
    a. Indent each paragraph to the first preset tab setting (^I or Tab Key).
    b. Enter the page offset dot command so that the file prints with a one-inch left margin (.PO10). *Note:* You must be at the top of the file.

Other Commands to Complete Exercise 3:

Insert Blank Line	^N (Do not strike ENTER/RETURN.)
Reformat Text	^B
Top of File	^QR

EXERCISE 4
(Relating to Lessons 7 and 8)

DIRECTIONS: In this exercise you will change the format of a file you copied from the Applications Exercise Disk that accompanies this text.

1. Edit the file named EXERCISE.4 (D Opening Menu).

2. Set the left margin at 15 and the right margin at 60 (^OL 15, ^OR 60).

Other Commands to Complete Exercise 4:

Reformat Text   ^B (Do not hyphenate.)

EXERCISE 5
(Relating to Lessons 7 and 8)

DIRECTIONS: In this exercise you will make changes in a file copied from the Applications Exercise Disk.

Note: Always exit WordStar before starting a new application exercise to reset the WordStar defaults.

1. Edit the file named EXERCISE.5 (D Opening Menu).

2. Enter the page breaks as indicated on the document on page 306 (.PA).

3. Go to the top of the file. Change the right margin to 50 (^OR 50).

4. Print the file with:
   a. a margin top of two inches (.MT12).
   b. a left margin of two inches (.PO20).
   c. no page number at the bottom of Page 1 (.OP).
   d. page numbers at the bottom of Pages 2 and 3 (.PN). Put this command on Line 1, Column 1 of Page 2.

Other Commands to Complete Exercise 5:

Insert a Blank Line	^N
Reformat Text	^B
Top of File	^QR

Our Solar System, one of many in the universe, consists of the Sun and all planets, asteroids, meteors, comets, dust, gas, and man-made satellites that orbit the Sun. The nine planets are Mercury, Venus, Earth, Mars, Jupiter, Saturn, Uranus, Neptune, and Pluto. Thanks to space exploration, our knowledge of the universe is expanding.

The Sun is just one of the many stars in a galaxy called the Milky Way. So much energy radiates from the Sun that a tremendous light is created. The Sun also emits gamma rays, Xrays, infrared rays, cosmic rays, and radio waves. Protons and electrons are released from energy called the solar wind. Another form of energy released from the Sun called a solar flare will disrupt radio communications.

———→ *New Page*

The planet Mercury orbits between the Earth and the Sun and is nearest the Sun. It is the smallest and fastest of all the planets. Because it is so close to the Sun, it is a very hot planet; its atmosphere consists mostly of helium.

The planet Venus is closest to the Earth and is the brightest object seen from Earth--the Sun and Moon excepted. A heavy cloud layer covers its surface. Unmanned spaceships have been able to see beyond the cloud layer and discovered that the surface of Venus is far more rugged than Earth's mountains and canyons. The temperature is around 869 degrees Fahrenheit.

———→ *new Page*

The planet Mars is much colder than the Earth's temperature, reaching about 80 degrees Fahrenheit at the equator. We landed on Mars in two unmanned spaceships called Viking in 1976. These ships sent back the first photos and data from the surface of the planet.   The photos revealed huge valleys and moon-like craters.

The planet Jupiter is the largest mass circling the Sun. Because Jupiter has areas of water vapor and temperature similar to Earth's temperature, scientists believe this planet can support life. Unmanned spaceship photos have revealed that a huge hurricane-like storm exists on the planet's surface that is 30,000 miles long and 7,000 miles wide.

Document for EXERCISE.5

EXERCISE 6
(Relating to Lesson 8)

DIRECTIONS: You will make format changes and add text to a file copied from the Applications Exercise Disk.

1. Edit the file named EXERCISE.6 (D Opening Menu).

2. Reformat Paragraph #1 with the left margin set at 10 and the right margin set at 60 (^OL 10, ^OR 60).

3. Reformat Paragraph #3 to match the margin settings of Paragraph #2. To do this:
   a. Place cursor at the beginning of Paragraph #2.
   b. Strike ^OF.
   c. Place cursor at the beginning of Paragraph #3 and reform.

4. Enter the paragraph below at the end of the file. Set the margins for this paragraph from a non-printing ruler line at 20 and 50 (^OX, ..^P ENTER/RETURN, ^OF, ENTER/RETURN, ^OX).

Other Commands to Complete Exercise 6:

Reformat Text   ^B

The songwriters Richard Rodgers and Lorenz Hart were the first composers to get equal recognition for both music and lyrics. Before their time, the music composer received top billing over the lyricist. This team was always known as Rodgers and Hart. When they collaborated on a musical score, each man received credit on the marquee. Richard Rodgers wrote the music, and Lorenz Hart wrote the words.

Document for EXERCISE.6

EXERCISE 7
(Relating to Lesson 8)

DIRECTIONS:

1. Edit the file named EXERCISE.7 (D Opening Menu).

2. Print the file with:
   a. a ragged right margin (^OJ).
   b. a margin top of three inches (.MT18).
   c. a margin bottom of three inches (.MB18).

Other Commands to Complete Exercise 7:

Reformat Text   ^B
Insert a Blank Line ^N

EXERCISE 8
(Relating to Lesson 9)

DIRECTIONS:

1. Enter the table below in a file named EXERCISE.8 (D Opening Menu).

2. Set the columns attractively across a 65-space line. Use a non-printing ruler line. Set tabs at Column Positions 14, 26, 37, and 48. Do not try to align commas or decimal points.

3. Print the file without a page number (.OP).

Other Commands to Complete Exercise 8:

Non-Printing Ruler Line	. .^P, ENTER/RETURN, ^OF
Insert Off	^V

MERCURY	3,100	0.056	5.13	0.36
VENUS	7,519	0.815	5.26	0.87
EARTH	7,926	1.00	5.52	1.00
MARS	4,218	0.108	3.94	0.38
JUPITER	88,732	317.9	1.33	2.61
SATURN	74,316	95.2	0.69	0.90
URANUS	29,200	14.6	1.56	1.07
NEPTUNE	27,700	17.3	2.27	1.41
PLUTO	1,900	0.06 ?	4.00 ?	0.3 ?

Document for EXERCISE.8

EXERCISE 9
(Relating to Lesson 9)

DIRECTIONS:

1. Enter the table below in a file named EXERCISE.9 (D Opening Menu).

2. Clear all the tabs on the Ruler Line and set new tabs at column positions 10, 30, and 50 (^ON A, ^OI).

3. Print the file without a page number (.OP).

Other Commands to Complete Exercise 9:

Tab　^I

```
WORD PROCESSING CHECKLIST

Software Considerations

        Preset Formats    Preset Margins      Preset Tabs
        Preset Pitch      Preset Line Space   Preset Margins
        Indent Function   On-Screen Help      Decimal Tab
        Center Command    Hyphenation         Page Endings
        Insert Text       Insert Pages        Delete
        Copy              Move                Stored Text
        Spelling Check    Footnoting          Superscripts
        Subscripts        Page Numbering      Calculations
```

Document for EXERCISE.9

EXERCISE 10
(Relating to Lesson 10)

DIRECTIONS: Enter a table with decimal points aligned in a file copied from the Applications Exercise Disk.

1. Edit the file named EXERCISE.10 (D Opening Menu).

2. Enter the table below at the end of the file. Align the decimal points. (*Hint:* Use the non-printing ruler line in the file. Make the necessary adjustments to the non-printing ruler line so that there are 6 spaces between the columns. Set dec tabs at Column Positions 29, 40, and 51.)

3. Omit page number (.OP).

Other Commands to Complete Exercise 10:

Match Non-Printing Ruler Line	^OF
Insert Off	^V
Dec Tab	#
Tab	^I

MERCURY	3,100	0.056	5.13	0.36
VENUS	7,519	0.815	5.26	0.87
EARTH	7,926	1.00	5.52	1.00
MARS	4,218	0.108	3.94	0.38
JUPITER	88,732	317.9	1.33	2.61
SATURN	74,316	95.2	0.69	0.90
URANUS	29,200	14.6	1.56	1.07
NEPTUNE	27,700	17.3	2.27	1.41
PLUTO	1,900	0.06?	4.00?	0.3?

Document for EXERCISE.10

EXERCISE 11
(Relating to Lesson 10)

DIRECTIONS:

1. Edit the file named EXERCISE.11 copied from the Applications Exercise Disk (D Opening Menu).

2. Indent each paragraph 15 spaces as indicated below (^OG three times).

3. Omit the page number (.OP).

Other Commands to Complete Exercise 11:

Insert a Blank Line	^N
Tab	^I
Reformat Text	^B

GUIDE TO A HEALTHY BACK

POSTURE

15 Whatever the cause of low back pain, part of its treatment is the correction of faulty posture. Good posture is not simply a matter of "standing tall". It refers to the correct use of the body at all times. In order for the body to function efficiently, muscles, joints, bones, and/or ligaments must not be strained. If the segments are well balanced, the muscles don't have to work to maintain balance. The body feels less fatigued and can work more effectively.

15 Proper alignment of the body when in a sitting position is vital to a healthy back. Maintaining the normal hollow in your low back when seated will keep your body in proper alignment. Avoid sitting with the legs straight in front of you. Sit with your shoulders square. Avoid prolonged sitting.

15 When lifting heavy objects, lift with your legs, not your back. Use a wide base of support. Keep the hollow in your low back as much as possible. Your feet should face the object as you pick it up. Your feet should face the object as you set it down. Avoid twisting. If the load is too heavy or awkward--get help!

Document for EXERCISE.11

EXERCISE 12
(Relating to Lesson 11)

DIRECTIONS: In this exercise you will reformat text in a file copied from the Applications Exercise Disk.

1. Edit the file named EXERCISE.12 as indicated on page 313 (D Opening Menu).

2. Change the right margin to 60 (^OR 60).

3. Reformat text. Hyphenate any word that does not fit on a line. (If you have been turning Hyphen Help off, turn it back on with with ^OH.)

4. Double space the text and reformat again (^OS 2).

Other Commands to Complete Exercise 12:

Center	^OC
Tab	^I
Reformat Text	^B

EXERCISE 15
(Relating to Lessons 16 and 17)

DIRECTIONS: In this exercise you will move, copy, and delete blocks of text in a file copied from the Applications Exercise Disk.

1. Edit the file named EXERCISE.15 (D Opening Menu).

2. Follow the instructions on the document on page 316.

3. Omit page number (.OP).

4. Make any necessary line space adjustments between paragraphs after the block commands.

5. Print with a one-inch left margin (.PO10).

Other Commands to Complete Exercise 15:

Insert a Blank Line	^N
Mark a Block	^KB, ^KK
Move a Block	^KV
Copy a Block	^KC
Delete a Block	^KY
Hide a Block	^KH

Move

OUR SOLAR SYSTEM AND THE UNIVERSE

Our Solar System, one of many in the universe, consists of the Sun and all planets, asteroids, meteors, comets, dust, gas, and man-made satellites that orbit the Sun. The nine planets are Mercury, Venus, Earth, Mars, Jupiter, Saturn, Uranus, Neptune, and Pluto. Thanks to space exploration, our knowledge of the universe is expanding.

THE SUN

The Sun is just one of the many stars in a galaxy called the Milky Way. So much energy radiates from the Sun that a tremendous light is created. The Sun also emits gamma rays, Xrays, infrared rays, cosmic rays, and radio waves. Protons and electrons are released from energy called the solar wind. Another form of energy released from the Sun called a solar flare will disrupt radio communications.

copy

MERCURY

The planet Mercury orbits between the Earth and the Sun and is nearest the Sun. It is the smallest and fastest of all the planets. Because it is so close to the Sun, it is a very hot planet; its atmosphere consists mostly of helium.

VENUS

Delete

The planet Venus is closest to the Earth and is the brightest object seen from Earth--the Sun and Moon excepted. A heavy cloud layer covers its surface. Unmanned spaceships have been able to see beyond the cloud layer and discovered that the surface of Venus is far more rugged than Earth's mountains and canyons. The temperature is around 869 degrees Fahrenheit.

MARS

The planet Mars is much colder than the Earth's temperature, reaching about 80 degrees Fahrenheit at the equator. We landed on Mars in two unmanned spaceships called Viking in 1976. These ships sent back the first photos and data from the surface of the planet. The photos revealed huge valleys and moon-like craters.

JUPITER

The planet Jupiter is the largest mass circling the Sun. Because Jupiter has areas of water vapor and temperature similar to Earth's temperature, scientists believe this planet can support life. Unmanned spaceship photos have revealed that a huge hurricane-like storm exists on the planet's surface that is 30,000 miles long and 7,000 miles wide.

Document for EXERCISE.15

EXERCISE 16
(Relating to Lessons 16 and 17)

DIRECTIONS:

1. Edit the file named EXERCISE.16 copied from the Applications Exercise Disk (D Opening Menu).

2. Make the changes indicated on the document on page 318.

3. Omit page number (.OP).

4. Print with a one-inch left margin (.PO10).

5. Make necessary spacing adjustments after the block moves. There should be one blank line between dates.

6. If the columns become uneven because of the block moves, use the non-printing ruler line to align them properly (^OF). If you want to begin this exercise again, save the file with ^KQ and edit the unchanged file again. To move the entire paragraph to the proper tab setting, move the cursor to column 1 before marking the block (^QS).

Other Commands to Complete Exercise 16:

Insert a Blank Line	^N
Center	^OC
Mark Block	^KB, ^KK
Move Block	^KV
Hide Block	^KH
Delete a Blank Line	^Y

(Center Title)

NOBEL LITERATURE PRIZES

1983	William Golding	Lord of the Flies	*— move to end*
1984	Jaroslay Seifert	The Casting of Bells	
1901	Sully-Prudhomme	LeBonheur	
1902	C. M. T. Mommson	History of Rome	
1903	Bjornstijerne Bjornson	The Fisher Girl	
1936	Eugene O'Neill	Morning Becomes Electra	
1937	Roger Martin du Gard	The World of the Thibaults	
1938	Pearl S. Buck	The Good Earth	
1904	Frederic Mistral	Mireio	
1940-43	No Award		
1939	Frans E. Sillanpaa	Meek Heritage	
1954	Ernest Hemingway	A Farewell to Arms	
1956	Juan Ramon Jimenez	Unidad	
1967	Miguel Angel Asturias	Strong Wind	
1958	Boris Pasternak	Dr. Zhivago	
1976	Saul Bellow	Herzog	
1977	Vicente Aleixandre	Swords of Lips	
1978	Isaac Singer	The Family Moskat	
1979	Odysseus Elytis	The Sovereign Sun	
1948	T. S Eliot	The Waste Land	*— move in chronological order*
1949	William Faulkner	The Sound and the Fury	
1945	Gabriela Mistral	Lagar	

move 2 lines below title —

The Nobel Prize for literature is awarded each year by the Swedish Academy of Literature. The awards were established in the will of Alfred Bernhard Nobel (1833-1896). He became wealthy through his invention of dynamite. Nobel left a fund of about 9 million dollars to encourage peace and progress.

Document for EXERCISE.16

EXERCISE 17
(Relating to Lesson 17)

DIRECTIONS: In this exercise you will write names and addresses from a mailing list into separate files.

1. Edit the file named EXERCISE.17 copied from the Applications Exercise Disk (D Opening Menu).

2. Write each name and address into a separate file. Name each file by the addressee's last name.

3. Print the File Directory. To do this in the DOS operating system:
   a. Exit WordStar (X Opening Menu).
   b. At the ⟩ enter DIR. Then type ^P ENTER/RETURN.

4. Circle the file names created in this exercise on the printed directory.

Other Commands to Complete Exercise 17:

Mark a Block	^KB, ^KK
Write a Block	^KW
Hide a Block	^KH

EXERCISE 18
(Relating to Lesson 17)

DIRECTIONS: In this exercise you will build a letter by reading a file copied from the Applications Exercise Disk and files you created in Exercise 17.

1. Create a file named EXERCISE.18 (D Opening Menu).

2. At the beginning of the file, read the file named MANSCH, created in Exercise 17 (^KR).

3. Insert a blank line after the address and read the file named LETTER1 copied from the Applications Exercise Disk.

4. Send the same letter, LETTER1, to Jill Sands, Jeff Barron, Jane Jones, Richard Harris, and Sandy Spencer. The addresses are in files you created in Exercise 17 under the names SANDS, BARRON, JONES, HARRIS, and SPENCER. Read all files into the same file—EXERCISE.18. Each address and letter will be read on a new page in the file named EXERCISE.18.

5. Print the file.

EXERCISE 19
(Relating to Lesson 18)

DIRECTIONS: In this exercise you will copy a column.

1. Edit the file named EXERCISE.19 copied from the Applications Exercise Disk (D Opening Menu).

2. Insert a centered title to read COPY A COLUMN three blank lines above the table.

3. Copy the column as indicated below to Column Position 60. Use the Space Bar to get to Column Position 60 (^KN, ^KC).

Other Commands to Complete Exercise 19:

Center Title	^OC
Mark Column Block	^KB, ^KK
Insert Blank Lines	^N

copy

2237	2425	6766	777
2238	2426	6767	778
2239	2427	6768	779
2240	2428	6769	780
2241	2429	6770	781
2242	2430	6771	782
2243	2431	6772	783
2244	2432	6773	784
2245	2433	6774	785
2246	2434	6775	786
2247	2435	6776	787
2248	2436	6777	788
2249	2437	6778	789
2250	2438	6779	790

Document for EXERCISE.19

EXERCISE 20
(Relating to Lesson 18)

DIRECTIONS: In this exercise you will move a column.

1. Edit the file named EXERCISE.20 copied from the Applications Exercise Disk (D Opening Menu).

2. Insert a centered title to read MOVE A COLUMN three blank lines above the table.

3. Move the column as indicated below to Column Position 10 (^KN, ^KV).

Other Commands to Complete Exercise 20:

Center Title   ^OC
Mark Column Block   ^KB, ^KK
Insert Blank Lines   ^N

2237	2425	6766	777	move
2238	2426	6767	778	
2239	2427	6768	779	
2240	2428	6769	780	
2241	2429	6770	781	
2242	2430	6771	782	
2243	2431	6772	783	
2244	2432	6773	784	
2245	2433	6774	785	
2246	2434	6775	786	
2247	2435	6776	787	
2248	2436	6777	788	
2249	2437	6778	789	
2250	2438	6779	790	

Document for EXERCISE.20

EXERCISE 21
(Relating to Lesson 18)

DIRECTIONS: In this exercise you will delete columns.

1. Edit the file named EXERCISE.21 (D Opening Menu).

2. Insert a centered title to read DELETE A COLUMN three blank lines above the table.

3. Delete the columns as indicated below (^KY).

Other Commands to Complete Exercise 21:

Column Mode	^KN
Center Title	^OC
Mark Column Block	^KB, ^KK
Insert Blank Lines	^N

2237	2425	6766	777
2238	2426	6767	778
2239	2427	6768	779
2240	2428	6769	780
2241	2429	6770	781
2242	2430	6771	782
2243	2431	6772	783
2244	2432	6773	784
2245	2433	6774	785
2246	2434	6775	786
2247	2435	6776	787
2248	2436	6777	788
2249	2437	6778	789
2250	2438	6779	790

Document for EXERCISE.21

EXERCISE 22
(Relating to Lesson 18)

DIRECTIONS: In this exercise you will format a two-column newsletter from text copied from the Applications Exercise Disk. Your printer must have microjustification to complete Exercise 22.

1. Edit the file named EXERCISE.22 copied from the Applications Exercise Disk (D Opening Menu).

2. Format the text in this file so that it prints in two columns as shown below. Do not hyphenate proper names.

3. The columns are three inches wide (^OR 30).

4. There are five spaces between columns (^OX).

5. Center the title GREAT AMERICAN COMPOSERS three blank lines above the columns (^OR 65, ^OC).

Other Commands to Complete Exercise 22:

Column Mode	^KN
Hyphen Help	^OH
Reformat Text	^QQ^B1
Write Block	^KW
Mark Column	^KB, ^KK
Move Column	^KV
Harden Hyphens	^QA, ^P^-, -, NG
Delete Hard Returns	^Y
Microjustification	.UJ0, .UJ1

George Gershwin not only composed beautiful music, but he was an accomplished pianist. Because of his expertise as a classical pianist, he was able to cross over from a composer of popular songs in the Tin Pan Alley tradition to a respected composer of concert and opera music.

Although George Gershwin started out in Tin Pan Alley writing songs for the popular musical comedy, he gradually turned toward serious composition. In 1922 Paul Whiteman asked him to write something for a concert that would feature American music. The result of that request was Rhapsody in Blue. Not only did he write this beautiful song, but he also performed it at the Paul Whiteman concert.

In a span of twenty years, George Gershwin wrote such hits as Swanee, Stairway to Paradise, Fascinating Rhythm, The Man I Love, Someone to Watch Over Me, I've Got a Crush on You, Of Thee I Sing, and the American opera, Porgy and Bess. He died at the young age of 38.

The songwriters Richard Rodgers and Lorenz Hart were the first composers to get equal recognition for both music and lyrics. Before their time, the music composer received top billing over the lyricist. This team was always known as Rodgers and Hart. When they collaborated on a musical score, each man received credit on the marquee. Richard Rodgers wrote the music, and Lorenz Hart wrote the words.

Document for EXERCISE.22

EXERCISE 23
(Relating to Lessons 21 and 22)

DIRECTIONS: In this exercise you will create a header and a footer in an existing file.

1. Edit the file named EXERCISE.23 copied from the Applications Exercise Disk (D Opening Menu).

2. Create the centered header and footer below (.HE space, .FO space).

3. The page number footer should include the number symbol. The page numbers will print PAGE #50, PAGE #51, PAGE #52, etc.

4. Print
   a. the page numbers, beginning with page number 50 (.PN50).
   b. the header five blank lines before the text (.HM5). (The text prints on the sixth line.)
   c. the header two inches from the top of the page (.MT17). (Header lines included in Margin Top command.)

Other Commands to Complete Exercise 23:

Center	^OC
Insert a Blank Line	^N
Move Cursor Left	^QS

HEADER

ROUGH DRAFT OF SCIENCE TEXT

FOOTER

PAGE \##

Document for EXERCISE.23

EXERCISE 24
(Relating to Lesson 22)

DIRECTIONS: In this exercise you will print page numbers at the bottom of the page, alternating the page number position between the lower right and lower left corner of the page.

1. Edit the file named EXERCISE.24 copied from the Applications Exercise Disk (D Opening Menu).

2. Enter a footer so that the page number prints alternately between the lower right and lower left corner of each page. The footer should read Page 1 of 6 Pages, Page 2 of 6 Pages, Page 3 of 6 Pages, etc. To do this:
   a. Enter .FO^P^K at Column Position 1.
   b. Space to Column Position 54.
   c. Enter Page # of 6 Pages.

Other Commands to Complete Exercise 24:

Insert a Blank Line	^N
Page Number Symbol	#

EXERCISE 25
(Relating to Lesson 23)

DIRECTIONS: To complete this exercise, your printer must be able to support bold print, superscripts, and underscores.

1. Edit the file named EXERCISE.25 copied from the Applications Exercise Disk (D Opening Menu).

2. Type the appropriate command to achieve the special print features indicated below. *Note:* Turn off Insert to add continuous underscore between column headings.

3. If the file becomes misaligned during the edit, use the nonprinting ruler line to fix the spacing (^OF).

Other Commands to Complete Exercise 25:

Bold Print	^PB
Superscript	^PT
Insert Off	^V
Continuous Underscore	^PS, Underscore Key (Shift Hyphen) in Place of Spaces
Word Underscore	^PS
Turn Off Print Display	^OD

Bold Print → **THE PLANETS**[1] *Do Not Bold Print Superscript*

PLANET	DIAMETER	MASS	DENSITY	GRAVITY
MERCURY	3,100	0.056	5.13	0.36
VENUS	7,519	0.815	5.26	0.87
EARTH	7,926	1.00	5.52	1.00
MARS	4,218	0.108	3.94	0.38
JUPITER	88,732	317.9	1.33	2.61
SATURN	74,316	95.2	0.69	0.90
URANUS	29,200	14.6	1.56	1.07
NEPTUNE	27,700	17.3	2.27	1.41
PLUTO	1,900	0.06?	4.00?	0.3?

Continuous Underscore

[1]SOURCE: Reader's Digest Almanac 1987, p. 760.

Word Underscore

Document for EXERCISE.25

EXERCISE 26
(Relating to Lesson 24)

DIRECTIONS: Print only Page 6 from the file named EXERCISE.26 copied from the Applications Exercise Disk (P ENTER/RETURN Opening Menu).

EXERCISE 27
(Relating to Lesson 25)

DIRECTIONS:

1. Edit the file named EXERCISE.27 copied from the Applications Exercise Disk (D Opening Menu).

2. Make the following changes as indicated below. The ⊗ is made by typing a capital O, the command ^PH and a capital X.

Other Commands to Complete Exercise 27:

Print Display Off   ^OD

OBJECTIVE: A JOB WITH RESPONSIBILITY IN EDUCATION/TRAINING

ABILITIES: ⊗ Research and negotiation experience.

⊗ Successful salesperson, presenter, and teacher.

⊗ Knowledge of the computer world.

⊗ Administrative experience.

⊗ Leadership ability.

⊗ Team player with demonstrated ability to accept responsibility and to take initiative.

Document for EXERCISE.27

Quick Reference

The following table is a quick reference guide to the WordStar commands and where they are discussed in this book. The first column describes the WordStar feature; the second column gives the command to execute the feature; and the third column indicates the lesson where the feature is discussed.

Feature	Command	Lesson
Abandon Edit	^KQ	Lesson 17, 19
Alternate Page Number Position	.HE^P^K	Lesson 21
Alternate Pitch	^PA	Lesson 25
Beginning of File	^QR	Lesson 4
Block Begin	^KB	Lesson 16
Block End	^KK	Lesson 16
Block Hide	^KH	Lesson 16
Block Menu	^K	Lesson 19
Bold Print	^PB	Lesson 23
Cancel a Command	^U Esc	Lesson 3
Center a Line	^OC	Lesson 11
Change Logged Disk Drives	L Opening Menu, ^KL	Lesson 2, 19
Change Ribbon Color	^PY	Lesson 25
Character Width	.CW	Lesson 6, 27
Column Mode On/Off	^KN	Lesson 18
Comment Line	.., .IG	Lesson 27
Conditional Page Break	.CP	Lesson 27
Continue Search	^L	Lesson 14
Continuous Scroll to File Beginning	^QW	Lesson 4
Continuous Scroll to File End	^QZ	Lesson 4
Copy Block	^KC	Lesson 17
Copy File	^KO	Lesson 19
Create a Document	D Opening Menu	Lesson 3
Decimal Tab	^OI, #	Lesson 10
Delete Block	^KY	Lesson 17
Delete Character at Cursor	^G	Lesson 5
Delete Character Left of Cursor	DEL	Lesson 5
Delete File	^KJ, Y Opening Menu	Lesson 19
Delete Line	^Y	Lesson 5
Delete Line Left of Cursor	^QDEL	Lesson 5
Delete Line Right of Cursor	^QY	Lesson 5
Delete Word	^T	Lesson 5
Double Strike	^PD	Lesson 23
Down by Line	^X	Lesson 4
Edit a Document	D Opening Menu	Lesson 3
End of File	^QC	Lesson 4
Exit WordStar	X Opening Menu	Lesson 2
File Directory On/Off	F Opening Menu, ^KF	Lesson 3, 17
Find Block Begin	^QB	Lesson 16
Find Block End	^QK	Lesson 16
Find Place Marker	^Q (0-9)	Lesson 14
Find Text	^QF	Lesson 14
Footer	.FO	Lesson 22
Footer Margin	.FM	Lesson 22
Get into WordStar	WS	Lesson 2
Header	.HE	Lesson 21
Header Margin	.HM	Lesson 21
Help Levels	^JH, H Opening Menu	Lesson 6
Help Menu	^J	Lesson 17, 29
Hyphen Help On/Off	^OH	Lesson 11
Insert Blank Line	^N	Lesson 5
Insert On/Off	^V	Lesson 3, 5
Justify Right Margin	^OJ	Lesson 3, 8
Left by Character	^S	Lesson 4
Left Margin	^OL	Lesson 6, 8